AF411967

“Colour'd Shadows”

"Colour'd Shadows"

Contexts in Publishing, Printing, and Reading Nineteenth-Century British Women Writers

Terence Allan Hoagwood
and
Kathryn Ledbetter

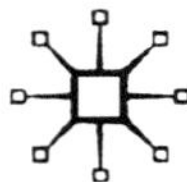

First published in 2005 by
PALGRAVE MACMILLAN™
175 Fifth Avenue, New York, N.Y. 10010 and
Houndmills, Basingstoke, Hampshire, England RG21 6XS
Companies and representatives throughout the world.

PALGRAVE MACMILLAN is the global academic imprint of the Palgrave Macmillan division of St. Martin's Press, LLC and of Palgrave Macmillan Ltd. Macmillan® is a registered trademark in the United States, United Kingdom and other countries. Palgrave is a registered trademark in the European Union and other countries.

ISBN: 1–4039–6637–0

Library of Congress Cataloging-in-Publication Data is available from the Library of Congress.

A catalogue record for this book is available from the British Library.

Design by Newgen Imaging Systems (P) Ltd., Chennai, India.

First edition: January 2005

10 9 8 7 6 5 4 3 2 1

Printed in the United States of America.

Contents

LIST OF ILLUSTRATIONS

ACKNOWLEDGMENTS

TERENCE HOAGWOOD

I would like to thank the Glasscock Center for Humanities Research at Texas A&M and its Director, Professor James Rosenheim, for a fellowship that I held while research and writing for this book were going forward. A Residential Fellowship at the Yale Center for British Art enabled me to examine rare materials that were important for this project, and I thank, too, Patrick Noon, Curator of that institution's Department of Prints and Drawings. At Yale, both the Beinecke Library and the Sterling Memorial Library were resources whose collections and whose hospitable staff were of substantial benefit to this project as well. Collections of rare books and periodicals at the following libraries, and the staffs of the following libraries, have been valuable resources for this book over a period of several years: Harry Ransom Humanities Research Center at the University of Texas in Austin; Cushing Memorial Library (Special Collections) at Texas A&M University; the Library of Congress; the British Library; the British Museum, Department of Prints and Drawings; the Newberry Library; and the Young Research Library at the University of California—Los Angeles. I thank Dean Charles Johnson of the College of Liberal Arts at Texas A&M and the Association of Former Students for an Outstanding Research Award that has been materially helpful as well. J. Lawrence Mitchell, long our inspirational Head in the Department of English at Texas A&M, has been helpful with financial assistance for travel for research and for releasing time for the work of research and writing, and Professor Mitchell's expertise—and likewise his enthusiasm—about the history of the book have been valuable. I was twice the recipient of research funds from the College of Liberal Arts Honors Plan at Texas A&M while working on this book, and I am glad to acknowledge the support in the form of funds and also the positive experience of the related seminars. Norman Mangouni and Scholars' Facsimiles have been excellent publishers of some of my earlier books, five of which—editions of Mary Robinson's *Sappho and Phaon*, Violet Fane's *Denzil Place*, Charlotte Smith's *Beachy Head, With Other Poems*, Mary Hays's *The Victim of Prejudice*, and *The Keepsake for 1829*—have been directly related and specifically helpful for the preparation of this book; in that connection, I thank my collaborators Becky Jackson (who worked with me on *Sappho and Phaon*), Nicole Stewart (who worked with me on *Denzil Place*), and Kathryn Ledbetter (who worked with me on *The Keepsake for 1829*). Neil Fraistat and Steven Jones, as editors of the outstanding set of scholarly resources on the

Web, Romantic Circles, were excellent editors for the hypertext and essays from *The Keepsake* that Kathryn and I prepared in 1999 and which helped us toward the conception and completion of this book. Learned and constructively critical audiences at several scholarly conferences have been helpful as this book was in preparation: the MLA, Keats-Shelley Association, Byron Society, Interdisciplinary Group for Historical Study (Texas A&M); North American Society for the Study of Romanticism; and Victorian Studies Association of the Western United States.

A version different from that presented in chapter 6, on Elizabeth Barrett's *A Drama of Exile* and Jean Ingelow's *A Story of Doom*, appears in *Victorian Poetry*, 42, no. 2 (summer 2004), and for permission to use that material in this book I thank the editor of *Victorian Poetry*, Hayden Ward; and West Virginia University Press.

Among numerous colleagues, in the broad and wonderful sense, I will mention two without whose expertise and generosity this book would not be, herewith, produced: Marilyn Gaull and Jerome McGann.

KATHRYN LEDBETTER

Research on parts of this book began as graduate work at the University of South Carolina, and I would like to thank my committee members who supported my dissertation on the *Keepsake* and taught me to consider the implications of text in literary scholarship. Thanks to Ezra Greenspan, Joel Myerson, the late William Richey, Lori Loeb, and, most of all, Paula Feldman, who introduced me to a lifelong obsession with literary annuals and rare book collecting. I also thank librarians in interlibrary loan, circulation, and rare book departments for valuable assistance and generous access to materials at the Thomas Cooper Library in Columbia; the Perry-Castañeda Library and the Harry Ransom Humanities Research Center at the University of Texas in Austin; the British Library; the Bodleian Library; and Alkek Library at Texas State University-San Marcos. Thanks to Terry Belanger of the Rare Book School at the University of Virginia for sharing much knowledge in his course on "Book Illustration to 1880." Many interested scholars contributed ideas and enthusiasm at conferences, and I am grateful for the organizations sponsoring these gatherings: Victorian Interdisciplinary Studies Association of the Western United States (VISAWUS); Research Society for Victorian Periodicals (RSVP); Society for the History of Authorship, Reading and Publishing (SHARP); Modern Language Association (MLA); and the Eighteenth and Nineteenth-Century British Women Writers Conference. I also appreciate the prolific and thought-provoking discussions on the NASSR, Victoria, and SHARP electronic discussion lists. I am grateful to Texas State University-San Marcos for supporting me in many ways, including a Research Enhancement Grant awarded in 2002 that allowed me to research Victorian periodicals at the British Library. Thanks to Lydia Blanchard, Chair of the Texas State English Department, Ann Marie Ellis, Dean of Liberal Arts, and my colleagues in the

English Department, for providing me with a positive environment where my scholarship is respected and supported intellectually, as well as financially. I am grateful to my English Department study group members, who read various parts of this manuscript or listened as I discussed my ideas: Libby Allison, Rebecca Jackson, Teya Rosenberg, Claudia Nelson, Robin Cohen, Marilynn Olson, and Priscilla Leder. I also thank my students at Texas State, especially the members of the undergraduate English honors society, Sigma Tau Delta, who twice asked me to give presentations from my work on this book. Thanks to June Hankins for sponsoring this wonderful student organization. The Center for Multicultural and Gender Studies also offered valuable feedback after inviting me to share my research on the *Keepsake*. I would like to thank my former colleagues at Oklahoma Baptist University, including Carolyn Cole and Bill Hagen, who pushed me to pursue my interests even when it meant that I would leave that excellent liberal arts institution. I am grateful to editors of these scholarly journals for publishing my work: *Victorian Newsletter, Studies in the Literary Imagination, Victorian Poetry, Papers of the Bibliographical Society of America*, and *Victorian Periodicals Review*. And finally, I would like to thank my friend and collaborator, Terence Hoagwood, whose encouragement after an MLA session resulted in my first graduate student publication in 1993. He is a model of mentoring excellence, and his brilliant scholarly record provides only a sampling of junior scholars he has helped. Many thanks to Alan Munde for being a good listener.

Introduction

Nineteenth-century British poets are frequently eloquent about their own means of production. To use the metaphor made familiar by M. H. Abrams, the mimetic poetry of earlier periods sometimes knew itself as a mirror, and the poetry that Alexander Pope produces and prescribes in *An Essay in Criticism*, for instance, takes its images for representations of other things; in contrast, the lamp is about itself. Two or three generations ago, the tendency of Romantic writing to refer to itself seemed ennobling in the rhetoric of important books by Abrams and others: Romanticism was about Imagination. From the Napoleonic wars through the Cold War, Coleridge's famous equation of poet with poem sloganized the admirable personalism of Romantic writing. That equation was a plank in the platform of "High Romanticism," when Abrams praised it, and when Anne K. Mellor later treated it more negatively as "male Romanticism." Much poetry, including many examples in this book, worked in a different way, directly or indirectly demystifying the self-reference of poetry by highlighting its manufacturing of illusions. Paradoxically, even while Letitia Elizabeth Landon's (L. E. L) sales doctrine remained the premise that the poem equals the poet, she developed a trenchant and skillful "art of disillusion."[1]

Having begun her career producing versified advertisements for figurines, L. E. L. not only suffered overwork and publication-relations crises, but she also wrote often about the manufacture of poetry in disenchanted terms. In *The Troubadour*, a young poet has "thoughts with their own beauty fill'd," and the thoughts "shed their richness over all," but

> Alas! for him whose youthful fire
> Is vowed and wasted on the lyre,—
> Alas! for him who shall essay,
> The laurel's long and dreary way!
> Mocking will greet, neglect will chill
> His spirit's gush, his bosom's thrill;
> And, worst of all, that heartless praise
> Echoed from what another says. (11)

The industry produces this disenchantment: "let him reach the goal, . . . Let his songs be on every tongue, / And wealth and honours round him flung"; he will throw down "the golden harp," and he will "sigh for all the toil, the care, / The wrong that he has had to bear" (12). In this narrative, in the age of commercial distribution poetry proves not to be about Imagination, and not about the poet's personality, but rather "mocking," "neglect," "honours," and "wealth," the pursuit of which is "toil" (11–12).[2]

L. E. L.'s poetry sometimes renders the nonequivalence of personal feeling and printed product with bitterness, but sometimes (in its more appealing sales moments) her poems represent that nonequivalence in opulent terms. A troubadour's workplace is not an inky desk in a rented room but a "festival" in a "castle hall." However, L. E. L.'s ornamental descriptions include tropes of disillusion: "With a thousand colours the tapestry falls," and oak panels are "Like dark mirrors"; rays of light from "pictured windows fall," making "colour'd shadows" (69–70). The dark mirrors of ornament are not about Imagination, and the colored shadows cast through painted glass are not about the poet's personality. *The Troubadour* is about the alienating industry, its lifeless and deceptive commodities (the painted glass), and the moving illusions (colored shadows), broadcast by the print media, which, in L. E. L.'s lifetime, had become big business in the modern and multinational sense.

Figure 3.1 displays an illustration entitled "Regina's Maids of Honour," reproduced from the January 1836 *Fraser's Magazine* and featured in chapter 3 of this volume. Several popular women writers from the 1830s gather here (left to right): Mrs. S. C. Hall (Anna Maria Hall); L. E. L.; Lady Morgan (Sydney Owenson); the Hon. Mrs. Norton (Caroline Norton); Lady Blessington; Jane Porter; Harriet Martineau; and Mary Russell Mitford. As I gaze, I might imagine that I am listening in, as the African servant standing to the left of Anna Maria Hall undoubtedly is, waiting for commands. I might wish to recreate the conversation between Lady Blessington and Caroline Norton at the far right of the image. Norton appears to be discussing her impressions of the recently published literary annual she edited, *The Keepsake* for 1836. Lady Blessington is listening thoughtfully, perhaps wanting to share a common experience with printers or publishers of her own annual, *Heath's Book of Beauty*, while Lady Morgan looks on with interest from Norton's left. Jane Porter and L. E. L. are having an entirely different conversation across the table, as Anna Maria Hall and Mary Russell Mitford attend. Harriet Martineau stares at Morgan, or perhaps the viewer, as if her deafness gives her extrasensory notice of our gaze.

Except for the anonymous figure primping at the mirror, these women are intensely serious—all business. Yet, in the accompanying article, "List the First," William Maginn wonders "What are they doing? what they should; with volant tongue and chatty cheer, welcoming in, by prattle good, or witty phrase, or comment shrewd, the opening of the gay new year."[3] His perspective accords with the satirical pose of the publication and likewise with the predominant gender codes of 1836. My perspective comes at great distance from these codes, and mine involves desire for knowledge about women's private and professional lives in the nineteenth century. However, Maginn and I are both creating fictions about women at a gathering that probably never occurred, represented in a mass-produced wood-engraving that copies a sketch drawn by Daniel Maclise. According to the essentialist fictions that still dominate literary study in English, there is a truth about these women, but I notice that it must lie somewhere beneath commodities fabricated by artists, engravers, editors, copy editors, publishers, proofreaders, investors, printers, binders, distributors, booksellers, writers, and readers. This truth takes shape behind newspapers, magazines, ephemera, letters, advertising, word-of-mouth, gossip columns, public records, literature, and (for me) over a century and a half of historical documents and scholarly discussion.

As Jerome McGann and others have clearly reminded us, the literature produced by these women was involved in complex relationships in a sometimes complicated commercial apparatus. Although nineteenth-century women writers faced difficult, painful challenges in their personal and professional lives, they participated in this commodification, releasing their work into market politics as did Tennyson and other male authors. Personal lives may be tragic and troubled, literature may reflect experience, and reputation may guide our reading, but words or images on a page do not feel, they are not themselves bourgeois or elitist, and persons other than authors manipulate them in a capitalist environment. As much as I want to hear the conversation in the *Fraser's* image, my imaginary script would only disguise truth, and a scholarly approach to literature deserves better. "*Colour'd Shadows*" seeks to recommend a scholarly approach based on the history of books, and to show in practice ways to unfold multiple meanings of literary work including meanings that the physical form of the work creates, and meanings that arise as the book circulates in material exchanges.

Donald Reiman, Jack Stillinger, Jerome McGann, and others demonstrated how the discipline of textual criticism, intimately involved in projects of scholarly editing, bears upon literary interpretation and understanding.[4] They showed how circumstances of production, distribution, and reception unpredictably and nonself-evidently affect and manufacture sometimes contradictory meanings. Without their revelations, this book would be inconceivable. The establishment of a text, however, is not, in itself, an interpretative goal, as Reiman, Stillinger, and McGann explain; and the relationship between bibliographical analysis and hermeneutics is never simple or resolved definitively. Nor is the problem a new one. Ian Balfour reminds us that J. G. Eichhorn's *Einleitung in das alte Testament* (Introduction to the Old Testament), a founding document of the Higher Criticism, concerns questions of text production and documentary transmission. Balfour notes that "the Higher Criticism has a little as possible to do with exegesis, but the consequences of the findings of Higher Criticism can be far-reaching for any understanding of the Bible."[5] For secular scriptures as well, the disciplinary divergences among production histories, editorial problems, and exegesis are also, as Balfour says, consequential.

A revolution in perspective has been occurring for twenty years, as scholars in the sciences and humanities reevaluate our world in terms of underserved populations, and the trend does not appear to be declining, if one can judge from the Modern Language Association's annual conference program and *International Bibliography.* Unfortunately, I may be doing a disservice to the very subjects I wish to uplift, as Margaret Ezell contends about feminist literary criticism:

> By unconsciously permitting our perceptions of the past to be shaped by unexamined ideologies, perhaps unwittingly carried over from certain privileged texts or theories, we may have infused the values and standards of those texts and theories in our constructions of the past. The result could be that we have unintentionally marginalized or devalued a significant portion of female literary experience.[6]

The chapters in this book show how a common assumption, widespread even among feminist critics, sometimes leads to a neglect of that literary experience: the notion that the feelings described in a poem can be attributed to its writer (e.g., Mary Robinson, or Felicia Hemans) is still widespread, often without interpretative anxiety concerning sincerity, mechanisms of exchange, or other realities of the author's life or the history of the book. We suggest that some scholars simply purchase the package of feelings that consumerism produces. While it may be comforting for feminist scholars to write about victimization, oppression, and misogyny evident in the lives of women writers such as Caroline Norton (and this is certainly a viable element of her oeuvre, as we clearly show in chapters 3 and 4 of the present volume), these writers participated, however unconsciously, in the creation of personae that scholars should recognize, whether the figment is named Sappho, Corinne, Byron, or Shakespeare.[7]

While Hartley Coleridge praises Caroline Norton as "The Byron of our Modern Poetesses," whose work expresses "intense personal passion," he advises her to "break through the narrow circle of personal and domestic feelings and adventure herself upon a theme of greater variety and less morbid interest. There is a great difference between writing always *from* the heart and always *about* the heart, even the heart of a beautiful woman of genius" (382). According to Coleridge, Norton places her feelings in the poetry as if it were an extension of her body, rather than a book that is for sale and which this prominent literary man is reviewing.[8] Another reviewer wishes that Norton would "confine herself to simpler themes, instead of plunging beyond the visible diurnal sphere." Perhaps no woman writer of the nineteenth century had more experience to draw from for themes deserving such comments, but Caroline Norton had a strong interest in a literary career; she did not keep her paper "feelings" locked in her desk drawer to avoid conflicts with her husband. Exploring Caroline Norton's poetry for clues about women's lives is valuable and rewarding. Considering biographical details of her cruel husband and divorce scandal while evaluating her fiction and poetry is critical to understanding the literature. But to ignore Caroline Norton's implicit poetic persona and its commercial marketability is to blindfold ourselves and to misinterpret literary evidence.

As Theodor W. Adorno points out, value (rather than content) governs cultural commodities. Further, Adorno places that principle in a historical frame: "The entire practice of the culture industry transfers the profit motive naked onto cultural forms. Ever since these cultural forms first began to earn a living for their creators as commodities in the market-place they had already possessed something of this quality."[9] In England, massive changes in printing arts and publishing trades took place in the nineteenth century—generally, mechanization, mass production, and popular commodification. These circumstances should affect the ways in which professional literary critics assess the meanings of literary commodities. With important exceptions that we will be mentioning in the chapters that follow, however, literary scholarship and criticism have largely persisted in the distribution of the critical fictions with which the mass-market commodities were endowed with sales appeal in the first place. These fictions include the premise of personal feeling, authorial or readerly: this fiction disguises commodity-production as personal feeling. A related critical fiction is the illusion that literary commodities are themselves thoughts and feelings, rather than manufactured objects.

Given the critical literature emphasizing cultural, political, historical, and bodily themes in professional literary study, in recent decades, this claim deserves some illustration. To survey the development and the character of the nineteenth-century printing industry, and its role in the production of what Guy DeBord calls "The Society of the Spectacle," will help to open a critical vantage on the still-popular fictions that we may call the supplement of personal feeling. In *The Essence of Christianity* (1841), Ludwig Feuerbach writes, "the present age . . . prefers the sign to the thing signified, the copy to the original, representation to reality." DeBord cites this remark in *The Society of the Spectacle*, in which he also says that "wherever representation takes on an independent existence, the spectacle establishes its rule." The use of the word "now" in DeBord's remark that "commodities are now all that there is to see" designates a historical difference between two centuries. He also expresses the shared historical determiner, which he calls "alienated consumption": "money," he says, "has dominated society as the representation of universal equivalence."[10] The foundational fiction of money is this fact that it represents an idea of value in an abstract scheme of equivalence. Reality disappears into the common denominator whose existence is nominal—that is, money. In contrast, the bushels of grain or buckets of milk traded in more primitive economies actually existed in the object-world of use. The weight of their material existence inhibited their flight into others' hands, and (to speed up the expropriation of life called "capitalism") these bulky entities dissolved into the more quickly shifting fiction of paper money, whose crisis of parturition, in the English-speaking world, was the late eighteenth century.

James Gillray's engraving *Midas Transmuting All into Gold Paper* (9 March 1797) memorializes one moment in the devaluation of exchange: owing to the expenses incurred in the war against the revolutionary French, Prime Minister William Pitt suspended gold payments; in Gillray's engraving, the P.M. is shown emitting paper bits orally and excrementitiously, while government place-holders at his side display a statement about the "Prosperous State of British Finances." During and after the war, political writers including William Cobbett, Samuel Taylor Coleridge, and Percy Bysshe Shelley wrote bitterly about the fiction of paper money, calling attention to its tendency to substitute a free-floating and manufactured signifier for the more substantive forms of value that had preceded it.[11]

In England, the consolidation of money as a way of life was the business of the nineteenth century, as its foremost documents of cultural criticism make plain. The deletion of reality was the cultural work of the twentieth century: "The real consumer...becomes a consumer of illusion," DeBord says. "The spectacle is the chief product of present-day society," and "the world is being transformed into commodities."[12] Nineteenth-century book production was central to this transformation of reality into its counterfeit. Book arts are a part of the machinery whereby capitalism transformed lived experience into its artificial spectacle. A book is no less a commodity than a plate or a vase (and all of them are artifacts of print), and they are similarly mass-produced and marketed in the nineteenth century. Even more readily than the plate or the vase, the book disappears into the illusion of its own exchange value. The book as an object in the material world of use vanishes, under the sponsorship of its sales staff, into the artificial idea of its supposedly spiritual, intellectual, or emotional meaning—that is, into its idealist illusion.

Instructive examples are easy to identify. Conventionally enough, in 1510 an anonymous woodcut *Fortuna and Sapientia* in the collection *Liber de Sapiente* depicts a blinded Fortuna holding her wheel and an open-eyed Sapientia beholding herself in a mirror. The engraving represents self-knowledge as the mirror represents the face of Sapientia. The frontispiece of a sale catalog for the Duchess of Portland, printed in 1786, includes "a fanciful representation of the [Portland] vase, engraved by Charles Grignion."[13] This copper-plate engraving includes the label, "Portland Museum," in a banner at the top of the design; beneath it is a pictorial simulation of artifacts for sale. One, a simulation of the Portland Vase, looks at a simulation of itself in a mirror. Obviously, the immediate purpose of the mirror is to show the imagery on the other side of the vase, to advertise it. The vase converts itself to its own two-dimensional replica. In this way, intentionally or unintentionally, the self-interested industry of advertisement provides an example of its own reductive tendencies and its own reliance upon simulation. This reflexivity is increasingly widespread in the nineteenth century: of course *Fortuna and Sapienta* was also for sale, but its pictorial referent (the wheel of Fortune) was not. In the Portland sale catalog, the condition of commerce is all that remains; the imagery can refer to nothing outside the commercial intent. Poetry—for example, L.E.L.'s *Troubadour*, Tennyson's "Palace of Art"— refers to itself, just as the mirror-image of the Portland Vase does, and this self-reference anticipates sales. One could object that the Wedgwood catalog is an advertisement rather than a work of art; but our point is that distinction disappears. This engraving (by Grignion) is now, itself, quite a treasure.

Early in the seventeenth century, Cassiano dal Pozzo commissioned drawings of several ancient objects, including a vase replicating a human head. The drawing is inscribed, "vase which served for ancient sacrifices." Near the turn of the nineteenth century, King George III bought the drawing—not the vase, which may or may not exist, but a drawing of it, which was a conveniently modern simulacrum in the seventeenth century. In the nineteenth century, it is already an antique artifact in its own right, valuable without regard to the lost original. Now, in the twenty-first century, the drawing is the treasure, rather than the record of one. Dawson's splendid *Masterpieces of Wedgewood in the British Museum* includes a photograph of the drawing, "reproduced by gracious permission of Her Majesty the Queen."

Nineteenth-century books frequently use ornaments in reproductions in ways that similarly erase the reference of books to anything outside themselves. For example, *Mrs. Hemans Illustrated*, published by Routledge (n.d., but after 1871), displays a lovely four-color cover, plus gilt, plus two-color stained and stamped leather. Not mentioning poetry or any sort of texts at all, the cover suggests that it is Mrs. Hemans rather than poetry that is illustrated within. This distraction from the poetry in favor of the ornament is more than the ordinary prominence of the package: an opening within the book shows an anonymous engraving illustrating a poem on the facing page, "Evening Prayer at a Girls' School." The engraving depicts eight kneeling girls, tightly herded together, heads bowed and hands clasped. The title of the engraving and poem, and likewise the way the picture represents feminine submission in adoration of patriarchy, express a theme, whether the poet intended it or not. The literary work has a rhetorical design on its real-world customers: it promotes the subjection of women. But the relation of the picture to the poem contradicts the doctrinal content of the book. Not only is the letterpress printed in such small font as to make reading unlikely; it is positioned at ninety-degree odds against the steel-plate engraving. To look at the picture makes it impossible to read the text. And if I ignore the superior interest of the engraving and turn the book around to read the poem in its tiny type, I discover that it is framed in a red box, ornamented at the corners, in a way that graphically contains the poem. That red box was printed before the poetry, and it was printed without regard to what its verbal content might be. The same red box appears around every page in the book, including advertisements at the back, such as one that says "How to Farm Profitably 2 shillings." The red boxes in *Mrs. Hemans Illustrated*, made by a quadrilateral rule, ostensibly imitate the typographical tradition of red-boxed poetic text: for example, nuns ornamented the first edition of George Herbert's *The Temple* in a similar fashion similarly.[14] In *Mrs. Hemans Illustrated*, without anyone's meaning for it to do so, the box becomes something else: it becomes a metaphor for the power of mass-production to contain and to overcome conceptual content, and to treat in the same way prayer and the prospect of profitable farming in the context of two shillings.

Mass reproduction tends to diminish or to delete conceptual content. A familiar icon from Albrecht Dürer's woodcut *Apocalypse* (1498) displays a bearded and enthroned deity who presides atop design after design: he spreads a benevolent hand over the Woman Clothed with the Sun when she confronts the Seven-Headed Dragon; he holds long trumpets over the heavenly war waged by the Four Avenging Angels; he spreads a star-laden arm over John's vision of the seven candlesticks. The icon is familiar in paintings as well: the bearded deity spreads his arms wide over the beatification in Vittore Carpaccio's *The Apotheosis of St. Ursula* (1491); his hands and his arms are alike spread open atop Jacobello Alberegno's tempera *Vision of St. John the Evangelist* (1360–90). William Blake's *Illustrations of the Book of Job* (1826) features this bearded deity, again with his hands open and his arms outstretched atop the design, nowhere more splendidly than the watercolor design, "The Morning Stars Sang Together." The same design is reiterated in a printed advertisement for Quaker Oats, a steel engraving that appears in the program of the 1899 National Women's Congress in Washington, DC. Here the patriarch is the familiar Quaker, of course, and he is positioned atop the page like Blake's Jehovah, and like the deity in the work of Dürer, Carpaccio, Alberegno, and many others, but here his omnipotence promises salvation in the form of relief from "fretful children."[15] Probably without anyone intending it, the meanings of this engraving include its freedom from any meaning whatsoever, free as it is to roam out of churches and into the sale of cereal. It can mean everything only by losing all meaning entirely.

Serious literature illustrates the same flight from meaning, for example, gilt ornaments the cover of *Golden Thoughts on Mother, Home, and Heaven*, a collection of prose and verse that the Reverend Theo. L. Cuyler assembled and published in 1878.[16] This book announces on its title page that it is a collection of copies—replicas, reprints, excerpts that the Reverend Cuyler reproduces out of context and jams into a new one. The apparently humorless Reverend reproduces passages from Byron's *Childe Harold's Pilgrimage* as if they expressed earnestly the pieties of Mother, Home, and Heaven; and of course the book reproduces several poems by Hemans as well. The frontispiece is an engraving entitled "Mother," and in its Victorian context the domestic stereotype is obvious (the print technology called "stereotype," in fact, is a nineteenth-century development). But this design is not a new one: the engraving carries a notice that it is "from a photograph of the original painting The Holy Family painted for the Empress of Russia by L. Kraus." The Holy Family of the painting is not the sanctified nuclear family of nineteenth-century America, in which blessed Mother bestows the blessing of Quaker Oats on her fretful children while Father is too busy undergoing workplace exploitation to be troubled with gilded toys such as this one. The Holy Family of the painting is of course the religious myth of the Blessed Virgin, but the icon loses that reference when it undergoes mechanical reproduction in the reference-free environment of the mass market, where it means something else. In the market, it represents shoppers to themselves, or it presents their idealized image.

In *The System of Objects*, Jean Baudrillard points out that "in order to become an object of consumption, the object must become a sign."[17]

Baudrillard is referring to commodified images in the televisual twentieth century, but the nineteenth century also furnishes examples, in print. A decorative vase, bearing a portrait of John Locke, was manufactured before 1862, in St. Petersburg, as a gift from the Tsar Alexander to the London museum. The vase acquires inutility by bearing the signifier (Locke's portrait), representing its own function in gift-exchange and commemorating the museumizing of England: and the institution of museums is itself a symptom of a spectacle society. Inutility qualifies an object for museum display, unless (as in the found art of Marcel Duchamp) the museum bestows inutility on an otherwise ordinary bicycle wheel or bottle-rack. The vase is not a vase, but a signifier of communication, a document referring not to philosophy but to diplomatic relations.

The gilt decoration and bronze mount also represent a convention. The Hetjens Museum (Düsseldorf) exhibits a circular porcelain plate, decorated after 1821 with an overglazed copy of Angelica Kauffmann's painting *Die Verlassene Ariadne* ("Ariadne Abandoned").[18] Over a brown-red background, the painting on the plate shows Ariadne, with one breast bared; this is a feminine pose soon to be conventionalized by the annual volumes of *The Keepsake*. Ariadne is robed in white and red (also like *The Keepsake*, which was bound in red silk and printed on white vellum). Emblematic ornaments in gilt encircle the plate, whose edge is also (like the edges of *The Keepsake*) gilt. In its painted front and gilt edges, this plate resembles *Mrs. Hemans Illustrated*. Like the gilt-edged vases that were so popular in the Victorian period, it also resembles the first edition of Tennyson's *In Memoriam*. Further, the painted plate resembles those ornamental books in being a copy rather than an original, despite the fact that the pictorial content is painted rather than printed. The decorative designs (trees, landscapes, mythological figures) on Victorian vases were copies too. Each painted vase from the Mintons, for example, represented a specific design number in the company catalog; factory workers used the printed designs to make the vases. The printed copy of the vase in the company catalog is the original, and the hand-painted vase is the copy.

That anomaly is common in nineteenth-century book art and handicrafts. A hand-painted cup, 1820–23, from the Derby firm of Robert Bloor and Co., is a copy of a page in a book of engravings by Tim Robbins, entitled *Human Passions Delineated* (Manchester, n.d. [Ca. 1790]).[19] In comparison with the hand-painted cup, the mechanically printed book is the original. The comical uselessness of both defines their value.

In his enduringly important social history of the nineteenth-century English reading public, Richard D. Altick points out "the emotionalizing of the very idea of literature" that tempered the utilitarian character of the business world that sold literature: "either because of their joy-bringing contents or because of some extrinsic appeal—rarity, physical beauty, the sentimental associations of certain copies—books, as objects, came to have a magical glamour about them."[20] Altick's book goes on to illustrate lengthily and clearly the discrepancy between that sentimental attitude about books and the actual conditions and practices of the trade. From an interpretative point of view, and not only a historical one, that distinction can unfold meanings of texts that were constructed to embellish those objects. The objects and the texts alike are subject to the public-relations of physical beauty and sentimental associations.

A covered vase and matching fruit-cooler made in Worcester by the firm of Flight, Barr & Barr, Ca. 1815, reproduces "scenes illustrating the works of Byron," painted by Thomas Baxter.[21] If these scenes appeared in celluloid or digital videotape, the question would arise whether the pictorial representation is "faithful" to the "original" works by Byron; I do not know whether anyone worries about whether the vase or the fruit-cooler is "faithful" to "the works of Byron." My point, rather, is that the commodity status of the vase, the plate, the fruit-cooler, and the book represents the common denominator of all of those items: universal (monetary) equivalence. This market-based equivalence of things for sale is the economic foundation of the illusions of desire and satisfaction in a world defined as a marketplace— for example, industrialized England in the nineteenth century.

Two teakettles, reproduced photographically by Antoinette Faÿ-Hallé and Barbara Mundt, represent reproductive practices in an instructive way. A kettle made in Nyon, Switzerland early in the nineteenth century displays a painted scene, which is an imitation of an engraving by an artist named Freudenberg. In contrast, an almost exactly contemporary kettle, made in Madrid in 1820, puts an engraving directly under its enamel. Wedgewood pieces had of course done something similar from the beginning. In many (but not all) cases, an artist in the Wedgewood factory would transfer a drawing by another artist in the factory onto a copper plate and thence, in wet ink, to damp paper, which would in turn transfer the imagery (typically a landscape) onto an already-formed plate, vase, bowl, or (aspiring to greater inutility) a plaque.

Again, books repeat the logic of commerce. The four-color cover of *The Poetical Works of William Wordsworth: The Only Cheap Edition* (Moxon: n.d., but after 1876) ornaments a gilded but cheap book, decorated as prettily as a vase. Within the book, an engraving illustrates the scarcely legible Book 8 of *The Prelude*, reproducing a drawing by Henry Dell entitled "A grove there is whose boughs." The stamped, gilded, and four-color cover, and the predominance of the illustration over the text, show the extent to which appearance wins and verbal reference loses in the 1870s poetry trade.

At the fortieth annual exhibition of the American Institute, in 1871, Walt Whitman read his poem, "Song of the Exposition": "You shall watch how the printer sets type, and learn what a composing stick is, / You shall mark in amazement the Hoe press whirling its cylinders, shedding the printed leaves steady and fast." Philip B. Meggs reproduces those lines of Whitman's and (photographically) a poster made by Forst, Averell and Co. in 1870, advertising the Hoe press. Meggs also points out that the machine was capable of chromolithography, and what made that capability important was not the production of works of high culture, but quite the opposite: the Hoe press was a device for reducing art to mass-produced advertisements. A poster for a production of *Macbeth*, made with the Hoe machine by W. J. Morgan and Co. in 1884, displays montage composition in ways that anticipate the formal fragmentations associated with modernism and the derivative art of MTV and broadcast commercials. The Hoe printing machine also made decorative labels for ads, for food and other commodities. A lovely poster (made by the Krebs Lithographing Co. in 1883) advertises the Cincinnati Industrial Exhibition with a design that imitates Pre-Raphaelite imitations of medievalism (a slender but regal character in crown and robes reaches tenderly and generously toward a yellow-haired maiden), while shifting the reference to industry in Ohio.[22]

The logic of industrial reproduction sometimes seems to affect even its most vocal opponents. Of course William Morris's Kelmscott Press linked the making of books to an oppositional social argument: Morris suggested handicraft as an emancipation from the alienated labor of factory workers. None of the Kelmscott Press books was more beautiful than the Kelmscott Chaucer of 1896, with wood engravings facing a beautifully designed and set letterpress. Free of reference to Chaucer, and publicly exhibiting its mobility as a free-floating signifier of nothing in particular, this style crossed the Atlantic and appeared in work by the Roycroft Press, which was not a site of small handicraft but a factory employing 400 persons at a time. The Roycroft Press title-page for *The Essay on Walt Whitman by Robert Louis Stevenson* (1900), designed by Louis Rhead, imitates some visible features of the Kelmscott style, but the Roycroft Press and its wageworkers mechanize it, mass-produce it, and commercialize it in a context alien to Morris and his press. What the imitative technologies produce, then, is work not so much void of any meaning as it is vivid in its single remaining meaning: it reduces objects to signs and commodities; it means reproducibility as such.

These examples make obvious the conclusion that the study of text production is the study of cultural artifacts, and it is inseparable from the study of literature. Scholarly critics are all bibliographers, as described by D. F. McKenzie: "the discipline that studies texts as recorded forms, and the processes of their transmission, including their production and reception." Like McKenzie, we extend the word "text" to mean "all forms of texts, not merely books," and this specification accounts for

> a history of the book and, indeed, of all printed forms including all textual ephemera as a record of cultural change, whether in mass civilization or minority culture. For any history of the book which excluded study of social, economic and political motivations of publishing, the reasons why texts were written and read as they were, why they were rewritten and redesigned, or allowed to die, would degenerate into a feebly degressive book list and never rise to a readable history.[23]

Literary critics charged with the task of exploring such histories will avoid the mistakes of others—including most of the contemporary reviewers of Hemans—who assigned or assumed subjective meanings and therefore personal feelings in the poet's often cagey work. Recent arguments defending the supposedly sentimental writing of British women in the nineteenth century, for example, became necessary only after a backdrop of two or three generations of New Critical selectivity.

This claim that the illusion I call "the supplement of personal feeling" threatens to hamper literary criticism may need some explanation, because for three or four generations, English and American literary studies have self-consciously eschewed the pathetic fallacy, the biographical fallacy, and other forms of interpretation that rest upon an equation of the page with the person. T. S. Eliot's announcement (in 1919) that "honest criticism and sensitive appreciation are directed not upon the poet but the poetry" voiced what became a powerful consensus for much of the twentieth century.[24] I. A. Richards's conception of practical criticism was as influential pedagogically as it was in theoretical discourses, promoting exclusionary rules to protect concentration on the poetic text "itself" rather than its ambient historical and biographical relations.[25] No poetry textbook was more influential in the United States in the twentieth century than *Understanding Poetry* (1938), which conveyed the anti-personalistic "New Criticism" into classrooms at almost every level.[26] From the 1960s onward in the United States, Hegelian and Marxian arguments of György Lukacs and others inspired antithetical forms of "realism" as opposed to the New Critical "formalism," but expressing an equal (though opposite) distrust of the personalistic and biographical fallacies.[27] The increasingly skeptical forms of language-based criticism that proliferated in the 1970s, including Paul de Man's *Allegories of Reading: Figural Language…* (1979), leave even less space for the category of the person of the poet than had *Practical Criticism* or *Understanding Poetry*, and the variety of contextual forms of thought that flourished in the 1980s, when the phrase "New Historicism" arose, tend toward anthropological and sociological forms of thought than individualistic categories of private experience.[28] Feminists from Mary Wollstonecraft to Virginia Woolf and Simone de Beauvoir argued powerfully about the prison of the personalistic reduction when gendered female. The supplement of personal feeling would seem to have been buried in obsolescence long ago.

To sample recent and current literary scholarship, however, is to find that illusion restored to its pre-New Critical sway, even among the languages of social (rather than personal) relations: in *Agnes Grey*, according to Dara Rossman Regaignon in 2001, the "image of the governess's pedagogical function as something which can be separated from her particular judgment and feelings is a premise which the whole of this novel questions"; according to Bruce Boehrer in 2002, in "Lycidas" Milton wants to "mediate between Christian and pagan literary traditions so as to emphasize the discomfort with feminine sexuality." Also in 2002, Ted Underwood writes that "the pleasure Romantic poems take in projecting historical difference onto the inanimate world is related to the pleasure of seeing (or imagining that one sees) a ghost." The personalistic form of rhetoric is not unusual in those examples: "Through personism…O'Hara strategically manufactures an alternative public sphere in which public individuals paradoxically meet as private persons"; "Hopkins uses nature in his poem as a way to justify the ways of God to humanity"; for Hopkins, beauty lies in the tension of opposites"; and "in 'The Leaden Echo and the Golden Echo,' the poet finds...beauty in present everyday objects."[29] In each instance, those sentences depend upon, and take for granted, the premise—associated with Wordsworth's Preface to the second edition of *Lyrical Ballads*—that the poet expresses the poet's own feelings; the meaning of the poem is the personal feeling, plus the pleasing reflection that the poet actually had that feeling. Despite the New Criticism and its more extreme successors in post-structuralist or historical-materialist forms, the everyday rhetoric of English literary study now, as we write this book, is the everyday rhetoric that, in the nineteenth century, trivialized the literary productions of women by treating them as "genuine out-bursts of feeling."[30] The supplement of personal feeling—the expressive fallacy—is the invisible common sense of literary criticism, which, like the emperor's new clothes, or the musical beauty in *The Music Man*, may prove to be locally profitable but need not, for that, exist. The truth-function of scholarly description may be served, in some instances, by study of the production, material form, and distribution of actual works in print. Even if we consider "nothing that is not there,"[31] but consider the printed and human work that produced and distributed it, meanings emerge.

Recovering the writings of many whose work fell outside New Criticism selectivity continues to be a project of the literary profession. As Yopie Prins notes in her study of the Sapphic tradition in nineteenth-century women poets:

> Popular poetesses throughout England and America were identified with a Sapphic persona that seemed to personify poetry written for the "personal" expression of "feminine" sentiment. Despite the publication of sentimental lyric in a nineteenth-century literary marketplace that capitalized on women writers, and despite the popular appeal of their verse to a wide range of readers, it was represented as merely private utterance unmediated by the publicity of print.[32]

Thus, women's poetry declined in critical appreciation and became lost in late-nineteenth-century literary scholarship, which banished sentimentality more generally and failed to separate feeling from text, sentiment from pose, product from work.

"*Colour'd Shadows*" demonstrates a scholarly approach that reads text as a complex web of meaning. As McKenzie reminds us, the word "text" derives

> from the Latin *texere*, "to weave," and therefore refers, not to any specific material as such, but to its woven state, the web or texture of the materials.... it is only by virtue of a metaphoric shift that it applies to language, that the verb "to weave" serves for the verb "to write," that the web of words becomes a text ... In each case, therefore, the primary sense is one which defines a process of material construction. (29)

The weaving of literary history involves "reading" the material book for what it has to say about the literature within.

The work of women writers and the reception of their work furnish sometimes the most valuable examples of the problem that we are seeking to explore, for two reasons: the nineteenth-century (and perhaps ancient) imprisonment of women's characters in a paradigm of unreasoned feelings, and the strange uniformity with which that limited presumption persisted despite the polemics of eighteenth-century and nineteenth-century women writers and despite the self-consciousness of academic feminism in the twentieth and twenty-first centuries.

We also contend that the repetition of old methods and assumptions hamper recent efforts by feminist scholars to reevaluate and justify the large corpus of literature written by women: these are the familiar habits and assumptions that marginalized women during the last one hundred years. We hope that an approach properly distanced from the supplement of personal feeling and acutely focused on material forms will help to ensure that the works we examine retain their permanent powers to question the conventions that repackage them in succeeding generations of readers.

"*Colour'd Shadows*" follows a loosely chronological ordering as it frames discussions of the publication, editing, and distribution phases of textual transmission by chapters concerning textual issues in particular literary texts of nineteenth-century British women writers. Chapter 1 examines bibliographical codes embedded in Mary Robinson's *Sappho and Phaon*, showing how Robinson's revolutionary and feminist politics conflicted with the military and conservative stance of her posthumous publisher, Minerva Press's wealthy founding proprietor William Lane. Minerva Press's advertising and marketing pose produced stereotypes of middle-class femininity and domesticity that opposed Robinson's anti-romantic, anti-domestic stance. The Minerva circulating library lists *Sappho and Phaon* among romantic novels, placing her work in a package that affects the meaning of her text, changing it from a critique of dependent domestic enslavement to a book of romantic sonnets, and associates Robinson's position in the marketplace with writers of romantic novels. Recent scholarship further confuses the meaning of the book by interpreting *Sappho and Phaon* as a delineation of leftover passion supposedly felt by Robinson for the Prince of Wales many years after their breakup, long after she had become an invalid consumed by worries of age and disease. To associate Mary Robinson with feminine weakness and domestic victimization is to defeat her revolutionary and feminist critiques of the literature that promoted such illusions. Mary Robinson provides an early example of a writer in conflict with male publishing entrepreneurs such as William Lane and later *Keepsake* proprietor Charles Heath, both of whom promoted stereotypes of women in books for middle-class women readers. Lane's legacy to literary annuals was the fictions of love that became the staple for *Keepsake* literary and visual texts; however, an examination of textual codes in these books reveal a subversive challenge to the dominating ideology promoted by Lane and Heath, suggesting a feminist perspective alternate to that of Robinson, Mary Hays, and Mary Wollstonecraft.

The dependent, abandoned female grieving for love is a conventional trope that Romantic-era poet Felicia Hemans marketed prolifically and which nineteenth-century readers and critics admired. However, bibliographical evidence suggests that Hemans maintained an ambiguous relationship with this theme. Chapter 2 demonstrates how the dependent-woman ideal promotes and publicizes ideology that damages rather than ennobles women, undercutting feminist attempts (e.g., the polemics of Mary Wollstonecraft and Mary Hays) that had already been made to liberate them from domestic ideology; yet recent scholarship often revives the supplement of personal feeling to identify personal loss in Hemans's *Records of Woman* where there is none and to interpret the poetry in terms of her abandonment by her husband Captain Hemans; we try to show that the notion of loss is central to her poetic persona, rather than an expression of feeling about her abandoned state. The personal reduction ignores the opportunities provided by the ambiguous nature of the Hemans text and denies an alternative and more empowering interpretation. To misperceive personal anxiety in Hemans's work is to ignore the commodity forces that market and replicate illusion, artifice, and unreality, and the repackaging of Hemans in literary annuals and other outlets make those meanings evident. To notice and to interpret Hemans's artifice *as* artifice is to appreciate her poetry for very different and excellent reasons, and not to propagandize servitude.

Although no one knows what Felicia Hemans or the women writers depicted in the January 1836 *Fraser's Magazine* illustration (Figure 3.1) thought or felt, we can collect a textual factbook to evaluate possibilities. The cultural implications of the picture are clear: over half of the women portrayed in this gathering had experienced serious, devastating scandal liberally publicized in periodicals sharing readerships with *Fraser's*. The proud display of such women as celebrated cultural heroes and models for other women professionals in *Fraser's* contradicts firmly defined codes of feminine decency and submissive humility. Chapter 3 describes the scandal that accompanies this visual text and suggests that periodicals participated in the commodification of personae crafted by women writers including L. E. L. and Caroline Norton. This collaborative fiction advertises the hypocrisy of domestic ideology. A short account of writings by L. E. L., Caroline Norton, and Lady Blessington demonstrates the gendered pattern of complaint while revealing the marketing pose of these and other women writers. As our study extends from the individual author's text to the professional producers of text, Chapter 4 explores the experience of women editors of literary annuals. Belabored by deadlines, pursued by debtors, and burdened by expectations of support from family members, these women confronted challenges not experienced by male literary professionals. In addition to meeting the publication demands of each yearly volume, women editors tried to conform to social demands for femininity and proper social behavior, with sometimes disastrous results. Misogynistic authors, proprietors, and publishers devalued and hampered their progress, as competition with each other fired a feverish race to enlist contributors each year. Publishers and editors underpaid, underappreciated, and overworked them; persistence sometimes reaped great rewards, sometimes moral and physical devastation. Women such as L. E. L. paid dearly for public exposure that invited gossip and heavy criticism. Yet women editors of literary annuals provide an early model of authorship and left legacies for later generations who would have fewer, or different, worries about public exposure.

Chapter 5 explores other phases of textual transmission with a study of visual images in *The Keepsake* Literary Annual. *Keepsake* proprietor Charles Heath and his various editors conducted literary business with most writers actively seeking publication during the period, from its debut in 1828 to the last volume in 1857. As mass-produced vehicles for literary and artistic matter focused on middle-class women readers, the *Keepsake* and other annuals exploited female desire for social climbing and romantic fantasy. Its poetry and fiction accompanied elegant steel-plate engravings of paintings by famous artists. Marketed in puff reviews and advertising to potential readers as a safe haven for domestic values, the engraved images countered domestic ideology by suggesting subversive themes and values. The *Keepsake* featured an ostentatious material display, with its brilliant red watered-silk binding, gilt-edged pages, and preference for presumed-elegant steel plate engravings over illustrations produced by faster mechanical image reproduction processes, and thereby found a solid following among its targeted readers as the most popular literary annual of the 1830s and 1840s, when the genre flourished. Thus the *Keepsake* reveals much about nineteenth-century middle-class women's fantasies and suggests that, at least in their intellectual, imaginary world, women had less oppression, prescription, and victimization than some historical accounts suggest. Sarah Stickney Ellis could write books about how young women should behave in an effort to control morality, but the relationship of a reader to a text is out of range; she can visit forbidden moral territory and explore silent fantasies at the turn of a page without ever leaving her chair.

Chapter 6 examines two biblically symbolic longer poems by Elizabeth Barrett Browning and Jean Ingelow that textually encode gender and exegetical politics that create self-reflexive meanings outside the poems. Barrett and Ingelow use biblical and Miltonic symbols as allegory for their historical moment. Barrett's poem *A Drama of Exile* appropriates the biblical tradition to create contemporary meanings implicating anti-patriarchal social and gender issues in 1840s England, and she proposes an alternate Edenic mythology that reverses the patriarchal diminishment of femininity, refusing guilt and making mother-love superior. The poem creates its own hermeneutic theme, displaying the making of its own meanings as something humans do with myths of any kind, whether biblical or otherwise. Jean Ingelow's *The Story of Doom* thematizes the fragmentary nature of the Bible and its ancient beginnings as versions of tales translated and retold. As in Barrett's poem, contemporary meanings collude with biblical stories to create a text partly about exegesis. The disjunctive form of the poem replicates the fragmentary assemblage of scriptures available in the Bible, and quotations within quotations within quotations demonstrate the problems inherent in biblical hermeneutics.

In a layered bibliographical display of paratextual matter similar to documentary apparatus found in Ingelow, Violet Fane's twelve-book verse novel *Denzil Place*, discussed in chapter 7, features complex "wrappers of citation" that encode social, historical, and religious issues, as well as a distinct intertextual Pre-Raphaelitism. Epigraphic verses and narrated viewpoints contribute to varied voices in the poem, providing an interesting display of textual meanings. Typography, language, allusions, imagery, and intertextuality produce a palimpsestic and ornamental narrative quite separate from the fictions within the poem.

Such observations about text and details about text-producers help us understand how literature as commodity integrates human society in a creative drive to communicate ideas and feelings to populations of readers. Yet the process from writer to reader involves a reconstruction of the space between them. Responding to Michel de Certeau's observation that a text can only exist "in combination: the expectation that organizes a readable space (a literality), and one that organizes a procedure necessary for the *actualization* of the work (a reading)," Roger Chartier suggests that

> To reconstruct in its historical dimensions this process of the "actualization" of texts above all requires us to realize that their meaning depends upon the forms through which they are received and appropriated by their readers (or listeners). Readers, in fact, never confront abstract, idealized texts detached from any materiality. They hold in their hands or perceive objects and forms whose structures and modalities govern their reading or hearing, and consequently the possible comprehension of the text read or heard.[33]

"*Colour'd Shadows*" does not claim to theorize or historicize reading. Nor does it attempt to outline the psychology of the imagination. However, we wish to direct attention away from methods of interpretation that do not take these theories into account. Featured in this volume are ways of reading texts that integrate available bibliographic codes rather than impose subjective personal fantasies.

C H A P T E R 1

SCHOLARLY FANTASY AND MATERIAL REALITY IN MARY ROBINSON'S *SAPPHO AND PHAON*

The feminist and anti-amatory sonnet sequence, *Sappho and Phaon* (1796 and 1813), offers an example of ways in which a book reveals important meanings when studied as a physical object. Literary definitions of the "text" or the "work" have not traditionally treated the book-as-object as essentially meaningful: in traditional accounts, the "text" is an arrangement of words that can appear in any physical presentation, and the "work" is an abstract mental entity in the mind of the author. Influential post-structuralist usages are equally abstract: Roland Barthes writes that "the Text is a methodological field";[1] Fredric Jameson writes of "textual structure" that "must be reconstituted, a deep-textual machinery whose characterization ranges from systems of tropes . . . to the narrative apparatus."[2] The physical book that is present is almost always understood as a vehicle for the conveyance of a text, a sign of a mental intention, imaginary object, or field of reproducible signifiers with which customers may play, if they like it, and buy.

In the traditional view, the literary "work" is merely an imaginary entity, lost forever but presumed to have existed once in the mind of the absent author. Recent standards of scholarly editing involve a reverence for this presumed mental entity so profound that scholarly editors were, for most of the twentieth century, actually *expected* to produce a text never produced by the author, combining readings of early and late versions, for example, on the theory that the fabricated text is perhaps closer to what the author intended, mentally (in contrast to the book that actually existed, physically). This logic is worth some thought: the long-ascendant theory and rationale for scholarly editing involve the principle that, for printed works, a text that never existed is a truer rendition of the work than any text that actually exists or existed. Underlying this principle is the belief that the author's invisible, irretrievable mental intention is better and more true than the book that actually existed and exists.[3]

This three-step abstraction, from physical book to lexical text to mental event, deprecates the physical book as mere vehicle. In the traditional view, the book contains "the text," but it is not to be confused with the book; in turn, the text (the words "themselves") conveys the mental or imaginary "work," which is not to be confused with its medium, the "text." More recently developed views of Barthes and Jameson understand the "text" as a reproducible piece of a signifying system; but the system remains abstract in comparison with the physicality of a particular book. If one decides *a priori* that meanings are all mental, by definition, the traditional view looks unproblematic: but this is clearly not the case. For example, the material medium of a gravestone bears meanings, even beyond the lexical "content" of its inscription. Words spelled in neon bear meanings imparted by the neon and not only by the mental content of its "text." The word STOP in a red octangle of metal bears meanings it does not bear elsewhere. These obvious examples of the meaning-bearing properties of physical media, meanings that are additional to the meanings of the lexical "text," might lead one to wonder about the willful attempt to erase consciousness of them, which has characterized much (though not all) of twentieth-century literary studies.[4]

Of course reproducible orders of words do circulate in networks of communicative action, and in a shifting variety of media; the same set of words on a page, on a CRT, and in an answering machine is, in some sense, the same, though not in all senses. It does not follow that the meanings of books are no more than what passes unchanged through the mediation of media. The material form frames and in part constitutes the text, and meanings change with the media. Much is lost in the transubstantiation that is textual reproduction. In terms of textual theory, the received view of "work"—that is, an imaginary event presumed to have existed in an author's mind—somehow remains dominant, yet this view contains little interpretative, philosophical, or practical utility.[5] Disablingly narrow in comparison with the concept of "work" that appears in discourse about other arts whose media are material, including painting and sculpture, the concept of "work" as the absent mental event (in the author's mind) is too far removed from every ordinary understanding of the word "work" in connection with human activities. A book examined as a material artifact often discloses meanings that are not merely ideational, not intensional (in the philosophical sense of "intensional reference").

Accordingly, my argument involves a larger sense of the word "meaning" than the merely mentalistic sense frequently indicated in modern hermeneutics. I want to suggest a method of materialist hermeneutics, a method that is not limited to concepts of authorial intention, and which is sometimes not even implicated in such concepts at all. Dark clouds mean rain. Books, in contrast to clouds, circulate among purposes. Using a material object within a network of social relations, in a system of exchange, complicates meanings beyond authorial conception. The publication of a long-dead author's work on CD-ROM, for example (rather than the World Wide Web) creates a commodity that is possible to sell; the format *means* something about its commercial character. As a product of human work and as an element in particular exchange networks, the book escapes the limits of privacy and mentality alike. Much of the published criticism of Mary Robinson seeks to mask certain meanings by treating the work as private and mental (or emotional), producing illusions rather than awareness, fictions rather than description, and sales rather than scholarship.

At the point of production, the manufacture of a work creates meanings that exceed authorial intention in the pragmatic sense, as well in as the sum of its effects. Sometimes with infinitely greater complexity, reception creates more meanings. A bibliographical analysis of a book as a product of human work often unfolds the social relations of a literary work, including truths of its production, distribution, and use. These latter activities, in contrast to the conventional and mentalistic sense of "hermeneutics," create additional meanings in a literary work.

The beautiful productions of William Morris and the Kelmscott Press and the wonderfully materialized artifacts of William Blake would be obviously relevant examples of ways in which a material book bears meanings beyond its lexical text, but their status as special cases on the margins of the ordinary modes of literary production makes them less illustrative in some ways than works in conventional typography, mass-produced for mass distribution. My first example, therefore, is a book of poetry first published in 1796 by Mary Robinson, entitled *Sappho and Phaon. In a Series of Legitimate Sonnets, with Thoughts on Poetical Subjects, and Anecdotes of the Grecian Poetess.*[6] Robinson was an important and widely known poet in her lifetime. Like Charlotte Smith, Robinson married in her teens—at fourteen according to Judith Pascoe or at fifteen according to her own *Memoirs* or at sixteen according to Ann B. Shteir.[7] Also like Smith, shortly after her marriage she lived in debtors' prison because of her husband's legal troubles. She was then an actress, playing successfully at Drury Lane, where the Prince of Wales saw her playing the part of Perdita in *The Winter's Tale.* Reportedly, the Prince's "importunities" were "unceasing" and "obliged her, with reluctance," to quit the profession of acting, and after a year as his mistress, she apparently insisted upon (and received) a promise of a lifetime annuity from him. She traveled to France, first in 1783 and several times afterward. She developed friendships with William Godwin and Samuel Taylor Coleridge. She and Coleridge wrote several poems to one another, many of which appeared as a sort of poetical correspondence in newspapers. Later, Coleridge contributed a "Tributary Poem" to her three-volume *Poetical Works,* which appeared some years after her death. Though she had published a collection of poems as early as 1775, her reputation as a poet developed in the years of the French Revolution: in 1790 she published "Ainsi Va le Monde," a poem in praise of the French Revolution, written in response to Robert Merry's "Laurel of Liberty" (*Memoirs,* 136); this poem appeared under the pseudonym "Laura Maria." By 1792, Merry was in Paris helping to organize a revolutionary army to invade Britain. Robinson was also in Paris in 1792; she left on 2 September, immediately before the arrest of all remaining British in Paris.[8]

The pseudonymous *A Letter to the Women of England, on the Injustice of Mental Subordination* by "Anne Frances Randall" (1799) appeared later in that same year with Mary Robinson's name.[9] Oddly with the encouragement of Edmund Burke, who was publishing her verse in the *Annual Register*, Robinson's two-volume *Poems* appeared in 1791–92. Its publisher, John Bell, was in 1794 a correspondent with the British Army in war-torn Flanders,[10] where Robinson also spent time: her explanation of her time in Flanders was that she sought relief from pain in the baths there, and she had been chronically ill since 1784, when she had lost the use of her legs (*Memoirs*, 123). However, the baths in Flanders were repellent to her: she called them "receptacles of loatheseome mud, and of reptiles" (*Memoirs*, 129). What she *did* do there is not a matter of record.

Robinson published several novels, two plays, and a fascinating poetry collection entitled *Lyrical Tales* (1800), a politically radical response to the *Lyrical Ballads* of Wordsworth and Coleridge. Robinson's poems often emphasize themes common among the democratic radicals in London in the 1790's: for example, she treats critically the power of custom, prejudice, and economic class to determine and inhibit character, which is of course a central concern in Godwin's *Political Justice* and in Mary Wollstonecraft's *Vindication of the Rights of Men* and *Vindication of the Rights of Woman*. Like Wollstonecraft and Mary Hays, Robinson criticizes the ideological illusions enslaving women of all economic classes and celebrates the outbreak of revolutions in the name of liberty.

Sappho and Phaon appeared in 1796, the year in which Robinson met Godwin. S. Gosnell printed the volume at Robinson's expense, and booksellers Hookham and Carpenter handled its London distribution. The frontispiece is an oval engraving of Sappho "Engraved for Mrs. Robinson's Sonnets from a Marble Bust in the Palace of the Prince Giustiniani at Rome," using both stippling and cross-hatching. The front matter also includes a preface, which is about poetry and politics, and an essay on Sappho, assembled from scholarly accounts. In the preface, Robinson writes about the form and the history of sonnets, especially by way of examples from Milton and from Charlotte Smith, and she politicizes her subject in this way: "It is the interest of the ignorant and powerful, to suppress the effusions of enlightened minds: when only monks could write, and nobles read, authority rose triumphant over right; and the slave, spell-bound in ignorance, hugged his fetter without repining" (14).

Robinson writes critically of the gender-specific reception that poetry received in her cultural time and place, in contrast with other settings: "the liberal education of the Greeks was such, as inspired them with an unprejudiced enthusiasm for the work of genius: and when they paid adoration to Sappho, they idolized the MUSE, and not the WOMAN." In the past, poetry was a "national ornament" and "princes and priests have bowed before the majesty of genius"; now, "the Poet's life is one perpetual scene of warfare: he is assailed by . . . concealed assassins." The language of "warfare" and "assassins" is not entirely metaphorical; Robinson visited the Queen of

France shortly before her execution, praised the democratic revolutionaries in Paris, and escaped from political imprisonment by unknown means at the time of the September Massacres.

Following the preface, the essay on Sappho treats that ancient woman writer as a sign of present possibilities: "I cannot conclude these opinions without paying tribute to the talents of my illustrious country-women; who, unpatronized by courts, and unprotected by the powerful, persevere in the paths of literature, and ennoble themselves by the unperishable lustre of MENTAL PRE-EMINENCE!" She writes of Sappho in ways that accord with what Mary Hays was writing in the same year of another character, the eponymous heroine of *Emma Courtney*: Robinson writes regretfully about an enlightened mind like Sappho's "yielding to the destructive control of ungovernable passions." Wollstonecraft also emphasized the evil and folly of submitting to the domination of sexually specific passion, an emotion or feigned emotion long conventionalized by the artificial and textualized role of the female as the slave of emotion. For Hays, Wollstonecraft, and Robinson alike, an ideological problem of literature is its power to contribute to patterns of domination by supplying conventional scripts of sexually specific characters (reasonable men, emotional women) and conventionally scripted lives (true love, ungovernable passion, and then marriage as the end of life). This issue is the center of Wollstonecraft's critique of Rousseau in *A Vindication of the Rights of Woman*, and it is the polemical theme of Hays's *Emma Courtney*.

Robinson's sonnets in *Sappho and Phaon* amount to a critique, via dramatic monologues and soliloquy, of the conventional script for femininity and its destructive effects on women. The book exhibits the deadly results of these illusions in the story of the destruction of a woman's life. In an antiromantic way characteristic of much "Romantic" period writing, Robinson's last sonnets in this volume condemn "Fancy's fev'rish dream"; the poet's lyre should "disdain love's dread control."

Another edition of *Sappho and Phaon* appeared in 1813. On the verso of the half-title appears the phrase, "Printed by J. Darling, Leadenhall-Street"; the engraved portrait of Sappho appears on the verso of another leaf, as in the 1796 volume; the new imprint changes the title-page from 1796 ("Printed at the/Minerva Press,/For A. K. Newman and Co./Leadenhall-Street./1813") and lists other Mary Robinson works—"*Vancenza; The Widow; Angelina; Walsingham; Hubert de Sevrac; Natural Daughter; The Sicilian Lover*, &c. &c." Apart from *The Sicilian Lover*, which is a five-act tragedy in verse, all of the works listed here are novels by Mary Robinson. In contrast, the title-page of the 1796 volume mentions only her *Poems*. This generic difference in puffery is important. The volume that she published in 1796 represents her as a poet; in the 1813 volume, twelve years after her death, the publisher's list represents her as a novelist: rather than the readership to whom she had displayed her classical learning and her political polemic, in 1796, the publisher's catalog now suggests a readership fond of sentiment and romance.

Another striking detail appears on the last leaf in the volume: "WORKS BY THE SAME AUTHOR" lists eight works and then "In the Press, *Hubert de Sevrac*, a Romance of the Present Century." This looks odd in 1813, because the novel *Hubert de Sevrac* appeared seventeen years before (in 1796). Furthermore, the title-page of this "New Edition" of *Sappho and Phaon* lists *Hubert de Sevrac* among the author's previously published works when the last leaf records it as "In the Press."

The obvious thing to suspect in a case like this is, of course, that the "New Edition" simply reproduces text, including the text of the back matter, from the first edition; and comparing them reveals that is exactly what happened. However, the comparison reveals more: the 1813 edition reproduces every printer's error from 1796 without a single exception. The collation is identical. The pagination is identical. The signatures are identical. The size of the paper is identical. The same double rule appears at the top of each page. The typography is identical, including at least one unusual character, a lower-case e with a relatively high horizontal bar. To understand the "New Edition" it is useful to know more about the printer (J. Darling) and the press (The Minerva Press) and its proprietor (A. K. Newman).

According to Dorothy Blakey, the Minerva Press was "the greatest single manufactory of fiction during the period,[11] but it was not esteemed highly in an intellectual way. Coleridge accused Scott's *Ivanhoe* of translating "the most common incidents of . . . romances" into "Minerva Library sentences."[12] Peacock's "Essay on Fashionable Literature" says that most Minerva Press books are "completely expurgated of all the higher qualities of mind."[13] Charles Lamb called "the common run of [Minerva Press] novels" "those scanty intellectual viands of the whole female reading public."[14]

The founding proprietor of Minerva Press was William Lane, who began a bookselling business in 1770,[15] and in 1773 sold an annual entitled *The Ladies Museum, or Complete Pocket Memorandum Book for the Year 1774*. In 1788 he became the proprietor of a newspaper, *The Star and Evening Advertiser*, the first evening daily in England. Its prospectus proclaims the paper's purpose: "to provide a reliable medium of advertising for their own products"—that is, Lane's publications (Blakey, 11). In 1789, Lane dismissed his newspaper's printer, Peter Stuart, for political reasons; during the controversy over the Regency Bill, the paper declared their wish to remain "palpably in favour of Mr. Pitt and his administration," and accused Stuart of accepting bribery "to support a Faction inimical to the Interest and Prosperity of this country." In a printed protest, Stuart blamed Lane and another publisher, John Murray, for his dismissal, alleging that he had been ordered "to support Mr. PITT through THICK and THIN" (13).

Simultaneously, Lane had a military career: he had been a member of the Honourable Artillery Company since 1767; in 1774 he was first captain of the Red Regiment of Trained Bands; and in 1779 he was Major General of a company. In 1780 he helped to suppress the Gordon Riots, and the city rewarded him with a present of two brass guns. In 1790 Lane began to use the name "Minerva" for his press; he published a description of the new enterprise referring to his "plan of a Literary Museum, or Novel Repository" for the distribution of "Novels, Tales, Romances, Adventures, &c." as well as "works of a general nature." In fact, most books published by Minerva Press were novels. For their distribution, Lane developed a system of circulating libraries, and in 1791 he claimed to make available "near *Six Hundred Thousand Volumes*" (14). In this business he made a large fortune, becoming one of the wealthiest booksellers in England. Clearly, Lane's politics and his militarism are in conflict with the radical feminism and democratic politics of Mary Robinson. Whereas Robinson, in Paris, celebrated the democratic revolution in France, Major General Lane led British troops to shoot the rabble in the streets, in honor of his Majesty. Whereas Robinson's *Letter to the Women of England* and Hays's *Appeal to the Men of Great Britain* articulate vigorous critiques of the ideology of sex whereby women's interests focus chiefly or exclusively on the fictions of love, the Minerva Press was very busy in selling those same fictions. Lane marketed stereotypes of passionate and unintellectual women while Hays, Wollstonecraft, and Robinson were warning British women of the dangers of those stereotypes.

Later chapters of this book discuss similar stereotypes in images of aristocratic women in the literary annuals and gift books designed for middle-class women readers. These genres created new contexts for women writers who owed much to Mary Robinson and other predecessors. Yet, while women writers such as Caroline Norton and L. E. L. practiced more control over the production process as editors, they continued to be hampered by the men who controlled the purse. Thus critiques of domestic ideology present in the annuals come by way of the type of material analysis articulated in this book, rather than in radical feminism as expressed by Robinson, Hays, and Wollstonecraft: the agency of women writers shows itself, in later years in the nineteenth century, less often in thematic or doctrinal content than in activity in the marketplace. Terror from the revolution's last days brought about a drastic change in attitudes in the next generation, and writers such as Felicia Hemans could not afford vigorous radical politics. Within fifteen years of Robinson's 1813 publication of *Sappho and Phaon*, Lane's legacy as a rich promoter of the fictions of love in the Minerva Press far outweighed the immediate political influence of Robinson, Hays, and Wollstonecraft, in spite of their important role as women working the writer's trade.

Blakey writes that "much of Lane's good fortune was probably due to his being on the right side in politics," consistently supporting the Pitt administration during the Regency crisis in 1788 and then again during counter-revolutionary war. His military career continued, too: in 1794, he became first captain of the West London Regiment; he joined together his military and publishing interests when in 1803 he published *The Soldier's Companion*, emphasizing the value of a "knowledge of the use of Arms, at a moment when we are threatened with Invasion" (quoted in Blakey, 20). He published sixty-five editions of this book.

In 1801, Lane made Anthony King Newman a partner in the Minerva Press. In 1809 Lane retired from the business, and he died in 1814. Blakey reports that "Newman, who succeeded [Lane] in 1809, made little change in policy during the next ten years" (26). Those policies involve some interesting business practices: in 1797, J. Fox, Jr., writes that many of the novels were simply rewrites, by anonymous writers in the press's employ, of novels previously written and published by others, and in some cases there was not even rewriting: "all that is original" in the case of some Minerva Press books, according to Fox, is the type and paper only."[16] Blakey adds that it was also common, "though Lane has not been accused of this particular deception, to tamper with the editions of a book," changing the title-page to claim that a book is a "new edition" when in fact it is not (29).

One example of Lane's sharp practice is the 1783 novel, *Female Sensibility; or, the History of Emma Pomfret. A Novel, Founded on Facts.* According to the *Monthly Review* (June 1794), this book "is literally the same with one entitled *Henry and Emma*, and which may be found in a work published by Noble, under the title of *Sketches from Nature*" (quoted in Blakey, 31–32). Blakey suggests that "Lane was not revising an old novel, but issuing remainder sheets purchased from Noble" (32).

Lane did sometimes issue remainder sheets with a new title-page: for example, in 1781 he published *Anticipation, or the Voyage of an American to England, in the Year 1899;* but it had previously appeared in 1769, under the imprint of J. Almon, with the title *Private Letters from an American in England.* In his resale of this book under another name, Lane did not even remove from the last leaf a list of other books " 'printed by J. Almon' " (Blakey, 32).

Lane kept up his political affiliations: in 1792 he published and distributed, free of charge, *Observations in the Particular Case of Captain John Kimber;* Kimber had been accused of murdering an African girl on a slave ship, and Lane wrote in Kimber's defense, accusing the eyewitnesses of perjury. At the time, Wilberforce was presenting a motion for abolition in parliament, and Lane was helping in the effort to sustain the institution of slavery in British dominions.

Meanwhile, the Minerva Press books—again, almost entirely novels, and most of them written by women—were distributed even more widely: for a time, Lane had an American agent in New York. After Lane retired, John Darling became sole proprietor of the Minerva Printing Office in 1813. Blakey says that "the printing practice at the Minerva was modeled on that of John Bell" who was an innovative printer: for example, he was the first to omit entirely the long s, in his collection *The British Theatre.* This is the same John Bell who was a correspondent for the British Army in France during the counter-revolutionary war.

Over a third of the Minerva Press volumes were issued anonymously; many bore pseudonyms (Mrs. Prudentia Homespun, Rosa Matilda, and most frequently "A Lady"). In 1798, Lane published a list of ten "Works of particular and favorite Authors"; all ten favorite authors were women. The political valence of the Minerva Press novels is not always straightforwardly clear: for example, the press published novels praised by *The Anti-Jacobin*

Review, a propaganda tool of the Pitt administration, including Mary Charlton's *Rosella; or, Modern Occurrences* (1799), but it also published Jacobin novels including Robert Bage's *Man as He Is* (1792) and *Hermsprong, or Man as He Is Not* (1796).[17]

Lane distributed periodicals under the arrangements of the Minerva Library, including *The Analytical Review*, a radical periodical that included Wollstonecraft among its writers and whose print run was interrupted in 1798 because Joseph Johnson, its publisher, was in prison for sedition.[18] It was during that year that Lane distributed the periodical.

John Scott engraved a Minerva Library catalog frontispiece, entitled "Genius inspiring literature," after a design by Henry James Richter. Scott's other works include "a series of profile portraits for Angus's *French Revolution*" (Blakey, 91n.). Lane issued this work at the same time that he was performing propaganda services for the Pitt administration and military service during the war against the revolutionary French.

For these reasons, it is surprising to find the Minerva Press issuing a "New Edition" of a book by Mary Robinson, who wrote in favor of the revolutionary French and who dedicated some of her work to a man (Robert Merry) who was in Paris conspiring to invade England. The odd bibliographical features of the 1813 volume are interesting in part because of their bearing on the production and use, including the rhetorical use, of the book. In that way, the meanings of the book are involved in its physical production, its commercial distribution, and its rhetorical use, even after its author's death.

The particular ornament that appears at the end of the preface of Robinson's *Sappho and Phaon* (the book printed by S. Gosnell in 1796) also appears in several other Lane publications: it appears on the title-page of *The New Sylph* (1788), and at the end of the preface of *Valentine* (1790), and at the end of chapter Ten of *The Fugitive of the Forest* (1801). The presence of this ornament, which belonged to S. Gosnell, in several books published by Lane suggests a connection of Gosnell with the Minerva Press. Though the Minerva Press had its own printing operation, Lane and his successor Newman did sometimes hire other printers. Gosnell was evidently among the printers hired but not acknowledged by the Minerva operation. Lane and then Newman acquired (by whatever means) remainder sheets from various printers, and, as I have said, issued them with a new title-page. In the case of the 1813 *Sappho and Phaon* that bears the imprint of the Minerva Press, the phrase "printed by John Darling/Leadenhall-Street" *seems* to refer to the entire book, which is accordingly called "A New Edition" on its title-page; but in fact, all that Darling printed was the title-page. Darling and Newman simply rewrapped existing sheets of printed paper, and sold them with the Minerva imprint. Thereby, they changed the meanings of the book.

For a specified charge, subscribers to the Minerva Press's circulating library received a certain number of books each year. A "General Prospectus" printed in 1798 lists four subscription rates, the highest being £3.30 for which a subscriber received eighteen books per year in town, and twenty-four in the country. Robinson's *Sappho and Phaon*, which is the only book of poems that I have found in the Minerva list, was thus presented among a set of romance novels. The representation of Robinson as a novelist, as added to the front matter by the Minerva Press, artificially exaggerates the continuity of this book with the press's other offerings.

The Minerva Press imprint provided a definition for its readership, in advance, of the sort of book that it was. The other books with which a Minerva Press volume arrived constitute a set: the package of books is a hermeneutic whole, which helps to define the interpretation of its parts. The Minerva Press published conservative political works, including *The Trial of Thomas Paine, for certain false, wicked, scandalous and seditious libels inserted in the second part of "The Rights of Man"* (1792); to publish works by a writer who celebrates Paine's cause seems like an odd choice for this press to make, but I think it becomes intelligible in connection with another set of sociopolitical issues.

The novels and romances the Minerva Press published and sent to its subscribers along with *Sappho and Phaon* represent the forms of sentiment criticized by Robinson, Wollstonecraft, and Hays for promulgating models of dependent (loving) characters that real women internalized, contributing to their enslavement. The sonnets in *Sappho and Phaon* corroborate the arguments of *Vindication of the Rights of Woman* by displaying, in the monologues and soliloquies of its heroine, the self-destruction that emotional submission to "love" entails. Like the preface and Robinson's account of Sappho, the sonnets cumulatively contend that women must set themselves free from the simulations of feminine weakness and feeling, which become the artificial roles in which they are enslaved: Sappho succumbed to the literature and life of sentiment, and Robinson warns readers to learn from her example that such literature and life are deadly. But the Minerva Press manages, in 1813, and probably without conscious intention, to reverse entirely these meanings of Robinson's book.

To consider the other Minerva Press books is to perceive quickly the reversal that Minerva Press achieves. In 1793, Lane published *A Tale for Misses and Their Mammas* by Prudentia Homespun, that is, Jane West, a Tory and a vigorous proponent of state religion who, in 1799, published *A Tale of the Times* representing as a vile seducer a villain who supports the evil cause of the French Revolution. The "humble duties" of women make her constant theme. Also in 1793, Lane published *Woman as She Should Be: . . . A Novel* by Mrs. Parsons, the author of eighteen novels advocating wifely obedience. In 1795, Lane published *A Dictionary of Love: wherein is the description of a perfect beauty;* also in 1795, *A Father's Legacy to His Daughters. By the Late Dr. Gregory. A New Edition.* Gregory's book is the work that Wollstonecraft mentions and condemns in the *Vindication:* "all the writers who have written on the subject of female education and manners, from Rousseau to Dr. Gregory, have contributed to render women more artificial, weak characters, than they would otherwise have been; and consequently, more useless members of society."[19] In 1813, Minerva presented to its readers one of the texts whose contentions about the subordination of women (via the myth of love) Robinson composed her book of sonnets precisely to attack.

Several other Minerva Press titles promulgate the picture of women criticized by Wollstonecraft and Robinson: for example, William Kenrick's *The Whole Duty of Woman* (1796), *The Ladies Miscellany, The Ladies Companion,* and *The Ladies Museum,* all issued annually. In 1809, Lane published *Celia in Search of a Husband,* an anonymous novel whose moral and rhetorical force exactly oppose Robinson's. Likewise, in 1811, the Minerva Press published *The Schoolmistress: A Moral Tale for Young Ladies* by Mrs. Hunter of Norwich. Again, Minerva Press books characteristically represent the artificial image of the subordinated and domestic female. Passion dominates women in the Minerva Press mold, resulting in their domination. The same is true of the didactic volumes and of the romances of feminine passion that arrived boxed with them in subscribers' packages, including Selina Davenport's *Donald Monteith, The Handsomest Man of the Age* (1815). In this context, the sonnets of *Sappho and Phaon,* which in 1796 developed a critique of feminine submission to passion, have become instances for prurient interest in such passion.

The marketing principle that people will purchase emotions that they wish they had forms sentimental and misleadingly personalistic responses to Robinson's work. Such misrepresentations of Robinson's work did not stop in the Regency, or even among the tearful readership of Victorian England, but persist in the present. Even critics who evidently want to make larger claims for the meanings of Robinson's work nonetheless repeat the belittling claims of sentimental and personalistic emotion. Thus, Linda H. Peterson writes in 1994 that "Robinson's sonnet sequence can of course be read as an autobiographical fiction, as a thinly disguised account of her agonies over her loss of the Prince of Wales"; and even the larger claims for the meanings of Robinson's work are personalistic and emotive at the level of the supposedly individual self: "While Robinson's sonnet may be read (and dismissed) biographically as an inflated tribute to the Prince of Wales and the power of her love for him, it is more interesting as evidence of her uneasiness about assuming this alternative feminine myth of authorship."[20]

Robinson's bitter experience with the Prince had occurred sixteen years before the production of *Sappho and Phaon.* In fact, by the time that *Sappho and Phaon* first appeared, Mary Robinson had been a paraplegic for twelve years; she was bed-ridden, tormented by bodily pain, solitary, afflicted with money troubles, and attended in her sick-room by her adult daughter, her first-born child; her second child had died in infancy in the same year in which she was exploited and lied to (in her view) by the Prince Regent. The odds that this aging victim of disease and abuse was writing about "the power of her love for him" are not good.

More extremely than Peterson, Stuart Curran writes (also in 1994) that *Sappho and Phaon is* "a sonnet sequence *a clef* on being deserted by Banastre Tarleton."[21] In her lifetime, politically conservative propagandists frequently attacked Robinson in print, consistently focusing on her supposed love life: engraved caricatures, satires, and forged confessions distracted attention from the intellectual significance of her work by offering cartoonish portrayals of her putatively amorous personal life, including the desertion by

Tarleton. Critics easily repeat these portrayals—even the printing of contradictions within one book, without discussion (the sonnets are about personal love for the Prince; the sonnets are about personal love for Banastre Tarleton). Such reductive representations is impressive, and so is the unargued consensus that, because Mary Robinson wrote the sonnets, they must be about personal passions and not ideas. Even in 1994, critics instruct readers to interpret Robinson's work in the terms of *A Dictionary of Love, Celia in Search of a Husband, and A Tale for Misses and Their Mammas*, rather than, for example, *Letter to the Women of England* or *The Victim of Prejudice* or *Political Justice.*

In *Reservoir Dogs* (written and directed by Quentin Tarantino, 1994), amidst senseless violence, two senselessly violent characters discuss their fondness for imitating the senseless violence of movies starring Lee Marvin. It would be possible to interpret that dialogue and that movie as an example of senseless violence, and it would be possible to interpret it as a satirical counter-example, referring to hosts of earlier movies rather than simply offering a spectacle. This circumstance applies similarly to books: Robert Frost did not say that "good fences make good neighbors"; Robert Browning did not say that "I gave commands;/Then all smiles stopped together." Instead, as everybody knows, satirized characters within these writers' critical fictions say those things. But there seems to be a tacit agreement among commentators that, if a poem is by Mary Robinson rather than Robert Frost or Robert Browning, it will surely be an expression of personal love rather than a representation of a critical idea.

More abstractly, the poetry expresses passion itself, rather than passion for Tarleton or for the Prince in particular, so long as (having been written by Mary Robinson) it is found to like it, want it, feel it, rather than criticize it. Thus, Jerome McGann argues that *Sappho and Phaon* is a celebration of sexual passion and bodily sensation, on the grounds that Sappho seems to be affected by those things at certain moments in the series; McGann suggests that *Sappho and Phaon* expresses an imagined union of feminine feeling with masculine reason: the "desired conjunction" is not only between Sappho and Phaon, but between physical passions and "the exalted power of thought."[22] That argument has the advantage of excluding no one and nothing from the putative meanings of the work, but the invalid Mary Robinson had worked hard to foster the faculties of critical intelligence and to repudiate the commercial and sexist illusions of "love's dread control." It may be helpful to understand McGann's argument as a way of bringing together the polemic of 1796 with the soap opera of 1813, in an ultimately incoherent mix that undermines them both.

Hollywood's version of women poets—for example, *The Barretts of Wimpole Street* (MGM, 1934; remake MGM 1957; remake again BBC 1961)—is now and will continue to be superior, in the court of public opinion, to Elizabeth Barrett Browning's abolitionist polemics, her lifelong commitment to the principles of Wollstonecraft's *Vindication of the Rights of Woman*, and the degradation of her having been sewn into one dress for months on end. However, for the critique or validation of claims concerning the production and meanings of works, whether by Barrett Browning or Mary Robinson, the site, the methods, and the time of manufacture are crucially important; these might be the meanings and the methods and the marketing of Hollywood, in the one instance, or of the Minerva Press, in the other.

CHAPTER 2

IDEOLOGY AND TEXTUALITY IN HEMANS'S
RECORDS OF WOMAN

A memorializer of Felicia Hemans's *Records of Woman* (1828) writes that, "to use her own words, 'there is more of herself to be found' than in any preceding composition.... [The "beautiful legends"] were not things of meditation, but imagined and uttered in the same breath"; the poems in which "her individual feelings are eagerly put forth" include those "wherein aspirations after another world are expressed, or which breathe the weary pining language of home sickness, or in which she utters her abiding sense of the insufficiency of fame to satisfy a woman's heart"; these poems are "genuine out-bursts of feeling."[1] In such descriptions, the recipe for enjoying the poem is to pretend that it is a person and not a printed work deliberately put on the market. Hemans's contemporaries Francis Jeffrey, Lydia Sigourney, and Henry Chorley write of her poetry as if the materials of which it is made were personal feelings, sanctified by patriarchal deity, and as if its destiny were personal feeling in the sensibility of its customer.[2] These nineteenth-century critics express no doubts about the author-function, about texts being made of other texts, or about the materiality of the text in real time and space. One could substitute a supposed personal feeling, which is not really present, for the text, which is present, and enjoy the illusion without doubts about its conventional unreality.

In fact, the generations of which I am speaking evidently preferred that which was absent (the supplement of personal feeling) over that which was manifestly present (the material text). In two of the most instructive examples of literary criticism in the so-called Romantic period—Joanna Baillie's "Introductory Discourse" in the volume entitled *A Series of Plays* (1798) and Wordsworth's preface to the second edition of *Lyrical Ballads* (1800)—the poets appeal to passion with the same concern for audience pleasure that now characterizes movie advertisements:

> What human creature is there, who can behold a being like himself under the
> violent agitation of those passions which all have, in some degree, experienced,

without feeling himself most powerfully excited by the sight? . . . The highest pleasures we receive from poetry, as well as from the real objects which surround us in the world, are derived from the sympathetic interest we all take in
beings like ourselves. . . . Eagerly as it is enjoyed by the rude and the young, to
the polished and the ripe in years [theatrical exhibition] is still the most
interesting amusement.[3]

It [the first volume of *Lyrical Ballads*] was published, as an experiment, which,
I hoped, might be of some use to ascertain, how far, by fitting to metrical
arrangement a selection of the real language of men in a state of vivid sensation, that sort of pleasure and that quantity of pleasure may be imparted, which
a Poet may rationally endeavour to impart. . . . I flattered myself that they
who should be pleased with them would read them with more than common
pleasure . . . a greater number have been pleased than I ventured to hope
I should please.[4]

These writers indicate thus that they are in the business of pleasing customers,
clearly stating that the rhetorical simulation of "passions" will be the means
whereby "pleasure" is to be produced for sale. In her lifetime and immediately afterward, Hemans's promoters (Sigourney, Chorley, and others)
offered the claim that the rhetorical constructions of her works arise directly
from "her individual feelings"; this belief induces "a greater number" to be
"pleased" by vicarious "passions," or so the promoters hoped.

After a few generations, professional commentary on Romantic-period
writing retains figments of personal feeling from these ancestors in criticism,
unwittingly devaluing the literature, as well as inhibiting feminist efforts to
recover women's writing.[5] A more comprehensive intellectual approach is to
embrace the "sentimental" aesthetic expressed in nineteenth-century literature as a viable material product, saleable as the emotional expression of
women's lives. Yet to say that poems are feelings, and to imply that authors
supplement the poems with endemic feelings to the extent that the poems
become biography, limit our ability to evaluate material meanings in a scholarly way that would extend our understanding of the literature, placing us in
a time warp that betrays important feminist criticism of the last twenty years.

To demonstrate an awareness of such temptations with the poetry of
Felicia Hemans, I use materials of two sorts—first, a set of stock textual
resources, and for *Records of Woman* these resources include narrative forms,
the anecdotal contents of Isaac D'Israeli's *Curiosities of Literature*, the
annotations published with Samuel Rogers's *The Pleasures of Memory*, an
anonymous book published in Amsterdam entitled *Fidelity unto Death*, a
French *Vie de Jeanne d'Arc*, and other repositories of reusable anecdotes.
Second, Hemans's resources include very conspicuously the devices of print.
The poetry's destiny was not personal feeling, but manufacture and commerce.[6] Susan Wolfson provides an example of such "consumerist" illusions,
stating that Hemans is "attempting to celebrate the domestic affections as a
universal foundation of bliss," but "she winds up exposing a socially specific
scheme so inwrought with suppression and denial for women as to evoke a
longing for death." Such questions of whether *Records of Woman* defends or

resists the oppression of women foster the illusion that the poem is made of feelings rather than typography.[7] I call this "consumerism" because the illusion is a commercial for the poetry, an advertising stance contrived to enable the customer to feel that the poetry is about her. At two levels— conventional literary materials and the features of the material book—*Records of Woman* is obviously a product, in the sense of manufacture for a market. The two forms of description, best understood together, are bibliographical and rhetorical.

In 1828, the volume's title-page announces *Records of Woman: With Other Poems by Felicia Hemans*, beneath which appears, as a verbal ornament, a pair of epigraphs, one from Wordsworth and one from Schiller (in German). The publisher's imprint reads "Blackwood, Edinburgh: and T. Cadell, London. MDCCCXXVIII." Facing the title-page is a page bearing the printer's signature: "Edinburgh: Printed by John Johnstone." A letter of 31 May 1827 from Hemans to Joanna Baillie (whom she never met) demonstrates the significance of the Edinburgh printing and publication:

> I have another favor to request; it is the permission to dedicate to you, of whose name my whole sex may be proud, a work which I shall probably publish in the course of this present year, and which is to be called "Records of Woman." If you do not object to this, I will promise that the inscription shall be as simple as you could desire. I very much wish to bring out the book in Edinburgh, provided my friends can make desirable arrangements for me with any of the publishers there; but I hope you will allow me to offer you, whether in your own country or mine, this little token of unfeigned respect. (Chorley, *Memorials*, 1: 118–19)

The "friends" who were in fact able to make those "desirable arrangements" for bringing the book out in the profitable Edinburgh market (and arranging its favorable reviews as well) were the agents of the London publisher, T. Cadell: hence the dual imprint. Hemans's letter makes it clear that she dedicates the volume to Baillie out of a concern for the market, and not a concern for Baillie. Nanora Sweet and Julie Melnyk demonstrate such concern by situating Hemans's works not among the domestic affections but rather in a "milieu of intense cultural merchandising," and Isobel Armstrong discusses Hemans's writings in the context of "the commodity culture of the post-Napoleonic period."[8]

Hemans's sister, Harriet Hughes (born Harriet Browne) contributed materially to the posthumous reception of her sister's poetry in her ably written memoir of Felicia Hemans.[9] As usual among accounts of women writers, Harriet Hughes writes in such a way as to promote a thematic match between the stories in the poems and the generic story told of the life. Thus, when Felicia Browne (at age fifteen) met Captain Hemans, "she speedily invest[ed] him . . . with all the attributes of the heroes of her dreams" (1:13). Harriet Hughes calls her sister's adolescent love an "illusion," and observes that their marriage was "little in accordance with the dictates of worldly prudence" (24). In a life of "uninterrupted domestic privacy" (26), Hemans, according to her sister, "created for herself a world of high-souled men and women, whose love had no outward glitter, . . . [men and women] to bear uncomplaining agonies—and, above all, to wait long, long days for the deceiver who will not return . . . and, at last to dedicate a broken heart to him who has crushed it" (28–29). This personal account in several of the narrative poems in *Records of Woman*, including "Properzia Rossi," whose eponymous heroine does wait through long days for the deceiver who does not return, and who, further, dedicates her heart and art to him who crushed the heart and trivialized the art. It is a conventional *topos* in discussion of *Records of Woman* to interpret her poems in terms of Hemans's forlorn life after her abandonment by her husband Captain Hemans. In an introduction to *Records of Woman*, Paula R. Feldman writes, "the loss of her marriage remained an intensely humiliating experience for the poet," an experience of which she "spoke" in her "imaginative work."[10]

However, according to Harriet Hughes, Felicia Hemans's poetry repeated the sad generic tale of the broken-hearted woman for several years before Captain Hemans left her; Harriet Hughes indicates that adolescent illusions about devoted and romantic love characterized her sister's imagination when she was fifteen years old, before her marriage. The masochistic tale of the grieving, abandoned, but still male-identified and dependent woman is a modular component in a machine, detachable and reusable in one work after another, in narrative poems, memoirs, gift books, magazines, and book publications. The memoirist as well as the poet understood the sales appeal of this anecdote and its heroine. Hughes writes that Hemans avoided any publicizing of her personal life, and so the memoirist confines herself to a rhetorical dwelling upon the narrative module of the broken heart—"that inward grief which pervaded and darkened her whole existence" (1). Thus the memoir thematically and tonally adjusts to the fictions of the forlorn devotion of the supposedly softer sex. The narrative module of the broken heart is itself publicity for the ideology whereby women are the softer sex, a politically potent falsehood all too powerful over real lives.

The 1828 volume *Records of Woman* includes nineteen poems in the series entitled *Records of Woman* and thirty-eight miscellaneous poems including the famous and infamous "Homes of England," discussed recently and in complicated ways by Jerome McGann and others because of militaristic patriotism expressed in the poem and its ally, domestic ideology for womanhood.[11] In the series of nineteen poems entitled *Records of Woman*, even before the module of the broken heart appears, some typographical facts confront the eye in a way that reveals much about the artifice (and artificiality) of the project. The reusable feature of the narrative components is not merely a thematic matter, but also a matter of bibliographical fact. Feldman points out that "at least forty-four of the fifty-seven poems were published by Hemans previous to their inclusion in *Records of Woman*" (xxxii). Hemans's own writing often states the same fact: the last line on p. 154 of the first edition, at the end of "The Queen of Prussia's Tomb," reads "originally published in the Monthly Magazine." On the facing page, before "The Memorial Pillar" and on a page of its own, in fine print, appears a fairly explicit indication that the supplements relevant to this book are textual and not personal feelings supposedly existing outside the language and the narrative: "on the road-side between Penrith and Appleby, stands a small pillar, with this inscription,— 'This pillar was erected in the year 1656, by Ann, Countess Dowager of Pembroke, for a memorial of her last parting, in this place, with her good and pious mother, Margaret, Countess Dowager of Cumberland, on the 2d April 1616'—See Notes to the '*Pleasures of Memory.*'" Of course *The Pleasures of Memory* is a precursor poem by Samuel Rogers, which, on the next page, Hemans quotes verbatim at the beginning of her poem "The Memorial Pillar." The text is about Rogers's text, which includes the text of a note referring to the text of an inscription, and all of these texts are the supplements that constitute the meaning of this new (1828) text inscribed to them.

Like the citational character and marketing of Hemans's poems, attention to their first public venues contributes to our understanding these poems as products. Hemans often published in the highly profitable literary annuals and gift books, sets of decorated commodities compiled and sold as a commercial venture so successful financially that it became the predominant venue of poetry in the "Romantic" period. Elsewhere we have tried to show how L. E. L. worked within this culture of mass-marketing by cultivating a poetics of double-talk, producing poems that dissimulate saleable sentiment on their engraved faces while, subtextually, registering bitterness, cynicism, and a critique of their own alienated *modus operandi*. In contrast, Hemans, who sold ninety-five separate poems to literary annuals, complies more totally with the conventional view of women in these publications.

Stuart Curran asserts that Hemans's poems generally present "other and darker strains in their voluminous production—a focus on exile and failure, a celebration of female genius frustrated, a haunting omnipresence of death—that seem to subvert the role they claimed";[12] but (in contrast to poems by L. E. L.) her poems in the annuals do not criticize but rather replicate the forms of sexual domination, propaganda, and exploitative simulation, in a straightforward manner.

In a strategy that was to persist throughout the nineteenth century, Hemans's poems in the annuals exploit their own secondariness: the poem can be secondary in relation to the corresponding engraving. Further, this secondariness of the poem makes imaginary women (characters) into metonyms of the (decorated) commodity.[13] The putative loveliness of the picture-plus-poem transfers to the putative loveliness of the woman character, and ultimately the woman poet. Aestheticized objectification detaches the woman from the world of action outside texts and outside her own subjectivity; she becomes the prisoner of her own supposed feeling-states, in the uncritical and even autistic condition designed for the customers of, for example, *The Literary Souvenir*.

Two poems that Hemans contributed to the *Literary Souvenir* for 1827 illustrate both this strategy of objectifying woman-as-ornament and the ideological content that, with or without Hemans's cognizance, it promulgates. Objectification reduces the woman to a figurine and then detaches her from the world to desire no more than her own incarceration in prefabricated feeling-states. In "A Spanish Lady. From a Picture by G. S. Newton," Hemans wrote the unheroic couplets to face an engraving by J. H. Robinson after a painting by G. S. Newton. Implicating further fragmentation, print sellers marketed the engravings without Hemans's poem, according to annuals editor Alaric Alfred Watts: "There was . . . a considerable sale of the engravings, published separately, without the letterpress, in portfolios."[14] The poem, which is also fragmentary, objectifies the "lady" and celebrates its own derivative character:

> She touched the silver strings, while her dark eye
> Grew to more perfect beauty, when the sigh
> Past from the chords, sweet as it loved the hand
> Ruling their music with such soft command.
> At first the notes were tremulous, like the break
> Of rising colour on her delicate cheek,
> And varying, till at last their timid tone
> Fixed on an ancient air; such ones are known
> To the dove's nest, or to the olive wood,
> Where hath the nightingale her solitude.
> Her song found words—it was like "the sweet south,"
> Breathing in odours from her rosebud mouth.
> And sang so touchingly that it betrayed
> Those sad deep thoughts which haunt a youthful heart
> By nature mournful.[15]

In the same volume, Hemans's "Corinna at the Capitol" versifies an already-popular moment from Madame de Staël's *Corinne* (1807),[16] the crowning of Corinne with laurels in Rome; but Hemans's poem does so only to repudiate even that much (poetic, ornamental) engagement in the public world: the honoring of Corinna's art looks first like a "day of glory" (I), and "Well may Woman's heart beat high" (III); but the triumphal music "dies" (IV) and Corinna cannot be "happy":

> Happier, happier far, than thou
> With the laurel on thy brow,
> She that makes the humblest heart
> Lovely but to one on earth! (stanza VI)

Like "A Spanish Lady," this poem manifests the unreality of its content in part by showcasing its derivative status. The title refers directly to de Stael's *Corinne*, the epigraph is a sentence from de Staël, and even in its verbal details the poem stitches together prefabricated materials (e.g., "Happier, happier far," alluding to Keats's famous phrase in the "Ode on a Grecian Urn"). Similarly, "A Spanish Lady" is less a poem than an advertisement of an engraving by J. H. Robinson of a painting by G. S. Newton, and the ideological force of both, like the ideological force of all of *Records of Woman*, is apparently not a matter of consciously critical thinking, but a two-step routine that (1) markets a gendered imprisonment in putative feeling-states, and (2) does so via the replication of tropes of replication. The poetic and rhetorical mission of such poetry is not to raise consciousness about figural and rhetorical forms, and their inherited power, but rather to extinguish critical consciousness altogether.

One of the poems in the 1828 *Records of Woman*, "Madeline: A Domestic Tale," also appeared in *The Literary Souvenir for 1828*, and, furthermore, in a note printed in *Records of Woman*, Hemans actually announces that it appears in the other venue as well. Her note to that effect does not mask, but actually advertises, the poem's utility as a multipurpose module. In that book, "Madeline" begins with an epigraph from Joanna Baillie's play, *Rayner: A Tragedy*. Like so many of Hemans's poems, this passage insists upon and even celebrates the enclosure of womanhood within homebound suffering and the cheerful acceptance of the twofold incarceration: architectural enclosure at home, and emotional imprisonment in one's own feeling-state:

> Who should it be?—Where shouldst thou look for kindness?
> When we are sick where can we turn for succour,
> When we are wretched where can we complain;
> And when the world looks cold and surly on us,
> Where can we go to meet a warmer eye
> With such sure confidence as to a mother? (*Records of Woman*, 144)

After the epigraph, Hemans's poem begins with a speech of an unnamed mother: "My child, my child, thou leav'st me!" In the first line, then, the mother conservatively resists a woman's escape from either the house or from the prescribed, domestic feeling-state. She imagines her adult daughter, now a bride: "along the moonlight sea, / With a soft sadness haply in thy glance . . . . sorrow not / For me, sweet daughter! in my lonely lot." This speech reduces the bride to weeping, and emblematically a "caged bird" sings "thro' the trellis'd rose-leaves." She leaves, thus mournfully, for America—"the youthful world / That glows along the West." Soon "tears" blot out whatever "bliss" might have been promised in the youthful land, and she is "widow'd in her marriage-morn." She turns "In weariness from life"; she is "heartsick." The resolution of the poem's narrative is a retreat into the dual enclosures of home and emotion from which she ventured when tempted by the gleaming reaches of the world; she cries to her mother, "Take back thy wanderer from this fatal shore, / Peace shall be ours beneath our vines once more" (144).

Clearly, "Madeline" repeats Hemans's most characteristic theme—the external world is a bad place, in contrast to the enclosures of house and of the autosphere of one's own emotions. Signifiers of its own unreality doubly frame the poem, including the epigraph from Baillie's play, and the note calling attention to the prior museumization of the poem in the ornamental *Literary Souvenir*. Another poem in the series, "Juana," is even more explicit in its repetition of Hemans's equally characteristic treatment of the topic of illusions. An unattributed headnote summarizes the story of "Juana, mother of the Emperor Charles V," of Spain. In spite of abusive treatment from her husband, "Philip the Handsome of Austria," Juana dons "a magnificent dress" and becomes "possessed with the idea that [his corpse] would revive" (123). Susan Wolfson points out that the historical "Juana la Loca" (Juana the Mad) "remained a virtual prisoner for the rest of her life."[17]

The poem's organizing principle, however, is not the dangers associated with madness, but the representation of reality as ugliness in contrast to beautiful dreams. An equally unattributed epigraph follows, whose theme is repudiation of the external or actual world in favor of Hemans's customary favorite, imprisonment within an interior feeling-state:

> It is but dust thou look'st upon. This love,
> This wild and passionate idolatry,
> What doth it in the shadow of the grave?
> Gather it back within thy lonely heart,
> So must it ever end: too much we give
> Unto the things that perish.

In the poem's loudly rhymed couplets, Juana is "the dreamer"; she accepts her husband's negative assessment of her ("I know thou hast not lov'd me yet; I am not fair like thee"), and consoles herself with the characteristic consolation of emotional confinement: "I have but a woman's heart." She articulates a fantasy: "In thy kind eyes this deep, deep love, shall give me loveliness . . . . my heart within me burns." This emotion-driven delusion contrasts with the ugliness of what the poem offers as actuality: "In the still chambers of the dust" Juana voices "The passion of that loving dream," until "the shadows of the grave had swept o'er every grace." Again, in the form of Hemans's customary binary opposition, the poem becomes a commercial for the beauties of illusion, set off by the sordid ugliness of its representation of actuality. The "fearful truth" is the bearing away of the dead and the leaving of "a woman's broken heart . . . in its lone despair behind." Lovelier by far the "festal halls" and the nonexistent "music of thy voice."

In Byron's "The Prisoner of Chillon" and, twenty years earlier, Coleridge's "The Dungeon," the incarceration motif involved a different sort of development, a trope of resistance and reform, and not an advertisement for the consolations of surrender. But in "Juana" as in "Arabella Stuart," Hemans develops the imprisonment theme with impressive consistency, in a Burkean retreat toward a celebration of chains. Women writers with political commitments ridiculed this trope of chains and the supposedly female preference for such chains as opposed to ugly realities. For example, Charlotte Smith wrote in 1793 of "degenerate triflers" who, "while they love / The glitter of the chains, forget their weight."[18] In contrast, Hemans's poems characteristically recommend (and express) desire for illusion. One form of the preferred illusion is psychological (fondness for illusion of the heart), and another is the artifice itself.

The headnote to the first poem in *Records of Woman*, "Arabella Stuart," is two pages of very fine print. Two verse epigraphs ornamentally precede the poem, quotations from Byron and from Pindemonte (in Italian). The typography of the poem exploits resources other than language. The last line in the separately numbered section five consists not of words but rather of a row of asterisks marking an ellipsis, though nothing is in fact omitted. The poem's fiction purports to be the manuscript fragments of Arabella, written in a grief-stricken but lovingly loyal incarceration. In the second poem, "The Bride of the Greek Isle," an asterisk keys the title to a footnote on the same page (21), referring to Hemans's source for this particular narrative module—D'Israeli's *Curiosities of Literature*. A verse epigraph (from Byron's *Sardanapalus*) precedes the poem.

A relevant feature complicates interpretation for all poems in the volume. Intentionally or otherwise, the poems make their artifice and unreality into a theme. Even while the narrative content of *Arabella Stuart* involves the emotions of its woman protagonist in a way that cultivates the sentimental aesthetic that critics such as Chorley praised and readers purchased, Hemans encases that narrative within a scaffolding of pre-narrative apparatus so conspicuous that it *prevents* suspension of disbelief, and another canyon of distance interposes between the fiction and its claim on even momentary credence: the poem begins, "Twas but a dream."

It is not my claim that Hemans emphasized the fictitiousness of her script for the purpose of causing her readers to feel distance from the retailed hearsay and the legendary materials. I have no contention to offer about whether Hemans felt as her fictitious heroine says she feels, and I make no claim about whether Hemans wanted (for whatever reason) to stimulate such emotions in the reading public. I do not say that Hemans intentionally makes visible the artificial textuality of the poem and its narrative, but I observe that the typographical fact of the headnote does reveal the artificial character of the work, and so does its referential meaning, making conspicuous the fabricated (rather than emotional) reality of the text and the work which is now (in 1828) for sale.

Similarly, in feminist terms to point out the poem's "enemy within"—its evident recommendation that women internalize the conditions of their own oppression—is not necessarily to assert anything about Hemans's conscious intention.[19] Rather, the poem manifestly *is* an ideological enemy within those very readers who most totally internalize its doctrines. What the woman in the poem desires, and what the poem offers as the focus of her being, is her subordination as prescribed by the mythic logic of true-love and nineteenth-century domesticity. The dream to which the first line refers iconizes the binary of thanatos and eros when, in Arabella's dream, Seymour, hunting a fawn, flings his spear away and retires with the dreamer. Later in the poem, Arabella represents herself as a stricken deer. The male/female binary clearly overlays the strong/weak binary, and a feminized illusion of the pleasure-principle (the dreamed retreat of the lovers) contrasts with the reality-principle and its constraints in the world of male machination and power. Arabella wakens from the dream, a captive. Her woman-spirit is said to furnish a lift from the earth (reality, bad) to heaven (dreamed, good).

The loveliness of illusion, already feminized in opposition to the masculine disagreeables of the actual earth, is reformulated as a love of the internal (subjective) as a resort from the offensively external world. In a way that used to be considered "Romantic," the real yields to the imaginary, and material externalities bow to the psychological interior. In this frame of mind, dying on thy breast (in the fourth verse paragraph) would be rich—the actual world is a bad place, but its compensatory opposite is the desire to *leave* the earth for the pleasure of dreams or an afterlife of bliss. There is no possible doubt that Arabella writes that *she* feels that way, though I see no warrant for ascribing these doctrines to Hemans.

Whether or not it feels like a doctrine to a subject under its sway, the notion that dreams are preferable to facts is doctrinal; Arabella professes it. The belief that the personal feeling (inwardly treasured true-love) is good, whereas political activity is disagreeable and bad, is also a doctrine; and Arabella professes it, too. In paragraph nine, Arabella represents bliss as a retreat from the reality of politics to a personalistic inwardness. In the same paragraph, she says that in contrast to dreams the actual earth is pitiless and cold. In the poem's concluding paragraph, the personal is *not* the political, but its binary opposite. A generation earlier, Mary Wollstonecraft and Mary Hays pointed out that removal of "woman's heart" from politics is itself a disempowering political doctrine. As Arabella dies, forlorn, suspicious that her beloved man traitorously chose the world in favor of her inwardness, it is not clear whether Hemans's poem promotes the ideology of disempowerment or whether it makes visible that doctrine's lethal effects. To attribute Arabella's incarceration in that ideological illusion of retreat to Hemans is no more warranted than to attribute to the poet Arabella's incarceration in the stone dungeon where (legend has it) Arabella writes. But in that writing and in its typographical simulation, another sort of verity emerges: scriptorial activity itself.

As mentioned, a row of asterisks simulates fragmentariness between paragraphs five and six, typographically replicating the supposed fragments of the inscribed sheets left in dead Arabella's cell. Obviously, this device of the typographically feigned fragment is not new or unique to Hemans's poem. Hays used it in *The Victim of Prejudice* in a similar but self-consciously critical way, but her heroine's narrative of her own death in prison is a critique of sexual injustice and class inequality, interrupted by a row of asterisks representing the truncation of her prison notebooks.[20]

The implications of this typographically symbolized illusion of omission in Hemans's poem is worth serious consideration: it marks the material truth of the ink-printed page, naked of its supposed referential relations. The ultimate opacity of the scriptorial evidence is the surviving verity of the text. The material word is the only actual presence of the poem, or of Hays's novel, however ardently readerly desire might wish to invest it with the palpability of heart, breath, and feeling, as Arabella does with the message from Seymour in paragraph four. Intentionally or otherwise, Hemans's poem represents and thus *means* these facts about its own material mode of existence, and it designates the distance between it and the putative reality of feeling.[21]

Just as they do for "Arabella Stuart," "Madeline," and Juana," headnotes precede most of the poems in *Records of Woman*. Each appears on its own page and cites its own sources. Hemans gives notes to key lines with asterisks that appear on the same page as the verse lines. Apart from these, Hemans gives additional numbered notes indicated by key superscript numerals to verse lines appearing on separate pages at the end of the series but before the portion of the volume subtitled "Miscellaneous Pieces." If we count only these four forms of paratextual matter by Hemans, already the poetry cloaks itself with headnotes, epigraphs, same-page notes to the verse, and end-of-the-series notes on their own pages. This evidence (which is as visible and present on the page as the poetry) identifies the poems' meanings precisely as textual supplements, and not fictitiously personal feelings. These textual supplements constitute the only extensional referent to which the poetry pretends.

On the unnumbered page 45 of the volume, opposite an entirely blank leaf, the title "Properzia Rossi" appears above a paragraph, written by Hemans, about that historical person:

> Properzia Rossi, a celebrated female sculptor of Bologna, possessed also of talents for poetry and music, died in consequence of an unrequited attachment—
> A painting by Ducis, represents her showing her last work a bas-relievo of Ariadne, to a Roman Knight, the object of her affection, who regards it with indifference.

Hemans does not identify her source, but according to legend Properzia de' Rossi (1490–1530) suffered an unrequited love for Anton Malvasia who reported in a court of law that he was not having a love affair with her.[22] When her work as sculptor could no longer support her, she gave it up, and became an engraver instead, and she died poor. Hemans very clearly imports in the headnote to her poem the narrative module of unrequited love, harmoniously with several other poems in the sequence and harmoniously, too, with what her sister said was a distinctly literary preoccupation *before* Captain Hemans abandoned the poet.

The printed appearance of the anecdote as headnote frames Hemans's poem as an artificial production, encasing it in a museum of words. What the poem then represents is a scene from a painting of Properzia Rossi by Louis Ducis, who also painted fictitious episodes about other poets including Tasso. In the painting, a Roman knight displays indifference to the broken-hearted (but supposedly true-hearted) woman artist, who supposedly dies after hearing his indifference to her last work in bas-relief, which represents the mythological figure Ariadne, abandoned by Theseus, thus achieving *her* broken heart. This is fiction, of course, despite the pseudo-historical headnote: according to Vasari, Properzia Rossi had given up bas-relief and worked at engraving on copper for some time before her death. Let's make a map of this hall of mirrors: a fiction posing as fact introduces a poem about a painting of a sculpture about a myth. To put a supplement of personal feeling at the end of that long and entirely artificial chain is to remove it from credibility. In just this way, "Properzia Rossi" is characteristic of Hemans's poetry in *Records of Woman*.

Paula R. Feldman and Susan Wolfson independently express perhaps the most currently influential and important perspective of "Properzia Rossi," the view of anxiety about professional reputation, or "fame." Summarizing Vasari's account of Properzia Rossi, Wolfson writes, "although she had some professional success, she had difficulties with her commissions.... The lovelorn female artist unfulfilled by her fame is a recurring figure in Felicia Hemans's poetry of the 1820s and 1830s."[23] Similarly, Feldman focuses on the anxiety of professional reputation: "In the depths of her despair, Rossi describes fame as 'worthless,' a statement some see as evidence that Hemans believed women should not pursue fame." Feldman repudiates that view, writing that "Hemans was a highly ambitious artist who worked tirelessly to build her reputation."[24] Feldman offers an account of professional anxiety as it is said to afflict Properzia Rossi (the figment in Hemans's poem) and similarly Hemans herself. The implication is a sort of psychological projection, whereby a woman who is anxious about her professional stature (e.g., Hemans) attributes that anxiety to a historically removed woman (Properzia Rossi) whom she represents.

Like Wolfson's observation about Hemans's character being "unfulfilled by her fame," this interpretation emphasizes the struggle for success in one marketplace or another, and distress attendant upon such struggle, whether she achieves fame or not. Another issue, however, seems to me both central to the poem and common among the poems in the volume. Strictly speaking, the poem is not about professional success or failure, but about a statue (artifact) of Ariadne (fiction) according to a painting (by Ducis). However, as the painting was located in Paris, Hemans did not see the painting that she describes; perhaps she saw a reproduction or imitation, so that her subject matter is already at four layers of removal before the poem even begins, becoming exponentially artificial, despite the rhetoric of genuine personal feeling that promoted her poetry in her lifetime.

Further, the poem's first line refers directly to the unreality of its putative passion: "One dream of passion and of beauty more!" Spoken by Properzia about the bas-relief she is making which she intends to be her last, the line is also an exclamation about the poem, "Properzia Rossi," itself, or perhaps "Arabella Stuart," or "Madeline," or "Juana"—one more artifact simulating passion and beauty. That reading, however, seems to me unsatisfactory, because the poem does not simulate passion so much as it takes such simulation for its subject matter. That is, one might read the poem as an expression of passion, of "unrequited attachment." Alternatively, one might read it as a piece of writing about the manufacture of passion as a commodity.

The impressive recycling of Hemans's poems from annuals and periodicals (principally the *New Monthly Magazine*) signals their commercial circulation and Hemans's action as an agent of commodity exchange. The following list records the republications in *Records of Woman*, though the vastly more numerous later reprintings of Hemans's poems has not been (and perhaps cannot be) tabulated:

"The Bride of the Greek Isle," *New Monthly Magazine*, 14 (October 1825).
("The Bride of the Greek Isle" is set in Scio, and Hemans's previously published "The Voice of Scio" in the *New Monthly Magazine* 7(1823), and after "The Bride of the Greek Isle" with its "Maids of bright Scio" she published "The Sisters of Scio" in the *Literary Souvenir* for 1830.)
"The Switzer's Wife," *New Monthly Magazine*, 16 (January 1826).
"Gertrude, or Fidelity Till Death," *New Monthly Magazine*, 16 (May 1826).
"The Indian City," *New Monthly Magazine*, 14 (December 1825).
"The Peasant Girl of the Rhone," *Literary Souvenir* for 1826.
"Joan of Arc, in Rheims," *New Monthly Magazine*, 17 (October 1826).
"Pauline," *New Monthly Magazine*, 19 (February 1827).
"Juana" (under the title "Joanna"), *New Monthly Magazine*, 20 (October 1827).
"The American Forest Girl," *New Monthly Magazine* 16 (April 1826).
"Costanza," *New Monthly Magazine* 14 (August 1825).
"Madeline, A Domestic Tale," the *Literary Souvenir* for 1828.
"The Queen of Prussia's Tomb," *New Monthly Magazine* 16 (December 1826).
"The Memorial Pillar," *New Monthly Magazine* 19 (June 1827).

Hemans's recycling of materials within the poems is evident at many levels. The first line of "Properzia Rossi" reads "One dream of passion and of beauty more!" and in the fifth line Hemans writes "Yes one more dream!" The recapitulation is not merely verbal: each of those lines is about replicating antecedent illusions; the second of them replicates the first's replication. Hemans's headnote represents the poem as a recapitulation of an antecedent legend about a replication by a painter of a statue imitating Ariadne.

I emphasize that I am not finding fault with this poetic practice, but pointing out its rhetorical and material forms to clarify and expand our understanding of Hemans's artistic texture. Internally, the poems in *Records of Woman* insist upon the trope of artificial replication (not personal feeling). Externally, via contracts with the editors of periodicals and annuals and the proprietors of the book publisher, and via the rapidly accelerating technologies of commercial printing, the poems replicate themselves in reprintings in other venues (more precisely, by Hemans and the men of business), as numerously as they replicate their signifiers within.

In their rhetorical forms, the poems are not only occasions for the anaphoric longing for "one more dream!"; they repeat and reframe Hemans's favorite two tropes: the bad-world / good-inwardness trope, and the trope of dual incarceration in home and in the inner feeling-state. This repetition and recycling within the poems, in their rhetorical form, repeats the repetition and resale *of* the poems, in their material forms and in their movements in the markets of exchange. The poems' commodity-lives are homologous with their internalized figments. The wholesale and retail facts of the matter outside the figments unfold the meanings of these figments.

C H A P T E R   3

S C A N D A L   A S   C O M M O D I T Y   A N D   T H E
" C A L U M N I A T E D   W O M A N "

The January 1836 monthly issue of *Fraser's Magazine for Town and Country* features an illustration titled "Regina's Maids of Honour" (figure 3.1), a Daniel Maclise drawing of celebrated women writers at tea, "every one a lovely she." The picture and William Maginn's accompanying article, "List the First," parallel the previous year's collection of male "Fraserians," which depicts *Fraser's* founder Maginn addressing a roundtable of the decade's best-known literary characters; twenty-seven men busily toasting the New Year include Samuel Taylor Coleridge, Theodore Hook, Barry Cornwall (Bryan Waller Proctor), Father Prout (F. S. Mahony), William Jerdan, Thomas Crofton Croker, John Gibson Lockhart, Thomas Carlyle, William Makepeace Thackeray, D. M. Moir, James Hogg, John Galt, Egerton Brydges, Allan Cunningham, Count d'Orsay, and William Harrison Ainsworth, among others. Like its male counterpart, *Fraser's* "List the First" formulates an intriguing, albeit smaller, canon of *Fraser's* contributors; its eight women writers include Mrs. S. C. Hall (Anna Maria Hall), L. E. L., Mary Russell Mitford, Lady Morgan (Sydney Owenson), Harriet Martineau, Jane Porter, Caroline Norton, and Lady Blessington. Predictably, Maginn identifies the women writers in gendered terms indicating domestic gentility rather than literary genius; Mrs. Hall is "fair and fine," L. E. L. is "painted con amore," Lady Blessington is "bright and fair, enchanting, [and] winning," and Norton is a beauty—"nobler, brighter, dearer, did ne'er on human eyeball blaze." While the men gather "o'er claret, punch, or ale, or what liquor could be found, they, with song, or chaunt, or tale, made the jocund night resound," but the women are "with volant tongue and chatty cheer, welcoming in, by prattle good, or witty phrase, or comment shrewd, the opening of the gay new year" over coffee and tea.[1] These women writers appear to be models of traditional propriety and femininity. However, that image distorts the reality of these women's lives and work, revealing the hypocrisy of the assembly and its social codes. The *Fraser's* illustration

Figure 3.1 "Regina's Maids of Honour." *Fraser's Magazine* (January 1836). Engraving after a design by Maclise

demonstrates the instability of visual texts in a display of conflicting signifiers that decenter ideological power. Such examples suggest that generalizations about literary history and dominating ideologies do not always correspond with contexts revealed within printed productions, whether they be volumes of poetry or (as in this instance) a monthly periodical. Furthermore, the literature these women produced and edited works from a distance to inform a reading of the image, supplying a layer of personal tragedy and suffering that became a theme in their work. This is not the "supplement of personal feeling" discussed in chapter 2, but a paratextual supplement available to one familiar with characteristic tendencies in literature written by these women writers. For a reader aware of the personal scandals of Caroline Norton, L. E. L., Lady Blessington, and Lady Morgan, biography gets confused with its marketable function as a literary product, and the picture converts to a story that makes scandalous women heroic. The textuality of their supposedly personal writings is an act of creative writing whose fictitiousness (Latin *fictus*, a made or shaped thing) is a covert theme that has sometimes been sold (read, interpreted, believed) by those who like to identify with the characters, or those whose stock in trade is profiting from that popular proclivity.

While the portrait itself disturbs the male literary profession by proudly displaying evidence of the invasion of women writers and competing commodities characterizing the nineteenth century, it upsets the domestic spheres by drawing the women toward a "Bluestocking" intellectual support group, where the sharing of ideas and accomplishments promotes further female independence and solidarity. Dorothy Mermin and others show how notions of propriety inhibited women's writing: "Women belonged only in the private sphere, where they were expected to be modestly unself-conscious and shun the gaze of men, while printed books were public and courted admiration. Any venture into public life by a woman risked being greeted as a highly sexualized self-exposure."[2] Mary Robinson experienced such prejudice, and, as noted by Linda Peterson, biographical details of her life helped to foster for future generations of women writers the Sapphic myth transformed into the myth of the poetess.[3] Yet William Lane promoted her in his list of novels for women, ignoring her revolutionary and feminist ideals. "List the First" also provides primary evidence of such public exposure and admiration and promotes it to readers of *Fraser's*. Alice Acland notes that, of these women, Caroline Norton, Lady Blessington, and L. E. L. "had tragic lives, and all were dogged by malicious gossip and scandal,"[4] and Patricia Marks studies individual companion illustrations of these eight women by Maginn and Maclise called "*Fraser's* Gallery of Illustrious Literary Characters," concluding that the portraits contain a "satirical, antifeminist commentary," revealing "a failure of critical acumen as well as a lack of intellectual generosity."[5] However, the irony of the visual text becomes more profound when we consider that over half of "Regina's Maids of Honour" are not honorable in the traditional sense; impropriety or scandal characterizes at least five of the eight women in the *Fraser's* illustration. The scandal was a valuable fiction: such celebrity enhanced their marketability, creating more exposure, while it deterred the effects of moral censorship and suggested lifestyle options for women readers. By promoting this particular group of women writers, *Fraser's* participates in scandal commodification while contributing to a profitable "calumniated woman" public persona for women writers who were, like Mary Robinson earlier in the century, victims of personal attacks from male reviewers from the periodical press, many of them represented in the 1835 gathering of Fraserians.[6]

In spite of novelist and Irish Nationalist Lady Morgan's illustrious place in *Fraser's* "List the First," her seat at the Maids' table appears to be nothing more than a conciliatory ploy by William Maginn to counteract a personal attack he delivered six months before "List the First" appeared, when *Fraser's* featured Lady Morgan in its "Gallery of Literary Characters," a monthly illustration and accompanying description that satirized and celebrated the most popular authors of the moment. In this illustration, Lady Morgan, " 'Author of 'O'Donnel,' " sits before a cheval mirror straightening her bonnet. Maginn's strangely cruel and personal description of the portrait begins with the blithe statement, "We leave it to our readers to decide whether she is fitting it on after having returned from boring some unhappy party to death, or is about to sally forth on a fresh mission of destruction." Maginn attacks Morgan's work ("*The Wild Irish Girls, Missionaries, Novices of St. Dominick*, and so forth, were mere stuff-stuff *sans phrase*"), not stopping before he slanders her husband:

> What has become of Morgan we do not know; when we last heard of him, he
> was proving some five pound debt against an unhappy magazine which he had

contributed to ruin. Colburn, with his usual sagacity, had turned him off long ago, and we have some obscure idea that he is dead.

Accusing her of connecting with "a quack French clique of the most ignorant and pretending praters in the world," Maginn claims, "on the strength of that acquaintance she thinks herself entitled to pretend to know gentlemen and ladies on the continent. She is sadly mistaken." According to Maginn, "Her excellent work on France, dedicated to prove that Napoleon Bonaparte was a most distinguished friend to liberty, and that his sole object in reigning was to propagate free institutions, has, we believe, descended to the grave."[7] Middle-class francophobia and conservatism combined with Maginn's hatred of Morgan as a Catholic sympathizer and an Irish Nationalist to produce a particularly harsh satire for a woman. According to Miriam Thrall, Maginn's habit in these features was "usually sharply disciplinary, a brisk wielding of the rod over the naked faults and frailties of his great contemporaries," and Lady Morgan does not escape because she is a woman writer.[8] In "List the First," Maginn writes, "Naughty fellows, we must plead, that with voice of angry organ once or twice we did, indeed, speak not civilly of Morgan; but we must retract, repent, promise better to behave. She, we are certain, will consent all our former feuds to wave . . . for your father's sake we are going never more to bother you."[9] Regardless of Maginn's claims of repentance, Morgan's appearance in this feature recalls the former abuse.

A recent altercation with Henry Colburn provides another context for the satire. Colburn was owner of the *New Monthly Magazine* and publisher of Morgan's highly successful books *France* (1817), *Italy* (1821), *The Life and Times of Salvator Rosa* (1824), and *The O'Briens and the O'Flahertys* (1827). With each publication, Morgan fought and won hard battles with Colburn over compensation; he gave Morgan a hefty £1,300 for the copyright of *The O'Briens and the O'Flahertys*, with an additional £100 each for the second and third editions, which were to exceed no more than 3,000 copies.[10] When Morgan prepared another book on France in 1830, she naturally applied to Colburn for publication, but when he failed twice to respond to her prospectus, she sold the book to Saunders and Otley. Colburn reacted by announcing in an advertisement that he had suffered great losses on Lady Morgan's books and therefore would be selling everything at half price. The ploy ruined Morgan's new project and damaged her literary reputation. Although she eventually continued her work, Lady Morgan suffered from this professional setback, while health problems and the loss of her husband burdened any progress she might make. As founder of *Fraser's Magazine*, perhaps William Maginn sympathized with Henry Colburn, a friendly competitor in magazine publishing who consistently fought battles against impudent, "manly" women writers who demanded more than their share of compensation. Nevertheless, when money could be made, the men accommodated them; Colburn published the first part of Morgan's *Woman and Her Master* in 1839, but by then she was unable to continue their arrangement because of her poor eyesight and failing health.

Many famous men praised Lady Morgan's work, including Byron, Sydney Smith, Leigh Hunt, and Sir Thomas Lawrence, making the heavy criticism strangely uncharacteristic of her reputation with these professionals. Yet Maginn's harsh critique is mild compared to some from Morgan's later years. The publication of Lady Morgan's *Memoirs: Autobiography, Diaries, and Correspondence* in 1863 (edited by Geraldine Jewsbury and Hepworth Dixon) unleashed more cruel personal attacks. An unidentified reviewer in the *Westminster Review* (April 1863) writes, "Lady Morgan's autobiography is much such a production as might naturally be expected from a very vain, indifferently educated, and strangely overrated woman, who, at an advanced period of her life, sits down to indite her own history."[11] This reviewer, while attempting to balance criticism with reason, surrenders to the assumption that

> at last, poor Lady Morgan, being neither an angel, nor a philosopher, nor a very superior being of any sort, did really and solemnly come to believe what she had so long been told—viz., that she was one of the most extraordinary and gifted personages of her time . . . The completing and editing of the work was an undertaking which it is probable both Mr. Dixon and Miss Jewsbury would have preferred to decline had they been able to do so.[12]

If the reviewer felt Morgan's work was detestable, why bother writing the review? G. H. Lewes writes of "old Lady Morgan" in *The Cornhill Magazine* (January 1863):

> To spectators and mere acquaintances, that was not a venerable figure: a little humpbacked old woman, absurdly attired, rouged, and wigged; vivacious, and somewhat silly; vain, gossiping, and ostentatious; larding her talk with scraps of French, often questionable in their idiom, always dreadful in their accent . . . this, we repeat, was not a venerable figure, nor did any one speak of Lady Morgan with veneration.[13]

Lewes cites opportunity as the reason for Morgan's popularity; it was "the temporal, not the intrinsic value of her books, which gave them success" (134). She wrote about France, Ireland, and Italy at a time of piqued interest in these topics, and this timeliness resulted in success for Lady Morgan, according to Lewes.

She appears to be an author critics loved to hate. As Harriet Martineau writes about Morgan's experience, if criticism against a writer persists, "the most unthinking public get the impression—they know not whence nor wherefore—that the writer in question is a person they have seen very often attacked in reviews . . . and therefore ideas of disparagement and contempt become associated in many minds with a name without reason or inquiry."[14] Beginning with John Wilson Croker's lambasting of Morgan's famous work, *The Wild Irish Girl*, in 1806, reviewers translated professional criticism into vicious personal judgments that seemed to build upon one another until Lady Morgan's death in 1859. Croker's review of Morgan's *France* (1817) treats her work under the following subheadings: "Bad Taste—Bombast and

Nonsense—Blunders—Ignorance of the French Language and Manners—General Ignorance—Jacobinism—Falsehood—Licentiousness, and Impiety," and ends by proclaiming that he hopes to "prevent, in some degree, the circulation of trash which under the name of a Lady author might otherwise find its way into the hands of young persons of both sexes, for whose perusal it is utterly, on the score both of morals and politics unfit."[15] Morgan felt that readers didn't care about the critics; after characteristically harsh treatment of her novel *The O'Briens and the O'Flahertys* in the *Quarterly Review*, she remarks in her diary (March, 1829): "So the *Quarterly* has let loose its dogs of war again on me, under the new groom of the kennel, Mr. Lockhart . . . I have been tried already before that truly Grand Jury, the PUBLIC, from which there is no appeal, and acquitted; and I have before me a letter from Mr. Constable, offering me the same terms as Sir W. Scott."[16] As long as she could demand high fees for her work and publishers made money, Morgan could withstand the psychological pressure of critics. Yet, whether it was because of her liberal views, her political affiliations in France, her radical Irish nationalism, or her personal habits, Lady Morgan must surely be the most maligned, calumniated woman author of the nineteenth century, and her presence with "Regina's Maids of Honour" contrasts sharply with mild, angelic domestic models provided by Jane Porter, Mary Russell Mitford, and Anna Maria Hall. A kinder observer from the 1863 *National Review*, Henry Stewart Cunningham, provides a thoughtful perspective of Lady Morgan in his review of the *Memoirs,* seeking a more realistic view perhaps available only to an observer later in the century, Cunningham confirms that Lady Morgan's faults are uncontradictable because

> she artlessly depicts them for us herself, and never for a moment asks us to take her for any thing but what she is, a shrewd, eager, rather clever woman, upon whom fortune imposed the vulgar necessity of making her bread, and whose high spirits, resolute ambition and imperviousness to petty slights, enabled her to succeed astonishingly well in a society whose pale she over-stepped, whose prejudices she shocked, and whose jealousy she ran every risk of exciting.[17]

For Lady Morgan, having a profession meant controversy, public attacks on her character, and daunting abuse of her talent by reviewers, but she remained in the public eye as a literary figure, inspiring a flurry of commentary, both positive and negative, until after her death.

Harriet Martineau does not exemplify one's imaginative vision of a "Maid of Honour." She was a prolific radical writer, early feminist, travel correspondent, and social reformer who was just attaining literary fame in the 1830s for strident social critiques of Anglo-Irish relations, the English tax system, the Poor Laws, and slavery in *Illustrations of Political Economy* (1832–34), *Poor Laws and Paupers Illustrated* (1833–34), and *Illustrations of Taxation* (1834). Three years before her appearance in *Fraser's* "List the First," Martineau had angered critics with her solution to Ireland's population problem in *Illustrations of Political Economy*, suggesting that the evils of overpopulation should be controlled by "restraining the increase of population."[18] The *Quarterly Review*'s Croker called her a "female Malthusian" in 1833, denouncing her as "A woman who thinks child-bearing a crime against society! An unmarried woman who declaims against marriage!!"[19] Croker found such an "unfeminine" woman unimaginable.

In "List the First," Maginn recalls Croker's public denouncement by depicting Martineau "with serious brow . . . meditating, grimly, how she can prevent the very bad use that people have in this sad earth of putting things into confusion, by giving certain matters birth, in spite of theories Malthusian."[20] According to Miriam Thrall:

> Those who were most roughly treated at these moments of ruthless hilarity were naturally the political economists and the writers who tended toward materialism in religion and philosophy. The staff viewed with such alarm any increase in the influence of rationalistic science and theology that they subjected even thoughtful work like that of Harriet Martineau to ribald scrutiny for being sacrilegious and immoral.[21]

Martineau's sin was the proposition of birth control and discussion of social issues she should not have been promoting as a woman.

Martineau later responded to Croker's method of criticism in an 1838 review of Caroline Norton's *A Letter to the Lord Chancellor on the Infants' Custody Bill* and two other controversial works promoting women's rights, printed in the *London and Westminster Review* in April 1839. Here Martineau complains about slanderous personal attacks on women in an article against what she labels "Crokerism":

> There are several clever and amusing writers of the present day who owe much notoriety, and sale, to the regularity with which they season their journals with attacks on men, and especially on women. The morality of controversy among these men, is a fear of the law of libel, and the rules of duelling, and nothing more. They hold, that in politics and literature everything is fair against an opponent that is safe; at least this is the only morality they practise, and, therefore, their only real morality.[22]

Martineau details the facts of slanderous attacks by Crokerites on Queen Victoria, Caroline Norton, Anna Jameson, and Maria Edgeworth, complaining that

> Women are not protected by law from the worst slander to which they can be subjected, unless they can prove special damages. They cannot have the miserable protection of the duel, because every affection of their natures rises up to make them use their influence to prevent their brothers and husbands from taking up their quarrels. They are the most piquant and the safest objects of abuse a reviewer can select. (460)

London and Westminster Review editor, John Robertson, agrees on the cruelty of such abusive attacks, recalling Martineau's public railing from

Croker: "She approved in 1833 of a measure which their slower appreciation approved a few years later. But, owing to this she was made the object of attacks in which every joke a coarse but stupid writer could invent in the subject of population was applied to her" (469).

While Robertson's response is appropriately apologetic in a periodical controlled by Martineau's sympathetic feminist Utilitarian peer, John Stuart Mill, he remains a representative of the status quo Harriet Martineau threatens as a single woman (she never married), living and working in the London literary profession. She was a woman who actively promoted women's rights through writings about political and legal equality, education, social expectations, treatment of prostitutes, the physical and emotional abuse of women, and the lack of career opportunities for women. Although middle-class domestic ideology and separation of the spheres gave women roles as social reformers, Martineau subverted the model by her lifestyle and radical intellectual activities. Her appearance as one of "Regina's Maids of Honour" therefore seems comically ironic. Oppositional framing of these women against the previous year's Fraserians makes Martineau and her female peers into opponents dueling with the Fraserians, defraying Maginn's joyful toast to the women writers: "Long may they flourish."

Her history does not chronicle harsh battles with literary critics, but the life and work of poet, novelist, and successful editor of *Heath's Book of Beauty* and other annuals, Lady Blessington, represent anything but traditional morality, supplying a heavy context of impropriety to the *Fraser's* illustration. Her alcoholic father forced the young Marguerite, then Margaret Power, to marry violent, insane Captain Farmer when she was only fifteen years old. She soon left Farmer but, finding herself unwelcome in her parents' home, Blessington left with a man of fortune named Captain Thomas Jenkins and became "that despised thing, a kept mistress."[23] She met Charles John Gardiner, Earl of Blessington, while living with Jenkins; when Farmer died, falling from a window during a drunken brawl in King's Bench prison, the Earl wrote a check to Captain Jenkins for the amount he had invested in Marguerite's jewels during their relationship, and they married in 1818. Margaret Farmer became Marguerite Gardiner, the Countess of Blessington. She and Lord Blessington extravagantly spent his fortune as they toured Europe, becoming friends with Byron. They traveled with dandyish Count d'Orsay, whom Lord Blessington liked so well he changed his will to exclude his only daughter unless she married d'Orsay, giving him a portion of inheritance. After Lord Blessington died, d'Orsay separated from his wife and lived openly with Lady Blessington in London, where she solidifed her reputation as a popular writer with her *Conversations of Lord Byron* in 1834.

Blessington's scandalous history was well known in London society; yet a long list of celebrated men who sought her company would include authors, politicians, and aristocrats from thirty years of British cultural history. A few of her closest friends were Benjamin Disraeli, Walter Savage Landor, Charles Dickens, Bulwer Lytton, Samuel Rogers, and Thomas Moore. As Benjamin Robert Haydon exclaimed, "Every body goes to Lady Blessington. She has the first news of every thing, and every body seems delighted to tell her . . . She is the center of more talent & gaiety than any other Woman of Fashion in London, Fashion of the highest kind."[24] Some people didn't care that she was living with d'Orsay, a married man. The nature of their relationship remains uncertain, but Moore recorded in his journal in June 1829 the gossip that "D'Orsay has never consummated with Lady Harriet" [d'Orsay's wife],[25] and noted in August, 1834, that the liaison between Blessington and d'Orsay was "too gross and bare-faced, even for London" (4:1623). Women would not visit Blessington's salon after dark, and she was not welcome at Almack's. As S. C. Hall remembers, "Her visitors were all, or nearly all, men. Ladies were rarely seen at her receptions. Mrs. Hall never accompanied me to her evenings, although she was a frequent day-caller."[26]

A woman with Blessington's history would seem unacceptable to readers of literary annuals, often touted as reading suitable for the family circle; yet she edited *Heath's Book of Beauty* from 1834 to 1849 and *The Keepsake* from 1841 to 1850. Other publications included a novel, *Grace Cassidy* (1834); *Conversations with Lord Byron* (1834); *Gems of Beauty* (1836), for which she wrote the entire text; *The Idler in Italy* (1839–40) and *The Idler in France* (1841). The *Sunday Times* serialized Blessington's work, and the *Daily News* featured her as a highly paid gossip writer in 1846. After her death, Jane Wilde writes in an 1855 *Dublin University Magazine* review of R. R. Madden's biography of Lady Blessington:

> The world has long associated with the name of Lady Blessington, beauty, wealth, rank, intellect, splendour of position, and the lavish homage of all the gifted minds of the age. Our interest, therefore, is excited to know what life an individual thus endowed wrought out of such rare and precious gifts. Besides, for twenty years she held a prominent position in the literary world of London; reigning there, indeed, as queen paramount of intellect; so that the mental history of the century would be incomplete without a page devoted to her remarkable career.[27]

Lady Blessington moved through the streets of London in her exquisite carriage embossed with the letter "B," while women publicly denounced her and publishers sought her literary work, knowing what one reviewer claimed in *Hunt's London Journal* on 9 November 1844:

> When a lady condescends to write, whose equipage arrests the attention of the thousands that throng daily the fashionable localities of London, she is all the time, as her carriage rolls on from street to street, creating a new class of readers. Struck with the appearance of her equipage, they are anxious to ascertain how its owner looks, thinks, acts, and writes; the circulating libraries gain new subscribers, and Lady Blessington extends in this way the reputation of her genius.[28]

Such accounts of Blessington's life ignore violations of propriety. The engraved image in *Fraser's* carries, like a code, the public persona touted by these diarists.

Incest, rape, and murder are the secret sins of a spoiled nobleman in Blessington's "A Tale of the Baptistry of St. Marks" (1847 *Keepsake*). A selfish rake, the man "deem'd the world was made/To minister to his voluptuousness." He was a man who cared little "whether ruin fell on those/O'er whom he triumph'd in his guilty love," and he attempts to rape a young woman he sees in prayer, chasing her into the river where she drowns.[29] Pulling the dead woman out of the rushing water he sees a locket around her neck containing a portrait of himself; he realizes the girl is his own daughter by a woman he abandoned long ago. The locket contains a message from her mother, "imploring him to guard his helpless child,/As he expected pardon from his God" (15). Rather than guarding the child he abandoned, the father becomes a power to guard against. Now he prays at St. Mark's for his secret sin "when conscience would be heard," but all the prayers and alms for the poor will not cover the sickness of his sins against the daughter and her mother (12). Blessington will not allow the double standard to excuse the nobleman for his "guilty love," and the man's pardon from God seems remote.

Blessington's 1834 *Keepsake* poem "The Storm" shows sympathy for a fallen woman who pays a heavy price for her passion when she and her bastard child drown on a convict ship in a storm. The woman, convicted of stealing food, becomes a victim of society's narrow rules of propriety. The child's birth "destroy'd for e'er a mother's fame," forcing her to become a thief to provide for her child.[30] Because the domestic ideology that requires women to be mothers does not allow them to be providers, women must go outside the law and the domestic sphere to survive; yet Blessington's woman suffers the punishment subscribed for those who resort to such desperate measures. Such textual examples challenged nineteenth-century social conventions as much as Blessington's notorious reputation; the more scandalous her public persona became, the more secure was her place in literary society. *Fraser's* could paint her as "gorgeous Countess" with "gayer notes for all that's charming, sweet, and smiling, for her whose pleasant tales our throats are ever of fresh laughs beguiling,"[31] but Lady Blessington's example personifies seductive social hypocrisy while providing trenchant social critique.

In its display of "Regina's Maids of Honour," *Fraser's* implicates yet more subversion in its inclusion of L. E. L. Her life was tormented by cruel gossip about a possible abortion, indiscretions with *Literary Gazette* editor William Jerdan, adultery with the article's writer and *Fraser's* founder William Maginn, whispers of an affair with Daniel Maclise (the artist who created "Regina's Maids of Honour"), and a broken engagement in 1835 with biographer John Forster. By January 1836, L. E. L.'s reputation had been so sullied by scandal that friends and observers wrote about her in pitying terms.

"Poor child, poor girl, poor woman, poor wife, poor victim—from the cradle to the grave, it was an unhappy life! I have seldom seen her merry, that the laugh was not followed by a sigh," recalls S. C. Hall in his *Retrospect of a Long Life: From 1815 to 1883* (1883). A close friend of L. E. L.'s during her lifetime, Hall writes, "I can not find space here to go into the history of the slander breathed against her; but Mrs. Hall is authority sufficient to brand as calumnies the whispers that pursued her during the later years of a grievous and mournful career." He repeats L. E. L.'s own assessment of her life:

> 'Weary, beset with privations, unkindnesses, disappointments, ever struggling against absolute poverty'—these were the mournful words 'L.E.L.' applied to herself. In one of her letters to Mrs. Hall she wrote: 'Envy, malice, and all uncharitableness—these are the fruits of a successful literary career for a woman'.[32]

If these be the fruits, L. E. L. reaped them fully, supporting relatives that sapped the hefty sums earned for her work in a brief, but prolific literary career that produced innumerable reviews and articles for various periodicals, poetry published in monthly magazines and literary annuals (she edited two annuals, *Fisher's Drawing Room Scrap-Book* from 1832 to 1839 and *Heath's Book of Beauty* in 1833), and highly popular volumes of poetry with sales sufficient to demand six editions of *The Improvisatrice and Other Poems* (1824) and four editions of *The Troubadour, Catalogue of Pictures and Historical Sketches* (1825). Other successful volumes of poetry included *The Golden Violet, with Its Tales of Romance and Chivalry, and Other Poems* (1826); *The Venetian Bracelet, The Lost Pleid, A History of the Lyre, and Other Poems* (1829); *The Vow of the Peacock and Other Poems* (1835); and *The Zenana and Minor Poems*, published posthumously in 1839. L. E. L. also wrote three novels, *Romance and Reality* (1831), *Francesca Carrera* (1834), and *Ethel Churchill* (1837), a short story anthology, *Traits and Trials of Early Life* (1836), and a play, *The Triumph of Lucca* (1837).[33] A successful literary career L. E. L. had, with the calumniated woman image at the core of her success.

Glennis Stephenson well documents the "construction" of L. E. L., clearly pointing to L. E. L.'s poetic persona as a business choice:

> Landon, by all accounts—including the evidence of her own correspondence— was actually a highly astute business woman who, as one of the first professional female writers, quite consciously set out to promote herself in the manner she felt would best assure her popular and critical success: she composed in accordance with society's idea of a poetess, and she carefully constructed the poetic self that became known as L.E.L.[34]

Fraser's "List the First" participates in L. E. L.'s commodification of the poetess, but it also provides an ironic reminder that scandal sells, regardless of our presumptions about Victorian propriety. Whether or not L. E. L. intentionally constructed her own tragic poetic persona, the gossip about her occurred, and her appearance in "Regina's Maids of Honour" creates an ironic subtext that subverts the sheen of domestic propriety.

Most observers eventually came to believe L. E. L. innocent in her affair with Maginn, but upon publication of "List the First" in January 1836, many remained suspicious. Actor Charles Macready recorded his concern in his diary in November 1835:

> It has lately come to light that she has been carrying on an intrigue with Dr. Maginn, a person whom I never saw, but whom all accounts unite in describing as a beastly biped; he is married and has four children. Two letters of hers and one of his were found by Mrs. Maginn in his portrait, filled with the most puerile and nauseating terms of endearment and declarations of attachment! I left quite concerned that a woman of such splendid genius and such agreeable manners should be so depraved in taste and so lost to a sense of what was due to her high reputation. She is fallen![35]

The 1836 volume of *Fisher's Drawing Room Scrap-Book*, edited by L. E. L. in 1835, provides curious textual propositions about L. E. L.'s situation. It features a poem about the death of Thomas Aquinas by William Maginn on page eight and nine, directly followed on page nine by "The Lily of the Valley," a poem presumably written by L. E. L., who was responsible for all "poetical illustrations" in the book. An accompanying engraving of a Frank Stone painting illustrates a young woman sitting with eyes downcast in an apparent melancholy mode. The poem's speaker grieves over a lost love and the ruination of her future hopes as she prepares to deliver letters that will finally sever their relationship:

> It is the last token of love and of thee!
> Thy once faith is broken, thou false one to me.
> I think on the letters with which I must part;
> Too dear are the fetters which wind round my heart.[36]

The woman indicates that she and her lover have public lives, but they have shared an intimacy that the others can't know: "The bitter concealings life's treacheries teach,/The long-subdued feelings the world cannot reach—/ Thy mask to the many was worn not for me" (10). Like so many of L. E. L.'s poems, this one is less about love than it is about the masks—social masks, such as the "calumniated woman" role, and poetic masks as well, including this one. The couple must continue to meet in their public lives, painfully cognizant of their former attachment: "You will try to forget me—you cannot forget./We shall hear of each other—oh! Misery to hear/Those names from another that once were so dear!" L. E. L.'s characteristic weary tone of lost love inflicts a depressed view of the future upon the speaker:

> Like others in seeming, we'll walk through life's part,
> Cold, careless, and dreaming,—with death in the heart,
> No hope—no repentance; the spring of life o'er;
> All died with that sentence—I love thee no more!

These stanzas written by L. E. L. in a book edited by L. E. L. and placed directly below William Maginn's printed signature suggests their secret relationship, or at least the public fiction of it.[37] The engraved illustration shows no letters that would initiate L. E. L.'s reference in the poem; the letters the speaker in the poem intends to deliver, while they are not "puerile and nauseating terms of endearment and declarations of attachment," might call to mind those found by Mrs. Maginn and shared with John Forster. The book's middle-class women readers would have received *The Drawing Room Scrap-Book* during the 1835 Christmas gift giving season, and this collection of clues serve as a reminder of the scandal at the same time the January issue of *Fraser's* appears featuring L. E. L. in Maginn's "List the First."

Gossip about L. E. L.'s affair with *Fraser's* illustrator, Daniel Maclise, provides further context to the scandal in "Regina's Maids of Honour." According to Greer, "By publishing a poem based upon his painting 'The Vow of the Peacock' in 1835, L. E. L. had also encouraged the linking of their names. Maclise made four portraits of her, on four separate occasions, one of which he kept by him until his death" (19). Thus "Regina's Maids of Honour" becomes a complex intertextual site, commodifying scandal involving the artist, his art and its reproduction, its writer/illustrator, the publication, its failing founder, the woman writer, her literary persona, and a competing popular literary commodity. While the poem seems to provide textual confirmation of the gossip surrounding L. E. L., it makes a luxury item of suffering in one of the finest and most expensive products of the gift book genre. When Maginn refers to L. E. L. in his "List the First" as "painted con amore," readers may not know of Maginn's inability to forgive his wife for passing along L. E. L.'s letters, and they may not know that drink and debt threatened his literary career (Father Prout would take over the editorship of *Fraser's* in 1836), and they may not know about suspicion of an affair with the Regina's artist Daniel Maclise that caused the final breakup of L. E. L.'s engagement with Forster, but they may have read the 1836 *Drawing Room Scrap-Book* poem by L. E. L., concluding once again that L. E. L. was the creator of poetic effusions expressing seemingly lived experiences that challenged their notions of propriety.

As Stephenson and others demonstrate, the truth about L. E. L.'s life lies somewhere behind a professional persona of disappointed love. Her portrayal of woman's lot dramatizes abuse, and optimistically one could suggest that such histrionics might imply a possibility of what they do not express: social possibilities such as independence, self-determination, and rejection of sphere separation for those who realize its abuse. As Jacqueline Labbé notes in her fascinating treatment of romance,

Landon wields the melodrama of defeat to expose the damage inherent in separating spheres, and she does so by allowing the violence intrinsic to a divided society to redound on its willing inhabitants. She poisons the spheres, renders them fatal to the opposite sex, and thereby hastens the demise of romance itself.[38]

Yet L. E. L. defends her depressive themes in poetic language that contributes to the persona's construction:

> If I have painted a state of moral lassitude, when the heart is left like a ruined and deserted city, where the winged step of joy, and the seven-stringed lute of hope have ceased each to echo the other; where happiness lies cold and dead on its own threshold; where dust lies dry and arid over all, and there is no sign of vegetation or promise of change—if I paint such a state, it is because I know it well. Alas! Over how many things now does my regret take its last and deepest tone—despondency![39]

In spite of L. E. L.'s insistence on presenting herself as the calumniated professional woman, her friends record a much different image. L. E. L.'s housemate and confidante Emma Roberts wrote in her "Memoir of L.E.L.," published in L. E. L.'s posthumous volume of poems, *The Zenana and Minor Poems of L.E.L.* (1839):

> While dwelling with apparently earnest tenderness upon the sorrows of love, its disappointments and treacheries, L.E.L. identified herself with the beings of her fancy, lamenting, frequently in the first person, over miseries which she had never felt, and to which she was by no means likely to be subjected, since both then and subsequently, she manifested an almost extraordinary want of susceptibility, upon all occasions when attempts were made upon her heart.[40]

One could view Roberts as trying to instill some respectability for L. E. L.'s reputation after rumors of her mysterious death in Africa; however, the rumors fired L. E. L.'s celebrity value, rather than detracted from it. Roberts is writing a subjective narrative of L. E. L. as a former member of her devoted circle of friends, "living under the same roof with her, and to whom all her thoughts and feelings were well known." According to Roberts, "these friends were sometimes amused, and sometimes provoked, by the various reports which gained universal credit" (11). Anne Katherine Elwood wrote:

> The truth is, that Miss Landon's disposition was peculiarly lively and cheerful, her conversation was playful, and her letters were so characterised by easy gaiety, as to induce her friends to wish that she had no other employment than that of chronicling passing events, and painting the form and fashion of the time.[41]

Jacqueline Labbé notes that a more modern observer, Anne K. Mellor, envisions L. E. L. as "entrapped" by the separation of the spheres that creates misery by the imposition of romance and its resultant pain; however, Labbé adds that "Mellor's entrapped poetess represents simply a persona employed by L. E. L. to demonstrate her poetic fitness—she writes what she knows (but don't believe all you read)."[42] Meanwhile, L. E. L.'s presence in the foreground of "Regina's Maids of Honour" gives readers room to speculate.

Celebrated writer and London society hostess Caroline Norton's case shows that notoriety was, in fact, a bonus and a natural companion to literature of the calumniated woman, a genre that became her specialty. A few weeks after *Fraser's* featured Norton in their "List the First," London newspapers began printing frenzied gossip about an affair between her and Britain's Whig Prime Minister Lord Melbourne. On 22 June 1836, Norton's husband accused Melbourne of adultery with his wife in a £10,000 criminal conversation suit. The trial was a comical display of hypocrisy and circumstantial evidence provided by servants who had been bribed and coached by Norton's Tory brother, Lord Grantley. The jury relieved Melbourne of guilt in the case without leaving the jury box, but the scandal permanently affected Caroline Norton's reputation. A reporter from London newspaper *The Age* commented a week before the trial (19 June 1836), the real victim of the case was Norton:

> The proceedings in all such cases bear peculiarly hard upon the lady, who not being a recognized party in the suit, cannot be represented by Counsel, although liable to the heaviest penalty that a verdict can inflict—nay, although acquitted by law, yet it is impossible to free her from the stigma of suspicion, or heal the outraged feelings of a calumniated wife.[43]

Calumniated she may have been, but the scandal did not permanently harm her literary career; indeed, a public image becomes evident from Norton's earliest published works that remains ironically consistent with the "outraged" woman from the scandal of 1836. Notoriety and the "stigma of suspicion" became a stimulus for success, helping to create Norton's public persona.

Two days after sensational, lengthy, special-edition reports of the trial appeared in the London newspapers, Norton's image was still a valuable commodity; on 25 June the advertising pages of *The Age* feature Ackermann print-sellers announcing: "The Hon. Mrs. NORTON—The most correct likeness published, painted by John Hayter, Esq., and engraved in mezzotint by W. O. Geller." A few months after the trial in late November, 1836, John Murray accepted her poem, *A Voice from the Factories*, for publication, and her political influence was still strong enough to persuade Serjeant Talfourd to introduce the Infant Custody Bill to the House of Commons on 1 February 1837, legislation that would allow mothers to see their children after separation or divorce. In the immediate years after 1836, Caroline Norton lobbied tirelessly for women's rights, publishing letters to Queen Victoria and others in the *Times* supporting the Infant Custody Bill, and she later wrote *English Laws for Women in the Nineteenth Century* (1854), a pamphlet that was to influence the passage of the Marriage and Divorce Act of 1857, which protected a wife's earnings against the demands of her husband. This legislation opened the door for the Married Woman's Property Act in 1870, which gave the same legal rights to all women, married or unmarried. After the 1836 scandal, Norton also contributed regularly to Victorian periodicals and published several novels and books of poetry, including *The Dream, and Other Poems* (1840), *The Child of the Islands* (1845), *Aunt Carry's Ballads for Children* (1847), *Stuart of Dunleath* (1851), *The Lady of La Garaye* (1861), *Lost and Saved* (1863), and *Old Sir Douglas* (1867). She served as editor and sole contributor of *Fisher's Drawing Room Scrap-Book* in 1846, 1848, and 1849. Her celebrity status influenced other authors to include her in their works; trial publicity inspired Charles Dickens's "Bardell v. Pickwick," and she later became the model for George Meredith's *Diana of the Crossways* (1885) because of her involvement in political intrigue. According to Micael M. Clarke, several of William Makepeace Thackeray's novels "reenact well-known incidents from Norton's life. *The Newcomes*, especially, supports the Marital Causes Act (pending before Parliament at the time of its publication) by recreating a 'criminal conversation' trial much like the one that made Norton famous."[44] Clarke notes that Norton was "a probable 'original' for Lady Lyndon, Becky Sharp, and Clara Pulleyn Newcome," providing Thackeray with "much material for his novels" (34). She was also rumored to be the model for Tennyson's Princess Ida. *The Dream and Other Poems* sold well enough to allow Norton to purchase her own carriage. American publishers Carey & Hart pirated the entire volume by 1841, and publishers Colburn & Bentley soon issued a second edition. As she reached age 50 in 1858, Victorian periodicals still published Caroline Norton's portrait. Her reputation remained a vital topic with diarists and biographers, who, until her death in 1877, kept the scandal alive by repeating her story as a scandalous woman. In 1893 Catherine J. Hamilton notes that the trial of 1836 "was the great event of 1836; to pass it over would be impossible, for all Mrs. Norton's future life is mixed up with it."[45] Indeed, literature of the calumniated woman sold books.

Well before the public embarrassment of an adultery trial, Norton's poetry demonstrated the wounded wife image. What kind of marriage Norton actually experienced we can only imagine; the most detailed descriptions of her marital battles indicate verbal and physical brutality. With the separation, Norton lost her three young sons, her inheritance, copyright earnings from years of publication, all her clothing, jewelry, letters, other personal possessions, and, for a while, her reputation. As in the case of Felicia Hemans, Norton's "realistic" picture of love and marriage gets replicated and repackaged throughout her professional career, beginning with poetry such as "Marriage and Love," published in *The Sorrows of Rosalie* just two years after her marriage (1829). The poem tells the tale of Laura, a young woman who finds that her new husband is "too cold to love, too mean to hate," a man who is "without a soul or mind/Too savage e'en to be in seeming kind—/ The slave of petty feelings, every hour/He changed his will to show he had the power."[46] The husband leaves her alone to regret the mistake of marriage, and the woman falls in love with another man, losing her reputation:

> Oh; it is wretched, when the loss of fame
> Hath left us but the shadow of a name—

> When all forget us, all refuse to own,
> And life is journeyed on alone—*alone*! (121)

Because she is now a fallen women, Laura's new love "consumed itself away" and Laura dies from grief and shame. Her lover goes to marry a "gentle bride/With gay light heart, and pure and placid brow,/Unused to grief, and impotent to chide" (122). The poem models a fictional persona that characterizes Norton's work; spoiled innocence, wounded pride, and disappointed hopes result from woman's attempts at love and marriage. The beautiful bride quickly falls into adultery or shame because of the careless, cold nature of man, and woman's lot is misery. Although there was no proof that Norton ever had an affair with Melbourne, one may read the poem from 1829 and wonder about it as a premonition of future scandals.

The Norton phenomenon, which, with a different theme, is also the Hemans phenomenon, and, without the poet's participation, the Robinson phenomenon. In Neal Gabler's formulation, "playing one was just as good as being one." This publicity-role is also and much more recently, the Zsa Zsa Gabor phenomenon. As Neal Gabler says, in the early 1950s she became "a household name," owing solely to publicity; and Gabor said, "I saw things not as they were but as a play within a play, in which I was always the heroine." This is also the Angelyne phenomenon: "a huge-breasted young woman named Angelyne posted billboard of herself around Los Angeles, but the billboards advertised nothing." Elizabeth Taylor speaks for all these women when she says, "I am my own commodity."[47]

Norton's work reveals women who are rejected lovers, abandoned mothers, disillusioned wives, or innocent virgins embarking upon their ruin by trusting foolish lovers. Men are crude, impatient, restless, unfaithful, manipulative, and ever fickle about love. Marriage is never constant and rarely happy in Norton's poetry. The future promises more pain and an early death for women who attach themselves to a man. The only hope for happiness is in a woman's love for her own family, or a mother's love for her children; but even that love is disappointed when the children (who are often sons) cause grief by becoming like their fathers, or are killed by men. Such is the fate of the illegitimate infant child in "The Haunted Wood of Amesoy," originally published in *Court Magazine* in 1833.

In this poem a young woman hides her baby in the deep forest of Amesoy because she is afraid of her brother's wrath upon the child. Norton gives the woman mythical status when she compares her to the Levite mother of Moses, "that mother of the east/Who laid her cradled child to sleep/Upon the water's changeful breast."[48] A wild dog leads her to the interior of the forest each day where the natural world of beauty and innocence surrounds the trio until nature is brushed aside by the impatient hand of her brother: "The slight acacia bends aside/Its trembling boughs and wavering form,/The larch o'erthrown, leaves passage wide—" (I:177). The loving serenity of motherhood is destroyed as the woman runs through the forest like a hunted animal until her brother grabs the infant and, in spite of her desperate pleas to spare its life, he murders the baby. Norton rails at the baby's father, "the false and faithless lover," asking, "Where was he . . . whose cold and coward heart/Refused to do a father's part?" (I:180). Norton's finish to this gruesome tale is a complaint about disloyalty, implying that men are never satisfied with one woman; the male is continually searching for a new lover: he "Plucks first the lily—then the rose" (I:181). While the male lover pursues another lover, the female lover is lost in her memories and, like the young mother in "The Haunted Wood of Amesoy," she sometimes becomes a madwoman, roaming the wild woods with a shaggy hound as her faithful guide to a hidden infant corpse. The woman is forever alienated from man by what appears to the male society as an unreasonable desire for constancy and devotion. Hopes for a family are destroyed by the lack of a responsible man willing to fulfill his duties in a mature partnership. Isolation or insanity are the only choices for a woman who looks to men for basic needs of human survival, a theme also familiar to L. E. L.. In "The Dream" (1840), a widowed mother recalls her youthful hopes for fulfillment in love and marriage, which she now bitterly views as unrealistic expectations as she watches her sleeping daughter. The girl wakes to retell her mother a dream she has had about a man she would like to marry, a mystery man who takes her to exotic Edenesque gardens and talks with her about science, history, and literature. She tells her mother, "We sate together: his most noble head/Bent o'er the storied tome of other days,/And still he commented on all we read,/And taught me what to love, and what to praise."[49] The man is a teacher, yet he is also a lover whose interest lies only in her. She says, "I was the living idol of his heart;/How to make joy a portion of the air/That breathed around me, seem'd his only care" (43). Through the girl's dream, Norton has painted a portrait of her vision of a woman's ideal companion: a man with whom she can share intellect and beauty, and who cares for her well-being without needing to control her destiny. Yet the mother of experience reluctantly tells her daughter that this mystery man is only possible in a dream world. She warns her to be realistic in her expectations of love, because a bad marriage means the acceptance of hardship and pain:

> Heaven give thee poverty, disease, or death,
> Each varied ill that waits on human breath,
> Rather than bid thee linger out thy life
> In the long toil of such unnatural strife.
> To wander through the world unreconciled,
> Heart weary as a spirit-broken child,
> And think it were an hour of bliss like Heaven
> If thou could'st *die*—forgiving and forgiven,—
> Or with a feverish hope, of anguish born,
> (Nerving thy mind to feel indignant scorn
> Of all the cruel foes who 'twixt ye stand,
> Holding thy heartstrings with a reckless hand,)
> Steal to his presence, now unseen so long,
> And claim *his* mercy who hath dealt the wrong! (58–59)

Like "The Haunted Wood of Amesoy," this poem provides a bleak picture of life which prefers poverty, disease, or death to an unhappy marriage. Norton displays the shameful yearning for a man who is incapable of love, and the pattern of many women who pocket their pride to return to their husbands again and again, admitting wrongs where there are none, just for the hope that the prideful husband will let them return to the hearth. The woman must devalue herself in return for the portion of security she receives from the man who controls her very livelihood.

Although this is the mother's vision of a bad marriage, her perception of a "good" marriage does not leave much hope for the girl's happiness. For happiness and fulfillment are not attainable in life through love and marriage in Norton's world. In the closing stanzas of the poem, the mother tries to comfort the girl with what she sees as a realistic vision of the relationship between men and women: "Not for herself was woman first create,/Nor yet to be man's idol, but his mate." With this union, woman should expect no joy except what comes from pleasing her husband: "doubt not thou, (although at times deceived, Outraged, insulted, slander'd, crush'd, and grieved;/Too often made a victim or a toy,/With years of sorrow for an hour of joy;/ Too oft forgot midst Pleasure's circling wiles,/Or only valued for her rosy smiles,—)" (69). This black view of marriage implies a life of slavery that includes total dehumanization, reducing the woman to an object of occasional entertainment and great spite for the man. Yet, by the end of the poem, the mother is satisfied that she has given her daughter a true picture of married life and she is now confident that her daughter is ready to go into the world "a youthful bride."

In another early poem, "The Future" (1830), a woman learns to be grateful for her life as a "childless, lonely wife." She remembers a childhood friend she once envied because of her wealth and beauty, who married against her will and went insane. The narrator then remembers her own first experience with love; she was rejected by a man who "changed, even as he did to me,/Thought something later; and he sought another/To please his fancy, far away from home."[50] She finally marries, but grieves about her childlessness until she watches a neighbor boy grow into manhood. The young man he has become is "so fierce,/So wild, so headlong, and so haughty too,/So cruel in avenging any wrongs,/So merciless when he had half avenged them!" (204). The man becomes a murderer, his mother dies of a broken heart, and his father dies soon after the sentencing.

Gendered complaints scold Norton for being too dramatic or depressing. In a June 1831 review of *The Undying One and Other Poems*, the reviewer writes, "We feel satisfied that, with a more congenial subject—one calmer, commoner, less ambitious—a very different whole would have been the result. It is strange how difficult it is to persuade ladies that their forte does not lie in representations of those dark passions, which, for their own comfort, we hope they have witnessed only in description."[51] The reviewer encourages Norton to "confine herself to simpler themes, instead of plunging beyond the visible diurnal sphere" (366). Highly charged emotional attacks evident in Norton's work subverted the domestic ideal and challenged notions of propriety for women. Although Hartley Coleridge dubs Norton "the Byron of our modern poetesses" in the *Quarterly Review* and praises her for showing "Byron's beautiful intervals of tenderness, his strong practical thought, and his forceful expression" in his 1840 review of *The Dream and Other Poems*,[52] Coleridge does not approve of her passionate themes; he hopes that Norton will "break through the narrow circle of personal and domestic feelings and adventure herself upon a theme of greater variety and less morbid interest. There is a great difference between writing always from the heart and always about the heart, even the heart of a beautiful woman of genius." Ironically, Coleridge also claims that Norton's suffering improves her poetry: "The last three or four years have made Mrs. Norton a greater writer than she was; she is deeper, plainer, truer" (376). Yopie Prins cites this as evidence that "Norton herself also seems to personify suffering womanhood."[53] In her late-century study, Catherine J. Hamilton bypasses Norton and scolds her predecessor for such themes: "To make poetry alive and bristling with our own personality—our own 'selfism'—is in reality a grand mistake, for which Byron has much to answer."[54] After Norton's death, James Hamilton Fyfe's obituary in the *Temple Bar* (January 1878) criticizes her fiction:

> The chief fault of these works is the melancholy tone which pervades them, which is apt to depress the readers, and make them rise more wearied and dismal than when they opened the book, which is obviously a mistake, as the essential object of fiction should be not exactly mere amusement, but an interesting relaxation of the mind.[55]

According to this writer, Norton's "Dedication to the Duchess of Sutherland" printed with *The Dream and Other Poems* "falls very glaringly into a tendency to the error pointed out by the *Quarterly*, baring her personal troubles too openly to the general gaze, and wailing in an undignified measure" (108).

Complain as they may, the image of Norton as a wounded wife became the standard interpretation of her life because, like L. E. L., she made her living by writing literature that articulated the wrongs of the calumniated woman. Two of Norton's popular *Keepsake* stories published for readers who may have also viewed "Regina's Maids of Honour" and read the newspaper accounts of Norton's personal troubles further demonstrate her despairing view of domestic harmony. Preacher Lawrence Bayley rejects his childhood sweetheart Mary Esdale for the temptations of a "painted lady of fashion" in "Lawrence Bayley's Temptation" (1834).[56] Before Lawrence confesses his love for Lady Delamere, Norton intervenes, becoming a preacher herself, ranting against false hopes of naive, but virtuous, maidens who hope for love:

> Shout, little children! . . . from you the angel nature hath not yet departed—
> in your hearts linger still the emanations from the Creator; perfect love and

perfect joy . . . the dark days are coming when ye shall see no light, and the hours when mirth shall be strange to you, and the time when your voices shall grow so sad that they shall mingle with the wailing of the winds, and not be distinguishable from them, because of the exceeding sorrow of their tones! (152)

Lawrence becomes one of Lady Delamere's many lovers, and eventually dies from his wasted life as a fashionable lady's toy. While Norton ennobles Mary for her angelic martyrdom, Lady Delamere's outright disregard for middle-class propriety presents an opportunity to consider the immense distance between values of the aristocracy and mid- to working-class social regions. Norton's portrayal of both lifestyles is problematic; Lady Delamere has sexual freedom and privileges of upper-class life, while Mary demonstrates righteous, but lonely, moral conformity. The reader can identify with Mary, justifying her own narrow position in middle-class society, while imagining what the permissive fashionable life of Lady Delamere would be like. As Eric Trudgill explains:

> She could revel in highly coloured pictures of fashionable vice, and yet keep in touch with the proprieties through the writers' nominal morality, their frequent diatribes against the immorality they depicted, their genuflections through the virtuous heroines towards the Madonna ideal.[57]

Norton nods to conventionality with Mary (the Madonna), and Lady Delamere is not an attractive model for a fashionable women, but both women are victims of a social system that depends on male attention and support. In Norton's scheme, neither Lady Delamere nor Mary will find happiness in love.

In one of Norton's interesting works of short fiction, "Count Rodolph's Heir" (1836 *Keepsake*), an Italian mistress jilted by her lover for an English heiress moves into a ruined castle on the Count's property where she can haunt Rodolph's new wife and curse their children. Leona's true enemy is the heir she unsuccessfully attempts to save from a shaky bridge leading to the castle ruins late in the story, for he represents the patriarchal regeneration which required the Count to marry a woman for title and money instead of his improper Italian lover. The mistress Leona goes insane and dies for her immoral obsession with destroying the Count's domestic harmony; but Norton clearly demonstrates the drastic results of woman's emotional or financial dependence upon fickle, disloyal men such as Count Rodolph. The madwoman Leona is a victim to society and male abuse; therefore, while she receives the punishment of death as a fallen woman, Norton allows her character the dignity of a hero when Leona sacrifices her own life in the attempt to save the Count's son.

Norton's heroines such as Leona are angry women, plotting intricate plans of cruel revenge and murder. These behavior patterns run sharply against domestic norms prescribed for women in the nineteenth century.

According to Deborah Gorham,

> The ideal woman was willing to be dependent on men and submissive to them, and she would have a preference for a life restricted to the confines of home. She would be innocent, pure, gentle and self-sacrificing. Possessing no ambitious strivings, she would be free of any trace of anger or hostility. More emotional than man, she was also more capable of self-renunciation.[58]

The women writers Mary Poovey discusses in her classic treatment of women and propriety, *The Proper Lady and the Woman Writer* (1984), found that indirection and accommodation best enabled their self-expression, but Norton's angry heroines go against the rules of propriety, becoming martyred avengers as they seek outright retribution for their abuse. This consistent presentation of disturbed women and domestic situations in her fiction and poetry combined with the cooperation of periodicals such as *Fraser's* to keep her before the public.

Norton's writings before and after the 1836 adultery scandal portray a friendless woman who sees herself completely devoid of the comforts of society, but guests at her popular salon at Storey's Gate before the trial record a starkly different version of the "calumniated" woman. Here witnesses describe a stunningly beautiful Mrs. Norton laughing and singing with luminaries such as Bulwer Lytton, Samuel Rogers, Thomas Moore, Disraeli, and Fanny Kemble. After the scandal, the Duchess of Sutherland invited Norton to ride through Hyde Park in her carriage, demonstrating her support and partially restoring Norton's position in London society. Norton thanks the Duchess in her "Dedication to Her Grace the Duchess of Sutherland," in *The Dream and Other Poems* (1840). According to Norton, the Duchess stood by her, against "bitter tongues . . . who hunt in packs the object of their blame."[59] The dedication publicizes private anguish, in a strategy that became even more conspicuous over time, until, in the twenty-first century, entertainment-hungry audiences expect (and get) best sellers in which public figures (perhaps wronged wives) candidly reveal their sorrows, under contract for millions. In 1840, Norton's volume exemplifies her secure place in the literary profession. Norton soon returned to London parties, although she was often the only woman among men whose wives would not accompany them to gatherings frequented by women such as Norton. William Brookfield's wife, Jane, refused to call on Norton, although Brookfield asserted in a letter to his mother on 26 March 1847 that "nobody in London believes a syllable of harm between Lord M. and Mrs. N.—nobody that is that knows anything at all about the matter."[60] He halfheartedly supports Norton: "And tho I should not approve of her as an intimate friend there is nothing against a mere slight acquaintance even for the most prudent. I believe her to be as entirely free from any impropriety as Miss Bates of Miss Harrison or Mrs. Best,—three as spotless virgins I should think as the chaste moon ever sees putting on their night caps" (210). The comment shows Brookfield mustering up a defense for Norton against pressures of middle-class propriety; nevertheless Jane Brookfield insists that keeping such company will taint her husband's reputation: "Cannot you call up visions of cosy little Sunday dinners with Mrs. Norton, Mr. Thackeray, and Mr. and Mrs. Wigan?" (11). Although Sidney Herbert was Norton's current companion, Jane's comment might also reflect a fear that Norton will interfere with her own designs on Thackeray.

Diarists often record her appearance at such parties; on 31 January 1845, Samuel Rogers invited seven men to his home for dinner, including Henry Crabb Robinson, Edward Moxon, Alfred Tennyson, and James Spedding. Rogers announced Norton a "mystery" guest and admirer of Tennyson's. Robinson writes about her arrival:

> A whisper ran along the company, which I could not make out. She instantly joined our conversation, with an ease and spirit that showed her quite used to society . . . And we had exchanged a few sentences when she named herself, and I then recognized the much-eulogized and calumniated Honorable Mrs. Norton, who, you may recollect, was purged by a jury finding for the defendant in a *crim. con.* action by her husband against Lord Melbourne. When I knew who she was, I felt that I ought to have distinguished her beauty and grace by my own discernment, and not waited for a formal announcement. You are aware that her position in society was, to a great degree, imperilled.[61]

Evidently Tennyson perceived Norton as a notorious flirt and behaved badly toward her, perhaps intimidated by her direct, flirtatious manner or disgusted by her attendance as the only woman at the party. Nevertheless, Norton continued to attract the best in English society, especially men.

Fanny Kemble remembers Norton as being vitally active in 1841, recalling that Norton "still maintained her glorious supremacy of beauty and wit in the great London world. She often came to parties at our house, and I remember her asking us to dine at her uncle's, when among the people we met were Lord Lansdowne and Lord Normanby, both then in the ministry."[62] Granddaughter of playwright and politician Richard Brinsley Sheridan and his first wife, singer Elizabeth Linley, Caroline Norton always had a sense for the dramatic. According to Kemble,

> Mrs. Norton was extremely epigrammatic in her talk, and comically dramatic in her manner of narrating things . . . I remember shaking in my shoes when, soon after I came out, she told me she envied me, and would give anything to try the stage herself. I thought, as I looked at her wonderful, beautiful face, "Oh, if you should, what would become of me!"

Lady Eastlake described Norton as "rather a professed story teller . . . a perpetual actress, consumma tely studying and playing her part, and that always the attempt to fascinate—she cares not whom."[63] Such accounts may show Norton's mechanism for carrying on in spite of personal pain, but they also suggest that the wounded-wife image depicted in her literary work was not necessarily bound with reality, in spite of many observers who wished to give her a Byronic temperament (whose pose was also, ironically, false).

In 1840 Hartley Coleridge called her "the Byron of our modern poetesses" in John Murray's *Quarterly Review*, citing her "intense personal passion" in passages that "sound like javelins hurled by Amazons."[64] Norton expressed ambivalence about Byron's work, claiming in a letter to Murray on 4 November 1837 that she had never finished *Don Juan*:

> It is a book which no woman will ever like, whether for the reasons given by the author, or on other accounts, I will not dispute. To me the effect is like hearing some sweet and touching melody familiar to me as having been sung by a lost friend and companion, suddenly struck up in quick time with all the words parodied.[65]

She resented Byron's occasional misogyny, accusing Murray of a similar attitude toward *Keepsake* editor Lady Emmeline Stuart Wortley, who had recently announced her engagement: "She is the truest, simplest woman that ever was bit by romance; but you are an infidel, and don't believe in women, because your Byron wrote some clever lines against the sex—yet how was so profligate a man to know good women?" (418). Yet, in her resistance she exemplifies the rebellion she supposedly inherits. In spite of Norton's disgust for Byron, around her name she constructed a public persona that imitated Byronic conventions. In 1883 William Bates would write of Norton's work: "There existed some fatal factor,—some lurking cypher, as it were—to mar the sweet equation of life; and domestic misery, wounded affection, and unmerited shame, was its well-known story."[66] In *Women Novelists of Queen Victoria's Reign* (1897), Anne Hector reports that "To this lovely and loveable woman, life was a long disappointment; and through all she has written a strain of profound rebellion against the irony of fate colours her views, her delineations of character, her estimation of the social world."[67] Such commentaries persistently recall complaints in Norton's work and newspaper accounts of her public battles.

Dorothy Mermin describes the Byronic tendencies in Norton, noting that "Like Byron, she made her notorious marital misfortunes the thinly disguised subject of verse, and her attacks on the legal system that empowered her husband exposed her, like Byron, to additional obloquy on the score of her personal life."[68] Byron "brazenly exploited the known facts of his life and his scandalous reputation" in his poetry, but most women writers avoided such "blatant self-exposure," according to Mermin:

> Female emulation of Byron in this respect would seem not just futile . . . but immodest, impure, unwomanly. For a woman to appear in public, to be publicly known or spoken of at all, was still, as it had been in England for centuries, morally suspect; for women, all fame was ill fame. (18)

Jerome McGann and others show that Byron's manipulations seemed like exposures, but were not; Jerome Christensen further describes the historical appetite for Byron:

> In the wake of the public failure of traditional metaphors to fit and enlightened ones to be fully adopted, a new figure merged on the contemporary scene as

the figure *of* the contemporary. That figure—the collaborative invention of a gifted poet, a canny publisher, eager reviewers, and rapt readers—became the culturally dominant and economically profitable phenomenon called "Byron."[69]

Andrew Elfenbein proposes that Byron's "representation of subjectivity meshed perfectly with a stereotypically feminine fascination with *"secret history*," and women readers (and writers) connected with a personal response, central to the aesthetic of sentiment in women's writing.[70]

Two generations of feminist scholars explore differing approaches to Byronism and women writers. Dorothy Mermin describes Byron as "a model on many levels—stylistic, political, moral, erotic—for the rebellion implicit in the fact of female ambition," and Mermin suggests that he "fed girls' restlessness, their desire for scope and freedom" while bringing them up "sharply against the barriers of gender." In Mermin's view, "Byron's obstinate self-assertion, his reckless defiance of tyranny and convention, gave an essential impetus to women who had to defy cultural authority and override the convention of feminine self-suppression in order to write."[71] More skeptically and more radically, Angela Leighton writes that Byronism "offered many of these women writers, not so much the cheap ideal of a dark, handsome husband, but the prospect of a transvestite emancipation from the restricting dress of femininity." Women explore "a drama of desire in which the woman seeks, not only a lover, but also her forbidden other self—the one who is experienced, worldy wise and, like Lélia, cynically unromantic."[72] Shifting perspective from personality to institutions and careerism, Yopie Prins contends that the "selling of women poets earlier in the century" established a "precedent for such identification" between author and audience and suggests that "a reversal of perspective might allow us to see how Byron's poetic career is modeled on female authorship as well."[73]

Nineteenth-century readers were less suspect of commercial fabrication than moral fiber, and, like Byron, Caroline Norton was morally suspect. Observers often commented on her "unwomanly" characteristics, and her aggressive printed rebuttals and lobbying efforts were clearly immodest. Although gossip enraged her, Norton repeatedly risked public exposure and, like Byron, she profited from it.

Critics and social commentators often described Norton in masculine terms, demonstrating her departure from feminine propriety and relating her more closely to the Byronic persona. According to S. C. Hall, "She combined in a singular degree feminine delicacy with masculine vigor; though essentially womanly, she seemed to have the force of character of man."[74] On 16 February 1839, American Charles Sumner describes her conversation as being "masculine without being mannish; there is the grace and ease of the woman, with a strength and skill of which any man might well be proud."[75] These comments show that, in spite of vehement protests about the way society treated her, Caroline Norton could not fit the gendered pattern dictated by domestic ideology. For she was an anomaly: married but single, a mother without children, a career woman without a salary, a tainted woman with influence, and an indomitable force for change in women's rights who refused to promote equality with men. Caroline Norton simply couldn't keep herself under the tight constraints required by traditional notions of femininity. According to biographer Alice Acland,

> In the almost flamboyant effect of her personality [Norton] was very far removed from the ideal feminine type of the day. The pure, gentle, timid, docile woman—a type soon to be crystallised in the person of Amelia Sedley— held a high place then in the public imagination. It was impossible for Caroline to model herself on the lines of such doves with folded wings. And because she could not pretend to be an Amelia Sedley, many people thought she must be a Becky Sharp instead.[76]

A letter to Lord Conyngham printed as a frontispiece in *A Plain Letter to the Lord Chancellor on the Infant Custody Bill* in 1839 displays the attitude that would invite such comparisons: "I may be a woman—and they may cut me to pieces,—but they shall find, like the worm, that every atom has life in it still, and if I have refused to turn their own follies against them, it has been out of respect to my own nature, not to them."[77]

This does not fit the model proposed by Prins and others who suggest Byronic analogies in Norton, Felicia Hemans, and L. E. L. in a sisterhood of sentiment positioned within the Sappho/Corinne myth described by Peterson:

> It tells the tale of an inspired poetess, half-Italian, half-English, who spends her daytime hours in solitude, awaiting inspiration, and her nights in company, per- forming for her audience and winning great fame . . . [The] Poetess sacrifices herself in performance for men: for their erotic pleasure, obviously, but also for their corporate benefit in that she does not interfere with (or intervene in) the patriarchal structures.[78]

Peterson traces the idea of poetess as improvisatrice and abandoned woman from Mary Robinson's autobiographical *Memoirs* (1801), although she excludes Norton from her curiously narrow desription of major nineteenth- century women poets: Mary Robinson, Felicia Hemans, L. E. L., Elizabeth Barrett Browning, and Christina Rossetti. Tricia Lootens and Yopie Prins argue that the construction of the Sapphic persona among nineteenth-century women writers was an empty pursuit, leading to "a conflation of poet worship and woman worship, constructing a generic idea of woman that shapes the reception of many Victorian women poets." "The Poetess proves to be the personification of an empty figure," thus ensuring the disappearance of their works in the canon.[79] According to Lootens:

> For while the glory of the Romantic poet-hero was believed to arise from purely individual genius, the "genius of woman" was often seen as both generic and radically ahistorical. Trapped between the demands of poet worship and "woman" worship, historical women writers became mythic impossibilities.

Efforts to accord them canonicity thus tended to split between casting them as honorary Great Men and lauding them as vessels of the unitary, eternal, and ultimately silent sanctity of womanhood. More like pâpier-maché than marble, the metaphoric figures of such canonized nineteenth-century women poets were shaped around vacancy: if their literary "relics" were revered, it was not as embodiments but as representations of a transcendent and definitively absent feminine glory."[80]

To ascribe feelings to the poetry inscribed by the poetic persona is to embrace the denial of art practiced in Lootens's model, and to believe that poetry is biography invites a regressive approach that history proves fatal for the canonization of women writers.

The image of Corinne persisted in biographical accounts of Norton and others, and Norton repeats the damaged woman trope in her literary work, but her private correspondence does not indicate such a submissive attitude toward men. Norton was a strong, rebellious activist for women's rights, spurred by personal resentments and disgust for the damage wrought by domestic ideology, and her work is sorely neglected. Norton shares with *Fraser's* Maids of Honour an indomitable spirit that kept the "calumniated" woman fighting for her professional status and personal integrity, in spite of the scandals that surrounded them.

While the paradoxical visual text placed before the public imagination in *Fraser's* creates an image of the Maids as fair and fine, literary texts and biographical records that often contradict them combine to war against the Fraserians' status quo. In his memoirs of the "Maclise Portrait Gallery of Illustrious Literary Characters," William Bates adds yet another pictorial image to "Regina's Maids of Honour." Recalling men throughout history who have been caught spying on women, Bates proclaims that "dire pains and penalties have been deservedly incurred by those rash individuals of the inferior sex who have dared to intrude upon the sacred rites and mysteries of the ladies in secret conclave assembled."[81] Bates claims that "there are here none of the symbols of secrecy. The rose is on the cheek instead of the ceiling, and a coffee-cup interposed between finger and lip" (356–57). His patronizing joke reverses the domestic spheres, making men the inferior sex who suffer when they try to invade the woman's circle; however, many symbols of secrecy encode "Regina's Maids of Honour." The Fraserians need only read the pages of *Fraser's* where Caroline Norton, Marguerite Blessington, L. E. L., Harriet Martineau, and Lady Morgan serve as examples of professionalism and the commodification of scandal that threaten to upturn the social order.

"THE VERY ROADS OF LITERATURE": WOMEN EDITORS OF NINETEENTH-CENTURY BRITISH LITERARY ANNUALS

Perspectives drawn from bibliographical analyses of the text as a product of human work must necessarily view the product from the enabling source and examine sociological environments that allow texts to circulate. Yet the history of scholarship on authorship, reading, and publishing is relatively new.[1] We emphasize our debt to such scholarship, as we explore methods of textual interpretation that view publishing history as part of the continuous link between material text and reader. The burgeoning middle-class consumerism that drove the nineteenth-century literary marketplace created early opportunities for women through the production of literary annuals and periodicals, and this moment in literary history provides an opportunity to examine gender politics informing women writers, editors, and texts in this moment of literary history.

By the 1830s, literature was clearly breaking genre and gender barriers. Women readers, writers, editors, engravers, artists, and other literary professionals encroached upon the male-dominated profession, creating new ways for doing business and capitalistic new formats for reading material. Dorothy Mermin writes that there were

> Periodicals at all levels, and for many audiences, intellectual or frivolous: for men, women, children, or particular religious groups . . . For many women, journalism served as an entrance to a literary career or augmented income from poetry or fiction. All sorts of journals were happy to accept poems from unknown writers, and Elizabeth Barrett and George Eliot first achieved publication in this way—not very prestigious, but encouraging to the young.[2]

According to Margaret Beetham, these opportunities for women in the periodicals "depended on the construction of reading as an essentially domestic activity, of writing as a task which could be undertaken at home, and of certain genres—notably fiction and improving or domestic articles—as potentially feminine in character."[3] The annuals had little to do with "domestic articles," but their literature and illustrations featured traditionally feminine themes, although, as we will show in chapter 5, the textual opportunities provided by such offerings connote domestic disfunction and ideological disarray. The professional model of a woman writer working within the confines of her domestic environment remained consistent throughout the early Victorian period, but the model caused problems for women such as L. E. L., whose mixture of public and private contributed to the scandal already accumulating in her name.

Male publishers and authors met the challenge of these new women workers in the trade with mixed responses; while quick to cash in on the promise of new prosperity, they were anxious about the turnover of power to women, as well as to the middle class, even though they were themselves middle class. By 1847 G. H. Lewes, reporting on the state of the literary profession, was expressing a paranoia felt by some male writers threatened by women and other undesirables entering the field in record numbers. He remarks upon the hordes of authors cashing in on profitable new outlets for writing in the nineteenth century: "Literature should be a profession, not a trade," he claims. When authorship is well-paid, it tempts "speculators" who dirty the profession with commercialism. According to Lewes, the next step will be "an innumerable host of hungry pretenders. It will be—and, indeed, is, now fast approaching that state—like the army of Xerxes, swelled and encumbered by women, children, and ill-trained troops. It should be a Macedonian phalanx, chosen, compact, and irresistible."[4] The military language invites a declaration of war on troops of bad writers and broadens the threat to include children and the "ill-trained" commoner working the grubby literary trade beneath him, presumably in both class and talent. Women writers encumber the efforts of real writers (men), who control the apparently chaotic classlessness now infringing upon his formerly secure encampment. The literary profession should be populated with a chosen few brilliant authors. As Julia Swindells notes, Lewes's comment "is about the reorganization of work and a fear that that reorganization will escape his control; and 'his' control signifies male control of a particular kind": an exclusionary men's club of "gentlemen" authors.[5] Unfortunately for Lewes, the notion of control was a long outdated reality. Women and other "ill-trained" troops had been working the writer's trade for centuries, but the nineteenth century's prolific shift to publishing periodicals and illustrated books created a bigger need for literary workers, whether they be of the chosen elite or not. The last twenty years of feminist criticism provides many examples of female professionalism from the early modern period to the present, and women writers and editors increased in record numbers since the late eighteenth century. The presence of women such as Mary Robinson, Felicia Hemans, L. E. L., Lady Blessington, Harriet Martineau, Lady Morgan, Caroline Norton, Mary Russell Mitford, and Elizabeth Barrett certainly justified Lewes's perception of a literary invasion.

Literary annuals of the 1830s and 1840s, in particular, created early economic opportunities for these women as writers and editors, who threatened to usurp male power by taking their place beside men in the publishing community. Victorian scholars often consider annuals in the same vein as other periodicals, but they were a distinctly different genre, sharing with other Victorian periodicals only the context of periodic printing and a "feminine" aesthetic common to much literature of the period, contributing to male fears of female domination. The appearance of the first literary annual, the *Forget-Me-Not* (1823), preceded by some twenty years the prolific growth of weekly and monthly magazines, and annuals deserve to be studied as a unique publishing phenomenon. Barbara Onslow writes, "The annuals like the silver-fork novels lost their glitter, but a small though significant legacy was that women had been visible as editors."[6] By the 1840s when titles of new periodicals began to appear weekly, the heyday of literary annuals was over, but women editors of the annuals served as early models for later women professionals and offered alternatives to prescribed domestic roles.

Of course, annuals editors did not work in a historical vacuum; their immediate ancestors were women such as Mary Robinson, Charlotte Smith, Joanna Baillie, Maria Edgeworth, Anna Letitia Barbauld, Hannah More, and a host of other "bluestocking" women writers whose texts and histories scholars busily work to make available for study. Judith Pascoe shows how Mary Robinson's career provides an example of literary professionalism as she "participated most fully and willingly" in a publicity stunt created by *The Morning Post* in the 1790s to market her as a literary commodity that would sell newspapers.[7] Poet and novelist Charlotte Smith provides another early example, beginning her career by sending compositions to the *Lady's Magazine* at the age of fourteen and later supporting nine children by writing ten novels in ten years. These predecessors to literary annuals editors showed that women could successfully work the writer's trade, and their examples, while outside the scope of the present book, provide fascinating case studies of how women negotiated gender politics as participants in a male-dominated profession. Literary annuals were elegant anthologies of original poetry and prose published during the Christmas gift-giving season. Their stunning display included steel-plate engravings of contemporary art and beautiful new binding techniques. Sometimes covered in sparkling crimson watered-silk or finely tooled morocco leather, annuals rapidly became a literary fashion from the first title in 1823. Annuals reported financial returns high enough to save many publishers from ruin during the depression of the 1820s, and they continued to enrich the publishing industry until competition between annuals and other periodicals forced most of them out of existence by the late 1840s. Until feminist scholarship of the last two decades created interest in women writers and women's books, scholars largely ignored literary annuals, viewing them as trite, sentimental examples of amateurism and literary fashion.

Historical accounts supported this interpretation; male writers such as Tennyson, Scott, Wordsworth, Moore, Lamb, and others blasted them as an inferior popular genre while they pocketed the high fees being offered to notable authors. J. G. Lockhart called annuals the "toyshop of literature" and "painted bladders" in his biography of Walter Scott;[8] Charles Lamb condemned them for their "ostentatious trumpery";[9] and Tennyson claimed in 1831 that he was so "beGemmed and be-Amuletted and be-forget-me-not-ted" that he would never again appear in annuals, calling them, by 1837, "vapid books."[10] Yet, most authors, celebrated or not, appeared in one or more of the many titles during the annuals craze. As frequent contributor Camilla Toulmin (Mrs. Newton Crosland) wrote, "Indeed everybody who was anybody in the close, introspective circle of early Victorian literary society was at some time or other seduced into contributing to the annuals—either by money, or by snobbery, or by ambition for notice, or by feelings of friendship, or simply because they feared that if they did not contribute people would think that they had not been invited to do so."[11] Despite the potentially prohibitive price of twelve shillings (*The Keepsake* was a guinea), S. C. Hall estimated the public spent 100,000 pounds each season for annuals during their peak in the 1830s.[12] In 1824 *The Literary Souvenir* sold 6,000 copies in two weeks; the following year their totals exceeded 15,000. According to A. Bose, "The number of English Annuals, rising from nine in 1825 and 1826 to forty-three in 1830, fell to eleven in 1850, and after 1860 the species virtually died out."[13] Troops of editors pursuing the same pool of writers for such a small piece of the marketplace could frighten writers accustomed to being courted by genteel publishers.

Already hampered by such resistance, women editors had to create unconventional ways to do literary business. Codes of propriety prevented respectable women from conducting business in an office like the male editors. Nigel Cross delineates the woman writer as working within

> a well-established ghetto for women writers; a cramped literary world where women wrote discreetly to each other courtesy of the General Post Office while their male colleagues enjoyed the privileged freedoms of the Garrick Club. The boundaries of this ghetto were well defined, they came into force before the woman writer put pen to paper.[14]

Many times editorial negotiations necessarily occurred during social events or late night receptions, and requests from hostesses came so frequently that authors began to avoid parties where editors would pursue them as contributors. Thomas Moore confesses in his journal (30 April 1833) that he "took the opportunity of escaping" during a concert because, "After all, all the Zoologicals of the Periodicals were there collected, Miss Landon, Jerdan &c &c."[15] Moore fears being asked for a contribution from L. E. L., editor of *Fisher's Drawing Room Scrapbook*, and *Literary Gazette* editor William Jerdan. Competition was fierce between annuals editors, who also competed with periodicals editors for contributors. A brief review of named editors in Frederick W. Faxon's *Literary Annuals and Gift Books: A Bibliography 1823–1903* reveals an incomplete, yet surprising number of women editors and the annuals they edited during the period (listed alphabetically):

Countess of Blessington (Marguerite Gardiner): *Heath's Book of Beauty* 1834–47; *Heath's Gems of Beauty* 1836–40; *Flowers of Loveliness* 1836–41; *The Keepsake* 1841–50.
Mrs. Ellet: *The Christian Keepsake* 1850.
Sarah Stickney Ellis: *The Juvenile Scrapbook* 1840–48.
Mrs. S. C. Hall (Anna Maria Hall): *Ackermann's Juvenile Forget-Me-Not* 1828–37; *The Book of Royalty* 1839.
Mrs. M. A. Jevons (Mary Anne Jevons): *Sacred Offering* 1831–38.
L. E. L.: *Heath's Book of Beauty* 1833; *Bijou Almanac* 1839; *Easter Gift* 1832; *Fisher's Drawing Room Scrapbook* 1832–38.
Eliza Leslie: *Juvenile Bijou* n.d., Ca. 1830.
Mrs. Milner: *The Juvenile Scrapbook* 1850.
Mary Russell Mitford: *The Iris* 1840; *Finden's Tableaux* 1837–44.
Caroline Norton: *The English Annual* 1834–38; *The Keepsake* 1836; *Fisher's Drawing Room Scrapbook* 1847–48.
Mrs. Maxwell Paisley: *Renfrewshire Annual* 1842.
Marguerite Power [Lady Blessington's niece]: *The Keepsake* 1851–57.
Louisa H. Sheridan: *The Comic Offering* 1831–35; *The Diadem* 1832–39.
Agnes Strickland: *Fisher's Juvenile Scrapbook* 1836–39 (with Bernard Barton).
Jane Strickland: *The Juvenile Scrapbook* 1849.
Charlotte Elizabeth (Charlotte Elizabeth Tonna): *The Protestant Annual* 1841.
Lady Emmeline Stuart-Wortley: *The Keepsake* 1837 and 1840.
Mrs. A. A. Watts (Zilla Maden Watts): *New Year's Gift* 1829–36; *The Talisman* 1831; *Le Keepsake Français* 1830.[16]

Most of these women were also contributors to other annuals and periodicals without apparent conflict between their roles as editors and writers, other than being overworked. Although the shift from editor to author complicates our distinctions of professionalism, women who wrote and edited annuals did not make such distinctions. It was all literary work, and the now-clearly defined positions of editor or writer were not immediate concerns. An editor's poetic persona became an editorial tool, just as it became the marketing tactic we describe in chapter 3.

Moore records in his journal the sense of competition between woman editors of the annuals. According to his journal entry on 17 December 1833, Lady Blessington bragged that her 1834 *Book of Beauty* "had beat Miss Landon's in sale by 2000 copies"; L. E. L. was the previous editor of the *Book of Beauty*, and Blessington took pride in her own success with the annual over any common ground she might have shared with L. E. L. as editor of the same publication.[17] On 24 February 1835, Moore called on Lady Blessington during his afternoon round of social visits and reported, "My Lady full of thanks for my contribution to her Book of Beauty, and emploring me not to give any thing to Mrs. Norton" (1665). His contribution for

Blessington's 1835 *Book of Beauty* was a poem, "The Boat of Life." But later that year, when Caroline Norton asked Moore for a contribution to her 1836 *Keepsake* volume, he wrote (14 October 1835): "A letter, a day or two since from Mrs. Norton entreating me to give her something for her Keepsake—I suppose I must" (1725). In spite of Blessington's previous request and an oath that he would never again appear in the *Keepsake* after its former (male) editors badgered him for contributions, Moore sweetly and easily gave Norton "The Progress of Painting" for her 1836 *Keepsake*, probably bending to an extreme last-minute personal appeal from Norton to rescue her on a deadline; many annuals were already available for sale in the book shops by October. The controlling force in this appeal was beauty; Norton enchanted Moore from the first time he first saw her as a young woman at Almack's, commenting that she was "the handsomest of any," and she was still banking on their intimate connections (3:943). The manipulation of male weakness for feminine charm and beauty was a powerful weapon for Norton, L. E. L., and Blessington.

Poet Lady Emmeline Stuart-Wortley took over as editor for the 1837 *Keepsake* volume during troubled years; literary annuals gorged the market and reviewers declared war on the genre, exhausted with annuals that diluted the original brilliance of innovators such as the *Forget-Me- Not*, the *Literary Souvenir*, and the *Keepsake* with cheap imitations. William Thackeray published a damaging essay in December 1837 titled "A Word on the Annuals," which is now much-quoted by critics scorning the annuals. Thackeray provides his description of an annuals contribution:

> Miss Landon, Miss Mitford, or my Lady Blessington, writes a song upon the opposite page, about water-lily, chilly, stilly, shivering beside a streamlet, plighted, blighted, love-benighted, falsehood sharper than a gimlet, lost affection, recollection, cut connexion, tears in torrents, true-love token, spoken, broken, sighing, dying, girl of Florence; and so on. The poetry is quite worthy of the picture, and a little sham sentiment is employed to illustrate a little sham art.[18]

Thackeray is satirizing the style of literature and art that some observers called the "Keepsake style," an affective aesthetic common in women's literature that expresses the language of the heart. Early twentieth-century critics inherited Thackeray's disgust for such sentimentality, assigning sentiment and the associated configuration of femininity as characteristic of everything distasteful about Victorian literature. Isobel Armstrong more intelligently describes the affective style as it appears in poetry of the era as being

> about wanting, about desire always in excess of its object, and which constantly redefines its object. Therefore it is always about knowing. To want more than the minimal experiences which keep us alive is perhaps to be fully human. Certainly this is not a private experience, for to know about wanting is to understand the social importance of desire, which is one of the vectors of change of affective emotions.[19]

Admittedly, many of the annuals crowding the market were derivative and poorly written, but Thackeray's agenda here also opposes the appearance of women in the literary profession, attacking editors as well as sentimental literature of the annuals. Jane Wilde, in an 1855 article in *Dublin University Magazine* characterized him as "the caustic satirist of women, the harsh denouncer of their follies, the author whose name, above all others, is hateful to the sex; whose theory of woman is expressed with the bitter irony in one formula: all clever women are wicked, and all good women are fools."[20] There was yet another reason for Thackeray's attack; as a member of the new group of middle-class writers filling the pages of literary periodicals, Thackeray and other reviewers were fighting in a competitive war for readers. Recently rendered destitute by the loss of his fortune, Thackeray was desperately trying to make a living in the same profession as the women of whom he complained. Yet Thackeray could bond with his *Fraser's* colleagues at the Garrick Club, where he met Charles Dickens, who one year later printed Thackeray's first story in *Bentley's Miscellany*. The existence of regular reviews of annuals in the periodicals suggests that literary annuals were too popular to ignore. Since men such as Thackeray could not ignore the annuals, they often satirized them, degrading the genre as silly and, of course, female.

As editor of the *Keepsake*, Stuart-Wortley courted a young new poet for the 1837 volume, touted by his Cambridge Apostles as the next great popular poet, Alfred Tennyson. As M. Shaw notes:

> From the time of his earliest volumes to the height of his fame in 1864, Tennyson was never allowed to lose sight of the ideal of 'a poet of the people'. To a large extent he came to share this ideal and it rebounded on him when the reaction to the tastes and values of the people for whom he spoke—the Victorian middle classes—set in.[21]

Writing for literary annuals would build Tennyson's reputation among the growing numbers of women readers. However, like many other male poets before him, Tennyson's need to attract a larger audience collided with his anxieties about appearing in a popular publication. He had already published three poems in *The Gem* (1831) and two in *Friendship's Offering* (1832, 1833). In spite of earlier decisions to stop responding to editorial requests from annuals editors, Tennyson needed money as well as readers. Stuart-Wortley wisely made her request for Tennyson's contribution through his Cambridge friend William Henry Brookfield. Tennyson sent a poem to Brookfield, writing in June 1836:

> I have sent you a little poem written some three years back: had there been any prospect of filthy lucre, or perhaps had the lady herself wooed me with her fair eyes, I might have sent something which would have filled a larger space in her annual . . . I trust that she will not take it in earnest of any thing to be sent her next year, for I have a sort of instinctive hatred toward annuals each and all.[22]

The tone here is deceptive; while trying to denigrate the quality of his contribution and show disgust for the *Keepsake*, Tennyson's contribution, evidently gratis, was an early version of one of his more popular poems, "St. Agnes' Eve." He sent a poem of considerable quality without remuneration, indicating a secret desire to appear before a largely female readership.

Yet Tennyson efficiently covered his tracks; writing to another Cambridge friend, Richard Monckton Milnes, in December 1836 when the *Keepsake* was for sale in the Christmas market, Tennyson quips:

> Three summers back, provokt by the incivility of Editors, I swore an oath, that I would never again have to do with their vapid books—and I broke it in the sweet face of Heaven when I wrote for Lady (what's her name?) Wortley . . . To write for people with prefixes to their names is to milk he-goats: there is neither honour nor profit. (146)

Tennyson wanted the female readership, but the gender attack implicit in his comment about "he-goats" reflects an anxiety about his participation in the invasion of women into the literary profession: to write for a woman is to upend sexual roles and disturb masculine honor.

When requesting submissions, Lady Blessington often sent a proof or a verbal description of an engraving to an author, asking him or her to supply a tale or poem for the illustration. The book had to be complete by summer, so they could be produced and shipped to America, India, and the Colonies in time for the Christmas season. By July, she was working frantically to meet deadlines, competing with other editors for production and sharing the same pool of artists, engravers, printers, and binders. Every year editors such as Norton, L. E. L., Anna Maria Hall, and Louisa Sheridan were involved in a massive public relations job, trying to out-flatter and out-pay each other, courting the entire publishing community for favors or contributions. Many times they desperately searched for additional works to fill their books in time to meet deadlines. Blessington writes to Dr. William Beattie on 24 July 1841, "I come a beggar to you at the eleventh hour for a few lines to illustrate a portrait of the Honorable Miss Forester, a very charming young lady."[23] Her requests were usually honored; indeed, Dr. Beattie's poem about Miss Forester appears in the 1842 *Book of Beauty*.

Authors of memoirs and letters throughout the nineteenth century are careful to note their encounters with Lady Blessington, as if this would be the one remembrance they would have to record, above all others. Much of their admiration was for her profound beauty. American writer N. P. Willis found Lady Blessington

> in a long library lined alternately with splendidly-bound books and mirrors, and with a deep window of the breadth of the room, opening upon Hyde Park . . . a woman of remarkable beauty half buried in a *fauteuil* of yellow satin . . . a delicate white hand relieved on the back of a book, to which the eye was attracted by the blaze of its diamond rings.[24]

Many men record being enchanted by her in this way, and Blessington took full advantage of their attraction to enlist contributors for her literary projects.

Alison Adburgham notes that "Charm was undoubtedly Lady Blessington's chief asset as an editor."[25] Editorial duties required Blessington's attention early every year as she began to enlist contributors for the next year's book soon after the previous year's volume appeared for the Christmas gift-giving season. Her niece, Marguerite Power, worked as secretary, writing notes to prospective contributors and answering the correspondence. Many times Blessington wrote long, tactful letters to authors whose participation in her annual took extra persuasion. She approached Charles Dickens through John Forster, hoping he could persuade Dickens to contribute. Dickens told her in April 1840 that she did not need to approach him through Forster; however, having an exclusive agreement with his own publishers, he was not free to contribute to the *Keepsake*, nor did he have time to get anything together for her. He added:

> I have always had an objection to write, and therefore have never yet written, in an Annual. But I assure you most unaffectedly that I could not have resisted your appeal, and would have cheerfully responded to it, had I been less firmly bound and less constantly beset than I am at this moment. Let me hope that next year I shall be able to devote a few mornings to proving to you how very sincere I am in what I say.[26]

Blessington held him to his promise, writing a lengthy letter on 2 June 1841 that is worth quoting at length here because it exemplifies the talent Blessington had for charming authors into contributing:

> Though you promised me last year, that you would kindly let me have something from your pen, for the Book of Beauty, or Keepsake for 1842, I really feel reluctant to intrude on you for the fulfilment of this promise because I know the value of a page from you too well not to be aware of the sacrifice you make in granting me one. If however, I did not remind you of the promise, I might appear insensible of its importance, so with great hesitation I venture to recall it to your mind and to add that even the slightest contribution from a pen that delights every class of readers, will confer on me a great obligation, and save you the repetition of an importunate request. (290–91)

Here Blessington bows to Dickens's pride as a rising literary celebrity by arranging her request in a tone of humility and flattery, while telling him that she will doggedly pursue him until he consents. Indeed, Blessington wrote on 17 November 1841 to remind him again of his promise:

> My dear Mr. Dickens: Will you pardon me if I venture to remind you of a promise the fulfilment of which before you leave England will confer a lasting sense of obligation on me. If I thought less highly of your writings I should not thus torment you; so you must consider this letter as one of the many unpleasant results brought on you by a genius of which no one is a more sincere admirer.[27]

In spite of Blessington's graceful series of reminders, Dickens left on a trip to America before responding to her requests, and his "A Word in Season" did not appear until the 1844 *Keepsake*. This time-consuming dance of propriety must have become tiresome to Blessington, who was always racing against a deadline and working to publish her own poetry as well.

Blessington's correspondence with Dickens exemplifies the differences between men and women editors. While male annuals editors could knock on doors or conduct business in a London office, Blessington had to work from her parlor writing flattering notes or inviting authors to a reception (at her own expense), where he could be entertained and charmed into contributing. Blessington's salary is unclear, but William Jerdan, editor of *The Literary Gazette*, estimated that her income ranged "somewhere midway between £2000 and £3000 per annum."[28] However, the financial status of annuals she edited affected Blessington's salary, and keeping up the extravagant social life necessary for getting contributors was a constant financial burden. She also supported several members of her family in London and back home in Ireland, according to Benjamin Disraeli: "She allows her father 200£ a year and has twice paid his debts, and has three or four nephews, young Powers at school and at very expensive ones."[29] Blessington's jointure after her husband's death was £2,000, a paltry sum considering her huge expenditure; many of her social events were necessary to business, for conferences with engravers or publishers often occurred at dinner parties. The immediacy of such concerns created pressure on Blessington to produce more and more. She repeatedly overloaded herself with work, trying to keep ahead of her debts. Blessington complained to Charles Heath, the proprietor of many literary annuals, including the books Blessington edited:

> I have no less than three works passing through the press, and have to furnish the MS. to keep the printers at work for one of them . . . which leaves me time neither for pleasure, nor for taking air or exercise enough for health. I am literally worn out, and look for release from my literary toils more than ever slave did from bondage. I never get out any day before five o'clock—have offended every friend or acquaintance I have by never even calling at their doors—and am suffering in health from too much writing.[30]

At this time, she was editing Heath's *Book of Beauty*, the *Keepsake*, and *Gems of Beauty*, a third volume of her travel reminiscences, *Idler in Italy*, and she was preparing a major poem, *The Belle of a Season*, for publication. She had also agreed to write the entire text for a new edition of *Gems of Beauty*, consisting of twelve poems describing twelve engravings of various subjects. Her friend Barry Cornwall (Bryan Waller Procter) was concerned about her feverish pace, saying, "How is it that you continue to go on with so untiring a pen? I hope you will not continue to give up your nights to literary undertakings. Believe me . . . that nothing in the world of letters is worth the sacrifice of health, and strength, and animal spirits, which will certainly follow this excess of labor" (277). Yet she also had to keep up her social schedule, for this was her source for contributions.

Michael Sadleir claims that her parties began to be less appealing to her friends because of constant requests: "Fond though most of them were of the witty and hospitable woman to whose house they gladly flocked, Lady Blessington's visitors began to feel disconcerted by the persistent cadging for contributions which she dared not relax, and which they could not escape . . . It is obvious that, with this undercurrent of editorial importunity, her evenings . . . had become faintly commercialised."[31] Financial ruin from the potato famine on Lord Blessington's Irish estates reduced her jointure in 1847, and in 1848 Charles Heath died bankrupt, owing her £700; Lady Blessington now faced overwhelming disaster. She had tried to write Heath's publisher to get sales figures of one of Heath's books in 1839 without success. She had no way of knowing Heath's financial status or how he was conducting his affairs. Blessington sold her beautiful home and all its contents. The public sale and final degradation of Lady Blessington was the sensational event of the season; biographer R. R. Madden sadly records the sale, writing that "This was the most signal ruin of an establishment of a person of high rank I ever witnessed . . . Here was a total smash, a crash on a grand scale of ruin, a compulsory sale in the house of a noble lady, a sweeping clearance of all its treasures."[32] In Blessington's case, her very existence was intricately tied to the literary annuals she edited; when Heath went bankrupt, it was the final disaster for its hardworking editor. She died soon after moving to Paris with her family and Count d'Orsay in 1849.

Other women were paid far less than Lady Blessington for their work. If women had been fairly compensated, life would have been considerably different for women editors such as L. E. L. who, like Lady Blessington, had to support family members as well as themselves on a salary unequal to those given to male editors. Charles Dickens also supported family members with literary work, but Robert L. Patten's description of Dickens's career would appear as cruel fiction to women writers and editors of literary annuals:

> From these modest beginnings Dickens rose swiftly to a commanding position in the literary and social worlds. He enjoyed an equally commanding position in the world of publishing: the history of his contracts is a history of agreements ever more favourable to Dickens, giving him increasing authority over all aspects of the issuing of his books, and an ever greater share of the profits . . . Dickens's eventual success provides a dramatic example of the changed status of the author in the nineteenth century, as compared to previous ages . . .[33]

As Patten makes clear, Dickens essentializes the model of a nineteenth-century male professional writer. In the 1830s when literary annuals editors were working at their most competitive steam, Dickens was struggling along with them, trying to make a living. But by 1847, because of the expensive lifestyle Blessington felt necessary for attracting contributors, and because of necessary dependence on the man who held the purse, Charles Heath, Blessington was facing bankruptcy while Dickens was receiving "the major share in the very large profits from the first four numbers of *Dombey and Son*" (10). As with Thackeray, the 1830s were difficult years for Dickens, fraught with financial worries, but eventually he was able to achieve literary stardom, certainly because his writing touched the pulse of middle-class readers and his combination of humor and sentiment helped to make him a popular author of fiction, but also because he had a degree of control over the legal details of his publishing and finances, while Blessington was a victim to expensive business practices and an overspeculating proprietor Charles Heath.

Although she had a room of her own, L. E. L. never made her fortune, either. Thomas Moore reports on 15 December 1838 that "the poor Newgate St. publisher" (probably Henry Fisher, the owner of the *Drawing Room Scrapbook*) had asked him to write and edit the *Drawing Room Scrapbook* after L. E. L., who had been editing the annual before she married George Maclean and mysteriously died at his home in Cape Coast, Africa on October 15. When Moore refused, he found that "the payment to poor L. E. L. for *her* 60 pages of verse (for such was the quantum required) amounted at first, only to £100, though afterwards to £120 or 30."[34] When Moore laughingly told the publisher that he had received 3000 guineas for *Lalla Rookh*, the publisher immediately responded with another offer: "We will, if you desire it, reduce the number of poems to thirty two to occupy from 50 to 60 pages and for this [*MS damaged*] you a cheque for Five hundred pounds—which taking into [*MS damaged*] quantity of matter, and this being we trust an arrangement to [*MS damaged*] many years, will not eventually be much less than the sum you [*MS damaged*] for Lalla Rookh. Moore later mentions that the "Scrap-Book man" declined a counter proposal and expresses regret that he will get £500 for a volume of history he has worked on for two years, when he would get the same amount "for a light task, which [he] could accomplish with ease in three months!" (2039). L. E. L. probably did not consider her task light and never earned £500 for any of her labors, except *The Troubadour* (1825), a book of poetry for which she received £600. William Jerdan claims that L. E. L. received £30 for editing the *Easter Offering* (1832), £300 for *Heath's Book of Beauty* (1833), £105 for *Fisher's Drawing Room Scrapbook*, and £200 total for 10 or 12 years in "other Annuals Magazines, and Periodicals."[35] Moore's celebrity garnered high fees, and he had been courted by the annuals to edit volumes or contribute poetry for several years. As recently as December 1836, Charles Heath had offered Moore £1,000 to write a volume "consisting of an Eastern or other Tale" and Rudolph Ackermann had offered almost £3,000 to write 12 poems for *Flowers of Loveliness*.[36]

L. E. L.'s celebrity brought her gossip, pity, and criticism. Rumors of adultery, a possible abortion, and a broken engagement plagued L. E. L.; nevertheless, she was able to find publishers and devoted readers for her writing for several years. She was a prolific contributor of reviews, articles, and poetry to various periodicals and annuals; several of the annuals required that she write the entire text for the volume. She also published highly popular volumes of poetry with sales sufficient to demand six editions of *The Improvisatrice and Other Poems* (1824) and four editions of *The Troubadour, Catalogue of Pictures and Historical Sketches* (1825). Other successful volumes of poetry included *The Golden Violet, with Its Tales of Romance and Chivalry, and Other Poems* (1826); *The Venetian Bracelet, The Lost Pleid, A History of the Lyre, and Other Poems* (1829); *The Vow of the Peacock and Other Poems* (1835); and *The Zenana and Minor Poems*, published posthumously in 1839. L. E. L. also wrote three novels, *Romance and Reality* (1831), *Francesca Carrera* (1834), and *Ethel Churchill* (1837), a short story anthology, *Traits and Trials of Early Life* (1836), and a play, *The Triumph of Lucca* (1837).[37] Lamon Blanchard recalls a friend's impression of L. E. L.'s working environment:

> It was her invariable habit to write in her bed-room. I see it now, that homely-looking, almost uncomfortable room, fronting the street, and barely furnished—with a simple white bed, at the foot of which was a small, old, oblong-shaped sort of dressing-table, quite covered with a common worn writing-desk heaped with papers, while some strewed the ground, the table being too small for aught besides the desk; a little high-backed cane-chair which gave you any idea rather than that of comfort—a few books scattered about completed the author's paraphernalia.

Blanchard calls this "an illustration of perfect independence of mind over all external circumstances."[38] It also provides a picture of a woman conducting business in the only office she was allowed. Such a collision of the public and the private became typical of this model of professionalism. Angela Leighton contends that "On the whole, women were less anxious than men about the taint to their reputations, perhaps because the annuals offered a context for publication which, being largely female, on the one hand presupposed a kind of literary modesty, but, on the other, offered a discreetly lucrative living."[39] L. E. L.'s independence and a room of her own cost her peace of mind and reputation as gossip relentless pursued her, but the scandal enhanced her marketability as a tragic poetic figure, as we show in chapter 3.

L. E. L.'s success attracted more than gossip about her personal life; it gathered charges of gender switching. Moore may call her "poor L. E. L." after her death, but he writes in his journal of 3 June 1830 that "The poetess L. E. L., whom I sat next, [proved] no exception to the bad opinion I entertain of all such literary hermaphrodites—this sort of talent unsexes a woman, and Miss L. E. L. though girlish enough in manner (affectedly so indeed) is no girl at heart."[40] To Moore, women who enter the literary profession are inappropriately, unattractively, and unacceptably masculine. Literary annuals provided women with the opportunity to earn their living writing and working in a man's world but, as Margaret Beetham notes, "The growth and professionalisation of the [periodical] press did not, however, produce a coherent discursive position for these women to occupy. Women writers—with few exceptions—were less successful than their male counterparts both materially and culturally."[41] L. E. L. provides a clear example of a literary talent who paid a heavy personal price for public exposure as a writer.

Frequently, and nowhere more clearly than in *A History of the Lyre*, L. E. L. makes her disillusionment with the business of poetry, or more specifically her disillusionment with the extent to which poetry is a business, into a topic and theme of her poetry. First the poet Eulalie is not seen live and in person, but in a "pencill'd sketch" (223),[42] calling attention to the artifice of representation and then, immediately, to the spectator's response to the image. This sequence of image and interpretation or misinterpretation is common in L. E. L.'s work, and it is a sign of what has been called "her artificial preoccupation with the artificiality of art."[43] L. E. L.'s series of poems entitled "Catalogue of Pictures" is another example, and similarly her contributions to annuals frequently take the form of verses about engravings of paintings; even earlier, her poetic career began as a paid writer for *The Literary Gazette*, mostly of versified notices of paintings, engravings, and commercially available figurines.[44] The ironies and disenchantments available to the manufacturers of spectacle (rather than its customers) characterized L. E. L.'s legendary life. Because she was the object of gossip, usually amorous in theme, on the basis of verses that she wrote for pay, L. E. L. was situationally equipped for critical distance on the conventional images of art. " 'You never think of such a thing as love,' asked the disappointed young man, 'you who have written so many volumes of poetry upon it?' 'Oh! that is all professional, you know!' L. E. L. exclaimed with 'an air of merry scorn.' "[45] Glennis Stephenson lucidly states that, "as one of the first professional female writers, [Landon] quite consciously set out to promote herself in the manner she felt would best assure her popular and critical success" (8); the ensuing ironies on the disenchanted emptiness of her own conventional performances is L. E. L.'s most trenchant and recurring theme.

In *A History of the Lyre*, when Eulalie appears in person, after the pencil sketch, the anonymous speaker of the poem introduces a series of tropes of antithesis, first by associating her with moonlight: "For moonlight, even when most clear, is sad:/We cannot but contrast its still repose/With the unceasing turmoil in ourselves" (223). The antithesis of that which is still, lovely and lifelessly cold against that which is alive and tumultuous is made a matter of art: the speaker views "statues, beautiful but cold,—/White shadows, pale and motionless, that seem'd/To mock the change in which they had no part,/Fit images of the dead"; and then L. E. L. describes Eulalie's "perfect loveliness" in those terms: "her robe/Was white, and simply gather'd in such folds/As suit a statue" (224). Among festivities in Count Zarin's palace, on the following night, "Her robe was Indian red, and work'd with gold,/And gold the queen-like girdle round her waist . . . her wit/Flash'd like the lightning: on her cheek, the rose/Burnt like a festal lamp" (225). When she appeared (peeping-Tomishly), Eulalie was colorless, simple, silent; on show, she is gilded (like the covers and the pages of the annuals to which L. E. L. contributed) and bright red. The binary of actuality and fictitious romance, or more generally the artifice of show business overlays the binary opposition of cold statue and festal flame:

>   'mid festival,
> Night after night. It was both sad and strange,
> To see that fine mind waste itself away,

> Too like some noble stream, which, unconfined,
> Makes fertile its rich banks and glads the face
> Of nature round; but not so when its wave
> Is lost in artificial waterfalls.

This passage—in fact, the entire poem—encourages the viewing of L. E. L.'s poetic work and its venues as "artificial waterfalls"—the simulacra of feelings, and not feelings.

Eulalie tells the poem's speaker her own intellectual history in just such terms, placing the binary of romance and reality in the narrative frame of youth and age. It is her career, or rather literary careerism in general, that furnishes the narrative content of false and true:

> ...how different I am from all
> I once dream'd I could be. Fame! stirring fame
> I work no longer miracles for thee.
> I am as one she sought at early dawn
> To climb with fiery speed some lofty hill....
> The way grows steeper, obstacles arise,
> And unkind thwartings from companions near. (226)

As all biographies of L. E. L. agree, the "unkind thwartings from companions near" were a leitmotif of L. E. L.'s letters and her business activities as much as they are themes of Eulalie's reminiscence. The extent to which the genres of writing about writing become reflexive—not only L. E. L.'s writing about writing, but writings about L. E. L.—is perhaps clearest in relation to the genre of scandal and gossip. According to Hoagwood and Ledbetter, "McGann and Riess report that Stephenson 'argues that a series of anonymous articles published in the *Wasp* in 1826 were the first public slander of L. E. L.'s reputation (35–36)' (30), whereas 'Grace and Philip Wharton' (i.e., Katherine and John C. Thomson or Antony Todd Thomson) claim that 'the first attempt to injure her character was made in the "Sun" newspaper' about the time of the publication of *The Troubadour*."[46]

But it is the nature and form of her poetic work, and not her personal life, of which L. E. L. writes:

> Yon Eastern tulip—that is emblem mine;
> Ay! it has radiant colours—every leaf
> Is as a gem from its own country's mines.
> 'Tis redolent with sunshine; but with noon
> It has begun to wither:—look within,
> It has a wasted bloom. (227)

Eulalie narrates her passage from youth, in which her "visions grew to thoughts" and thence to poetry; her juvenile rapture when "The flowers were full of song"; to her adult life in the trade:

> this world is
> A northern lime, where ev'ry thing is chill'd.

> I speak of my own feelings—I can judge
> Of others but by outward show, and that
> Is falser than the actor's studied part.
> We dress our words and looks in borrow'd robes:
> The mind is as the face,—for who goes forth
> In public walks without a veil at least. (227)

The imperatives of marketing are the reality concealed behind the illusion of romantic sincerity: " 'Tis a false rule: we do too much regard/Others' opinions" (227). This is what befalls the once-elated but juvenile poet: "worldliness/Has crept upon his spirit" (228).[47] Neverthless, L. E. L. did suffer for her professional status. Leighton claims that L. E. L. provided a dubious model for other women writers:

> The example of L. E. L. stands both as a dread warning to the women poets who come after, but also as a figure whose mistakes may become the measure of the possibilities of their own art. In either case, echoes of her life and work reverberate in women's poetry long after her death.[48]

The grind of a literary career could be discouraging and debilitating when woman editors were working for bread money. Fiction writer and *Finden's Tableaux* editor Mary Russell Mitford writes to her friend Mrs. Partridge on 2 November 1849: "I confess that, for a friend's own happiness, I would never persuade her into writing. It is not a healthy occupation. I always detested it; and nothing but the not being able to earn the money wanted by my parents in any other way could have reconciled me to the perpetual labour, the feverish anxieties, the miserable notoriety of such a career."[49] In spite of her complaints, one wonders if Mitford is not trying to belittle her literary ambitions to winnow the competitive field of authors even more. In a letter to Richard Hengist Horne in June, 1840, Mitford's confidante and *Finden's Tableaux* contributor Elizabeth Barrett claims that " 'annualizing' brings an important part of dear Miss Mitford's income . . . She works upon the very roads of literature, in heavy stone-breaking labor, for hire & his [her father's] sake."[50] Yet Mitford was graceful about her hardships, conducting business in a professional manner, even when her own works as a writer suffered in the publication. Pleased by her first volume in 1838, Mitford writes to her friend Miss Anderson:

> I hope you will like the "Tableaux." They are said by many eminent critics to be greatly better than last year; and I think so myself. By having been limited by Mr. Tilt to the exact number of pages of the former volume, my own stories were cut up on the proofs—to use the printer's language—Anglicè, after they were actually set up in type—within an inch of their lives: so that I feared they would appear bald and thin, as well as brief. I, however, preferred that risk to the damage that I should have done to my contributors by cutting away their poetry."[51]

Elizabeth Barrett's appearance in the *Tableaux* helped Mitford sell the publication to potential contributors and readers, and she counted on her participation. Barrett's contributions included "India: a Romance of the

Ganges" (1838), "The Romaunt of the Page" (1839), and "The Dream" and "Legend of the Brown Rosarie" (1840).

In addition to serving as editor, Mitford sometimes acted as a teacher and advisor to novice women writers; in a letter to potential contributor Henrietta Harrison (later Mrs. Acton Tindal), she writes (20 July 1837):

> What I have to request of you is a poem, not shorter than forty or fifty lines, and as much longer as you choose, with a motto from any English poet that you like, on the subject of the enclosed plate—which seems to me to represent a Georgian selling two beautiful girls for a Turkish harem. You may make a story to it if you like, or dwell merely upon their being torn from their country and sent to an unknown land. The terms which my proprietors have enabled me to offer, are £5, and a copy of the work, a two-guinea book. (267)

Mitford then promotes the annual as "the most splendid of these works," promising to Harrison that she will be in a small group of the very best poets, in a book that will be seen on the tables of "almost every rich person of taste in England; so that it is the very best possible introduction to authorship" (267–68). Mitford's strategically flattering comment about class should appeal to the relatively unknown woman writer, convincing her that a contribution to Mitford's annual will place her among wealth and class. As a folio edition, *Finden's Tableaux* was indeed a fine specimen of the genre, the largest, most expensive literary annual ever published. Its huge, green tooled leather binding opened to elegant engravings, certainly earning the right to lie upon the drawing room tables of rich, upper middle-class readers. This would have been a selling point to contributors such as Harrison.

Yet, in spite of its expensive format, Mitford's work was the same as other annuals editors; she still had to find contributors in a highly competitive literary marketplace and race to produce the volume for the gift-giving season. Mitford leaves until the end of her letter to Harrison a frantic appeal to deadline: "The whole of the copy must be delivered to Mr. Tilt, the publisher, by this day fortnight" (268). With low fees to offer, Mitford would have to depend on a novice, who would be willing to write quickly and for a limited sum, but she treats Harrison with respect and follows up the next month with a letter praising her contribution to the 1838 volume, "Georgia, The Georgian Sisters." Here we see Mitford as a mentor who is teaching Harrison how to write. Harrison contributed another poem for the 1841 volume, "Returning from Milking." By December 1841, Mitford is already working with Harrison on another writing project:

> I have marked two or three words that should be altered—or rather phrases—because you can do so very well; that you should always do your best, correct again and again; write as slowly as you can—(not to lose ideas by mere dawdling)—and be very particular in diction and versification. The introduction to the Tales is very charming . . . but I should earnestly advise you to write the tales in the old heroic couplet—the measure of Pope and Dryden—and, let

> me add, of Crabbe . . . Make the story, too, as pleasing as possible; generosity, gratitude, nobleness, happiness, form a truer and finer source of tears than the common one of sorrow. (284)

Mitford is patient and supportive as she guides Harrison into the revising process; however, the 1842 volume does not include Harrison, nor does she appear in any other literary annual except *Finden's Tableaux*. Perhaps Mitford's experience in 1842 gave Harrison a glimpse into the realities of the writing life for women.

That year, in spite of her impoverished circumstances, *Finden's Tableaux* publisher Charles Tilt cheated Mitford on their copyright agreement. Mitford was to keep the rights to the prose she wrote for the volumes she edited; however, after contracting with Colburn to publish three volumes of her prose from the *Tableaux*, Mitford found that Tilt was already publishing it in monthly parts. She writes to Harrison on 1 June 1842:

> I have just written above a dozen letter upon this subject, and am sick at heart when I think upon it, the money for which I had thus contracted being absolutely required. My poor father is become sadly feeble—forced now to be wheeled about in a chair, and so blind that I read to him seven or eight hours a day. (295)

Mitford's experience shows a woman untrained to meet the challenges of a value system dominated by commercial competition, one that men such as Tilt knew well. He could take advantage of Mitford because she was a woman living within a gendered ideology that drove her to care for her father as nurse and daughter, while trying to support him financially with literary work encoded by a rigid, masculine system. Mitford was a woman editor, writer, and model for other women wishing to enter the field, but she depended on literature for her living, seldom a viable financial solution for women, especially when faced with shrewd business tactics of the men in charge.

In 1843, Mitford again complained to Harrison about the unresolved issue, saying, "There was no use in going to law with persons so situated." By this time, her situation was desperate: "This, and the terribly expensive and lingering nature of my dear father's last illness, occasioned the debts; and I have just this pension—bread and no more!" Mitford follows with a request to Harrison to sign a petition to Robert Peel to increase her pension and contribute £50 (2:2). Now Mitford is making a request to a benefactor who was once her protégé. If there had been other opportunities for women, Mitford's case might not have been so severe. As for Harrison, she evidently surrendered her writing for marriage; Mitford congratulates her on the upcoming event on 27 February 1843, as updates on subscription amounts replace talk of the writing process in Mitford's letters to her. One doesn't wonder at Mitford's complaints about her life as a woman writer after the age of fifteen (2 November 1849): "Then came the writing for bread, the thirty years of drudgery, and toil, and harassing, over which nothing but the strong sense of duty, the overwhelming necessity, could have borne me alive" (253).

Her life's labors produced several books of poetry, *Miscellaneous Poems* (1810), *Christina, the Maid of the South Seas* (1811), and *Narrative Poems on the Female Character* (1811) and a collection of plays in two volumes (1854). She is now best known for her collections of tales of village life: *Our Village* (five volumes, 1824–32); *Belford Regis* (1834); *Country Stories* (1837); and *Atherton* (1854). In 1857 she published her memoirs, *Recollections of a Literary Life*.

Nineteenth-century literary annuals provided women with opportunities to make their mark on literary history. Yet, as Julia Swindells reminds us, these women "entered, as writers, into a particular process and means of representation," with "its own gender and class terms":

> Women who make the entry to professional work are therefore required to negotiate conflicting and potentially conflicting subjectivities. Soon, we must look at individual writings and individual writers to see what is made of these conflicting subjectivities in action . . . Before that, though, it is necessary to look back to the nineteenth century to glimpse some of its articulations of literary professionalism.[52]

Editors such as Lady Blessington, L. E. L., Mary Russell Mitford, and hundreds of unknown women who worked the writer's trade in nineteenth-century literary annuals and periodicals created models for professionalism. Gatekeepers created insurmountable conflicts and gendered restrictions for some women, but some managed to carve out a self-supporting, creative life in the literary business, however brief. Their path was necessary for later generations; the "New Woman" of the 1890s and dreams of careers for women in the twentieth century could not have been possible without these early professionals. Yet middle-class consumerism created these early opportunities through the production of literary annuals; thus the annuals, too, belonged to the "host of hungry pretenders."[53]

VOLUPTUOUS OPPORTUNITIES: VISUAL IMAGES IN THE *KEEPSAKE*

Analysis of the sort that *Sappho and Phaon* and its history call forth illustrate a methodology of literary criticism that is the larger purpose of *"Colour'd Shadows."* That method involves analyses of a process of production and reception: William Lane's Minerva Press captured Mary Robinson's 1813 edition of *Sappho and Phaon* within a canon of romance novels, where the fictions of love and stereotypes of women as frail, dependent creatures conquered revolutionary ideology textually encoded in Robinson's previous 1796 edition. Lane's militaristic, conservative politics intervened when he, as a publisher and proprietor, issued Robinson's text because its presence among Minerva books imprints conservative views upon the readings of the poems. Marketed by Lane as domestic products to engage women reader's emotions, the poems are draped with anti-intellectual meanings by the Minerva Press, and not by Mary Robinson. Paradoxically, this industrial depersonalization of literature, of which *Sappho and Phaon* is a telling example, coincides historically with the Romantic rhetoric that personalizes the concept of literary meanings; this relationship is paradoxical because, as Max Horkheimer and Theodor Adorno have said, under conditions of industrial productivity "the individual disappears before the apparatus which he serves"[1] The apparatus manufactures and bears meanings, in the web of paratextual matter described by Gerard Genette as materials that "surround [a text] and extend [it], precisely in order to *present* it, in the usual sense of this verb but also in the strongest sense: to *make present*, to ensure the text's presence in the world, its "reception" and consumption in the form (nowadays, at least) of a book."[2]

Whereas the arguments of Horkheimer and Adorno sometimes suggest a total fatality of subjection (as in the passage we have just quoted), local insurrections in artistic production suggest otherwise, as Jean-Francois Lyotard pointed out.[3] A study of the illustrations and literature of the *Keepsake* Literary Annual, published each fall from 1828 to 1857 as fashionable literary Christmas gifts, provides an opportunity to explore the ways texts can work against dominating ideology such as Lane's and later conservative proprietors who published books encoding domestic harmony and feminine propriety. Rather than conquering revolutionary ideals as in Lane's 1813 Minerva edition of Mary Robinson's *Sappho and Phaon*, the *Keepsake* textually subverted the conventional notions about women which dictated women's lives by the time the first literary annual appeared for sale in London booksellers' shop windows in 1823. Within the *Keepsake* context, sensuality and sexual fantasy release women from social strictures. Disregarding the warnings of Hays, Wollstonecraft, and Robinson that such ideas betray women's independence, *Keepsake* texts display sensuality in the face of what twentieth-century critics of the period often characterized in stereotypes of "Victorian" as prudish, evangelical propriety. Analysis of the printed works reveals an alternate form of feminism, consciously or subconsciously available, whether it be for you or for the *Keepsake*'s first readers in 1828.

The traditional view of nineteenth-century literary annuals identifies the genre as a "pretty, glittering book for use in drawing-rooms where parents and children and visitors—prim ladies, clergymen, and evangelical gentlemen— might sit together, read from the Annuals, and discuss their literary merits without the slightest embarrassment."[4] Elegantly bound and illustrated anthologies of poetry and prose published as gift books during the Christmas season from 1823 until the 1850s, literary annuals rapidly became a popular, expensive fashion in literature soon after Rudolph Ackermann's debut volume, *The Forget-Me-Not*, appeared in 1823.[5] Anne Renier, a respected early scholar and collector of literary annuals, says: "young ladies found them much more to their liking than the manuals of conduct, stolidly bound in leather, presenting an ideal of womanly behaviour and offering advice on how to achieve it, which had hitherto been regarded as adapted to their needs."[6] The *Keepsake* departed considerably from the conduct books Renier mentions; far from delineating bounds of morality, the *Keepsake* explored female sexual fantasies in elegant steel-plate engravings of sensually suggestive love scenes, titillating poses of fashionable ladies, and naked nymphs carrying mythical gods into primeval forests. To quiet evangelical protestations of impropriety, artists distanced their subjects by making them exotic eastern maids, mythological characters or medieval rustics.

Another paradox arises: this sensual emancipation is of course a commercially distributed mirage of emancipation. The partially covert subtext of sexual liberation is a semblance for sale, and its sellers are devotees of exploitation rather than emancipation. In this way, the *Keepsake* and other literary annuals and gift books in the transitional years between the Romantic and Victorian periods anticipate a central feature of postmodernity as Slavoj Žižek explains: "The authentic twentieth-century passion for penetrating the Real Thing (ultimately, the destructive Void) through the cobweb of semblances which constitutes our reality thus culminates in the thrill of the Real as the ultimate 'effect.' "[7] The construction of that cobweb of semblances, that optical illusion with its reality-effect, warrants some analysis.

Keepsake proprietor Charles Heath knew what appealed to his middle-class female readers and marketed vigorously toward their loyal patronage. A testament to the success of his formula is the fact that the *Keepsake* was a highly successful publication during a time of economic depression in the literary marketplace. Pictures of women and children, animals, nature scenes, and romantic embraces in the *Keepsake* seem innocent, but they frequently suggest contexts that threaten to disturb the domestic fabric.

Keepsake editors and their proprietor, engraver Charles Heath, chose images that displayed the unique blend of female sexuality and social grace distinguishing the *Keepsake* style. Sensuous portraits of fashionable women suggest a casual disregard for modest convention, while romantic narratives and accompanying pictures portray illicit love encounters, the frank sensuality of peasant women and young girls, violent scenes in which men become potential rapists or murderers, and apocalyptic situations where tormented women contemplate their desperate fate. These pictures, designed to excite the middle-class female reader's desire for romance and satisfy her yearning to demonstrate a sophisticated knowledge of art, depicted female sexuality and women's inferior position in the domestic hierarchy. However, the images and accompanying stories also encode the dangers of woman's vulnerability and widen a reader's imaginative possibilities toward democratic notions, as Margaret Linley shows:

> annuals necessarily announce, both materially and textually, the ambivalent effects of the beautiful forms they celebrate. While at first glance the annuals may appear simply to mirror aristocratic values, a closer look reveals a fluctuating cultural market whereby social positions, and the political outlooks they imply, are in the process of being formed and differentiated through continual negotiation.[8]

The unstable social context evident in *Keepsake* illustrations demonstrates another disturbance in the domestic fiber as middle-class women readers became social climbers through textual fantasies.

Heath knew his readers were not looking for domesticity and propriety; instructing *Keepsake* artist Kenny Meadows to adjust a drawing of a mother and her daughter to make them look the same age, Heath exclaimed:

> I don't care about her maternity, or Shakespeare, or anything else. You must not make her more than twenty or nobody will buy! If you won't I must get Frank Stone to do her instead. All Frank Stone's beauties are nineteen exactly, and that's the age for me![9]

Not all *Keepsake* readers were nineteen, but Heath knew his women readers wanted to see youth, beauty, and romance in *Keepsake* illustrations more than instruction, maternal glory, or religious inspiration.

The sensuousness of *Keepsake* images often offended evangelical middle-class reviewers such as William Makepeace Thackeray, who scolds Meadows and other artists for their contributions to the sensuous *Keepsake* style (December 1837):

> Who sets them to this wretched work?—To paint these eternal fancy portraits, of ladies in voluptuous attitudes and various stages of dishabille, to awaken the dormant sensibilities of misses in their teens, or tickle the worn-out palates of elderly rakes and roués? . . . Why not condescend to be decent, and careful, and natural? And why should Miss Corbaux paint naked women, called water-lilies, and paint them ill?[10]

Thackeray's vigorous lambasting of annuals in *Fraser's* indicates the perception of moral dangers inherent in illustrations of the *Keepsake*:

> "How sweet!" says miss, examining some voluptuous Inez, or some loving Haidee, and sighing for an opportunity to imitate her. "How rich!" says the gloating old bachelor, who has his bed-room hung round with them, or the dandy young shopman, who can only afford to purchase two or three of the most undressed; and the one dreams of opera-girls and French milliners, and the other, of the "splendid women" that he has seen in Mr. Yates's last new piece at the Adelphi. (758)

Thackeray's critique implies sexual deviance in the woman reader admiring a freeloving sensual eastern maid, as well as the perverted old bachelor and lower-class shopman who uses the engravings for pornographic pinups. Both male and female viewers become willing participants in the supposedly subversive exchange between image and imagination, while the site (the shop) makes visible the exchange in which the volumes are actually counters.

By 1850 reviewers were expressing relief that literary annuals and their sensuous illustrations appeared to be going out of fashion. In a review of the *Keepsake* (17 November 1849), *The Literary Gazette* complained, "Indeed, we are getting rather fatigued with the constant repetitions of languishing, amorous-looking women . . . From Landseer, and the others, 'every dog has had his day,' and after the run on the soft, voluptuous ladies, it is time the public should have some changes of subject."[11] The *Keepsake*'s many years of financial success long after other annuals ceased publication testifies to the popularity of this type of sexual display with women readers; regardless of protests from moral critics, Heath continued to feature art that portrayed women as sensual beings in portraits and romantic story pictures, countering middle-class notions of propriety. Richard Altick contends that such portraits were

> the quintessence of the age's notorious sentimentality, in which the preceding century's *sensibilité*, a prized affectation of the élite, was coarsened for, and by, the middle classes. It would not be too daring to suggest that pictures of her were icons secularized for Protestant homes, hung and reproduced in places where, in Roman Catholic societies, images of the Madonna and female saints could be found. They were the most familiar visual manifestation of the Victorian cult of woman worship.[12]

Altick's comment characterizes the narrow view of sentiment common in twentieth-century scholarship, while articulating the power that *Keepsake* images held in the middle-class woman's imagination, precisely the outcome to which *Keepsake* proprietors and editors aspired. Altick reluctantly testifies to the "staying power of the Keepsake-beauties branch of literary art," adding that the *Graphic* reproduced them again later in the century, distributing them as supplements throughout the world, increasing their paper sales:

> Thus from their inception in the late 1820s as an ornament to the luxurious life of the drawing room to their final Victorian incarnation late in the era as a circulation-stimulant for an illustrated paper, engravings of young women exemplified the way in which artistic taste was standardized by the sheer repetition of subject and style. (91)

Thus *Keepsake* visual texts continued to proliferate and recontextualize meanings about domestic ideology to varied audiences throughout the Victorian period. The contradiction between overt signs (faux aristocratic and faux exotic materials) and the lasciviously covert semblances of passion replicates, at the literary and visual meanings, the contradiction between merely imaginary desire and the actual commerce of the shops.

Because art was largely the production of male artists, the *Keepsake*, as a book for women readers, furnishes examples for reflection, in terms, for instance, of Luce Irigaray's description of the male gaze and the male scopic economy. Irigaray represents women within that economy as products of masculine desire, mere images of the masculine, as men project their own desire on women.[13] Linda Nochlin writes accordingly:

> As far as one knows, there simply exists no art, and certainly no high art, in the nineteenth century based upon women's erotic needs, wishes, or fantasies. Whether the erotic object be breast or buttocks, shoes or corsets, a matter of pose or of prototype, the imagery of sexual delight or provocation has always been created *about* women for men's enjoyment, by men . . . Thus there seems to be no conceivable outlet for the expression of women's viewpoint in nineteenth-century art, even in the realm of pure fantasy.[14]

Nochlin's discussion of nineteenth-century erotica addresses images far more overtly sexual than *Keepsake* illustrations, but her views on female desire and art in the period are clear: "Those who have no country have no language. Women have no imagery available—no accepted public language to hand— with which to express their particular viewpoint" (139). However, these notions narrowly define female desire as heterosexual. In her discussion of images from works by Tennyson and Rossetti, Lynne Pearce summarizes a post-structuralist, feminist way of reading, a "symptomatic approach to reading visual and verbal texts initiated by Althusser and Macherey" that reveals the text as "a shattered surface whose cracks and fissures represent the ideological gaps into which the feminist may, if she chooses, insert herself."[15]

Pearce discusses these writers and the artists who illustrated their books as "against the grain": their "web-like complexity militate[s] against any monolithic notion of Victorian ideology" (11).

Feminist film critic Mary Ann Doane notes: "even if it is admitted that the woman is frequently the object of a voyeuristic or fetishistic gaze . . . what is there to prevent her from reversing the relation and appropriating the gaze for her own pleasure?"[16] A modern example would be the proliferation of fashion magazines featuring female models displaying varying levels of nudity; the *Keepsake* offered similar opportunities for vicarious sensuality.

Edward Snow mentions a problem with critiques of the gaze:

> Under the aegis of demystifying and excoriating male vision, the critic system-atically deprives images of women of their subjective or undecidable aspects— to say nothing of their power—and at the same time eliminates from the onlooking "male" ego whatever elements of identification with, sympathy for, or vulnerability to the feminine such images bespeak.[17]

Snow prefers to examine art "in a different spirit, resisting ideological (fore)closure and treating one's initial terms—'male' and 'female,' for instance—as subject to revision." Peter Brooks concludes:

> However well-defined our gender and our sexual preferences may be in the prac-tice of our social lives, we are, I believe, capable of responding—and responding erotically—to depictions of male and female bodies in a great variety of ways as seer and seen, as voyeur and actor, in objectification and participation. Although the male gaze is inscribed in our cultural ideologies, its privilege is precarious— merely ideological—and subject to imaginative twists and reversals.[18]

This essay situates a discussion of *Keepsake* art with each of the above perspectives in mind, acknowledging that the *Keepsake*'s male artists objectify women in a cultural system that supports the double standard of domestic ideology. The strategies and forms that ideology takes are functions of a soci-ety of exchange value. Illustrations in the *Keepsake* also license female desire, inviting women readers to identify with or explore the female sensuality portrayed in the engravings: the illustrations sponsor local and imaginary insurrections of sense in the context of commercial exploitation, in ways that anticipate the desire-driven character of the avant garde in Lyotard's descrip-tion (71–82). Lynne Pearce reluctantly establishes the validity of such an approach: "my experience, as a teacher and in writing this book [*Woman/ Image/Text: Readings in Pre-Raphaelite Art and Literature*], has forced me into the uncomfortable position of admitting that in the practice of looking at images of women, the most ideologically discomforting concepts are borne out. Where women viewers ought to feel alienated and indignant, they are constantly seduced."[19]

Although this essay discusses *Keepsake* engravings thematically, artistic styles and themes varied throughout the *Keepsake*'s long history between 1828 and 1857. The smaller early *Keepsakes* tended to feature more narrative pictures, sweeping landscapes of foreign places, historical scenes, and greater tolerance for nudity in mythical settings. From about 1840, *Keepsake* engravings began to demonstrate social concerns, portrayals of motherhood, family, and children, and a more muted and normalized depiction of sensuality in female models, without the total nudity of former years. These engravings reflect the increasing power of domestic ideology in British culture during Victoria's reign, while continuing to simulate female sexuality and display domestic disfunction.

Because the engravings were the most expensive part of the *Keepsake* production, editors often asked their contributors to write a story or poem to go with the illustration. Sometimes the text has little in common with the picture except a title, but together they produce a subtext in two languages—first the engraved art, and then the textual after-image of the visible object.

Nochlin warns us that nineteenth-century illustrations may engage with domestic ideology at several different levels; we must go beneath the surface of the image to appreciate its meanings:

> Ideology manifests itself as much by what is unspoken—unthinkable, unrepresentable—as by what is articulated in a work of art. Insofar as many of the assumptions about women presented themselves as a complex of commonsense views about the world, and were therefore assumed to be self-evident, they were relatively invisible to most contemporary viewers, as well as to the creators of the paintings.[20]

J. Hillis Miller adds, "Illustrations are always falsifying abstractions from the ungraspable idea they never adequately bring in to the open. What they bring to light they also hide. Like all illustrations, they leave the idea still out of sight, grimly reposing in the dark."[21] In contrast to the uncognized "idea" to which Miller refers, the erotic implications of some *Keepsake* engravings are evident enough.

In the 1828 *Keepsake*, "Hylas" illustrates the story of a young companion of Hercules, abducted by water nymphs while fetching water for the Argonautic expedition; the *Keepsake* engraving shows three semi-naked women seducing Hylas in a river. One woman strokes Hylas's hair while the others reach for his well-shaped torso; Hylas looks up in orgiastic surrender, helpless to resist the rushing waters and the touch of the nymph hands on his body. The exotic river emerges from a mystical wood, the flora on the riverbank suggesting aphrodisiacs in a garden of sexual delight. At a distant clearing in the forest Hercules searches for Hylas, his muscular naked body accentuating the picture's eroticism.

The engraving's mythological setting permits its appearance in the *Keepsake*, circumventing moral censorship. Ronald Pearsall cites the British Museum exhibit of the Elgin Marbles in 1816 and the discovery of the Venus de Milo in 1820 as two events influencing the public's toleration of nakedness in art: "The acceptance of Greek nude statues as great art made it almost impossible to carry out a campaign against them, and throughout the nineteenth century the nude in art was reluctantly accepted—if it was served up in a religious, classical or mythological setting";[22] Rozsika Parker and Griselda Pollock add that, "despite their manifold disguises and the elevated obscurantism of their classical, historical or literary titles, women's bodies are offered as frankly desirable and overtly sexual."[23] Yet the scene in "Hylas" offers more than a mythological male fantasy; the picture demonstrates the seductive power of female sexuality, inviting the female viewer to fantasize about overcoming the male with her mysterious sexual powers. The engraving provides an opportunity for women to gaze upon ink that dissembles a naked male body, and to do so without societal restrictions.

"The Enchanted Stream," from the same volume, looks neither enchanted nor mythological as naked women enjoy an outing in a stream. A few women on the bank not yet swimming wear contemporary fashions that anchor the scene in a realistic setting rather than one of enchantment, but the anonymous poem accompanying the engraving makes the women into "Fairies or nymphs of a haunted dell" in a magical vision that disappears upon the discovery of a man watching from the woods;[24] here the man and the woman reader become co-participants in the gaze. Although the engraving's title and poem attempt to distance the scene mythologically, the naked women in this engraving are a realistic representation of women bathing, offering a frank display of female sexuality for the viewing of women readers. Parker and Pollock note the frequency of such portraits:

> The female figures are frequently asleep, unconscious or unconcerned with mortal things, and such devices allow undisturbed and voyeuristic enjoyment of the female form . . . All present woman as an object to a male viewer/ possessor outside the painting, a meaning sometimes explicitly enforced by the gaze of a subordinate male onlooker in the painting itself.[25]

In this example, the painter Thomas Stothard, the engraver Charles Heath (or one of many on his staff who engraved separate elements of his book illustrations), and the man in the picture watching from the woods constitute the male gaze objectifying the bathing females, but what of women readers? Parker and Pollock contend that art "mediates and re-presents social relations in a schema of signs which require a receptive and preconditioned reader in order to be meaningful. And it is at the level of what those signs connote, often unconsciously, that patriarchal ideology is reproduced" (119). However, female sexual fantasies do not necessarily correspond with generalizations about preconditioning or patriarchal codes, and sex does not necessarily require or imply dependency on men. Although the perceptions of any book's readers are unknowable, human imagination consistently, chaotically, and unpredictably refutes expectations. If one's interest is in subjective responses to books' pages, one can imagine that the active imagination of women readers of the *Keepsake* might have had the same local and interiorized freedom in illusion that may be available to women in any era, in spite of their patriarchal conditioning.

Sensuality is the central focus of the *Keepsake*'s frontispiece engravings of aristocratic ladies by artists of the Royal Academy. Characteristically, elegant shiny gowns envelop bejeweled bared shoulders and décollettée, while stilled, barely discernable smiles speak to the reader, as if interrupted from a private conversation. Thomas Lawrence's "Selina" provides a frontispiece example from the debut *Keepsake* volume in 1828 (figure 5.1). The model's satiny ruffled empire dress pushes up and emphasizes her partially exposed breasts, accented by a four-strand pearl necklace that dips from her long neck nearly to the upper line of her cleavage. Such fashions as the empire dress and

Figure 5.1 "Selina." *The Keepsake* for 1828. Engraving by Charles Heath from a drawing by Corbould

the exposed bosom were remnants of the classical fashions of the Napoleonic Era, according to Stella Blum:

> The bosom, which nearly had been laid bare in the opening years of the nineteenth century, was chastely covered and concealed under layers of trimmings, though still placed high . . . By 1828 the age of Josephine and her circle was gone and, although Victoria was only nine years old and would not be queen for nine more years, the seeds of the Victorian era had already been sown.[26]

Yet *Keepsake* portraits show a reluctance to surrender the bare-shouldered bosomy look, in spite of the fashion's passing.

In Lawrence's frontispiece portrait of "The Viscountess Beresford" from the 1835 *Keepsake*, the dress falling slightly off the woman's left shoulder suggests a casual disregard for modesty, as if the wealthy Viscountess, literally draped in a chain of jewels, cares little for the restrictive controls of middle-class morality. The engraving's delicate shadowing accentuates curves in the Viscountess Beresford's neck, shoulder, and breast. Her feminine curls peek out from beneath the fashionable oriental turban, uncontrolled by artificial restraints, and the look in her eyes suggests a self-confident aura of independence that transcends her position in the hierarchical order. These aristocratic women represented the ultimate social climbing fantasy for middle-class women, and their appearance in the *Keepsake* every year taught other women the dress, graceful pose, and proper aristocratic expression for success in the social world. As Susan Casteras writes, in portraits such as these, the model's "sartorial style was a means of communicating with others within the social hierarchy."[27] What the women in these portraits communicate is frank display of upper-class sensuousness, inviting readers to mimic their disregard for middle-class mores. Frontispieces in later *Keepsakes* translated the same codes about sensuality and class; well into the mid-Victorian period, *Keepsake* artists were still featuring full-shoulder views with partial breast exposure and the added attraction of the corseted waist.

The 1840 frontispiece by A. E. Chalon displays the new style on a woman standing in a garden holding a sketch; layers of crinoline and a huge feathery bonnet accentuate the model's full white shoulders. Again the dress falls loosely off its proper place at the top of her left arm, and her shawl hangs carelessly at the elbow, leaving the other shoulder appropriately covered. A beribboned blooming rose tucked between her breasts attracts attention to the forbidden territory beneath the ruffles on her chest. The garden scenario around the model symbolizes a sexual environment, described by Casteras as the "lines of sexual and social demarcation, enshrining the ideal middle-class female in a pure, secluded interior or a walled garden . . . a cultural symbol of female innocence and unavailability" (57). Yet the woman's bared shoulders suggests a sensuality inappropriate for daytime fashion and invites the reader to step outside the rigid construction of feminine virtue, perhaps to envision a lover standing just outside the picture's range, anxious to approve the sketch and touch the woman's bare shoulder.

The later *Keepsakes* provide many examples of candidly sensuous portraits quite different from the formal poses of fashionable society women in the frontispieces. These later pictures look into the model's intimate private space, inviting the viewer's imaginative participation in the woman's fantasy world. "The Wild Rose" (1850 *Keepsake*) features a woman barely draped by her flowing dressing gown, combing lustrous, long curls with her fingers (figure 5.2). In Anna Maria Hall's accompanying story, "The Wild Rose of Rosstrevor," a Londoner delayed by an ankle sprain on a journey through Scotland finds the portrait of Rose in an abandoned summerhouse, and the

Figure 5.2 "The Wild Rose." *The Keepsake* for 1850. Engraving by Eyles after a design by Wright

image takes on a glimmering, supernatural appearance. Here the man in the story duplicates the gaze of the portrait viewer, and the image of Rose enchants him. An innkeeper later tells Rose's story, describing her natural innocence: "wild enough she was, poor darling! and bitterly she paid for it, full of innocent wildness and mirth."[28] The tale takes a fictional turn common in the *Keepsake* style when the traveler admits to being Rose's former love, described by the innkeeper as "one who loved her less than his pleasures,—pleasures cursed by God, and ruinous to man." The text portrays Rose as a victim of male neglect. The visual image depicts a natural sensuality as Rose's hair, a symbol of sexual power, envelops her in a mass of loose waves as if she has just come from sleeping. The distant look in her eyes suggests she is still in a dream state where social rules hold no power; her name "Wild Rose," suggests sexual deviance, and her natural appearance implies an Edenic innocence that liberates sexuality from its rule-laden inhibitions. The male gaze may theoretically appropriate the pictorial woman in a patriarchal structure as Parker and Pollock suggest, but the story textually converts the illustration into a complaint about such a structure and promotes female sexuality as woman's preferable native state.

A temptation arises to regard the apparent erotic appeal of such pages and the conceivable erotic response of its customers as some sort of subversion of prudery and gendered constraints. Janice Radway made a similar suggestion concerning Harlequin romances.[29] However, as Jean- Christophe Agnew pointed out, such internalized experiences occurring in a context of commerce represent "repressive desublimation" (Herbert Marcuse's phrase) and not emancipation at all. In effect, they, and the desire for such imaginary indulgences, serve the interests of exploitative institutions and social structures, impeding critical consciousness and inhibiting the praxis of social change.[30]

Many *Keepsake* pictures feature sensuous little girls or young women barely beyond puberty with the dress and look of older women. In "Mary Danvers" (figure 5.3, 1839 *Keepsake*) the little girl squats on an open plain in a pretty dress that falls off her bare shoulders remarkably like the sensual portraits of the frontispieces. Her hands close onto her chest, emphasizing her undeveloped breasts, and short hair flows wildly around her pixie face; the girl's fashionable shiny dress and shoes suggest that she comes from a middle- to upper-class home. Ralph Bernal's accompanying story about Mary assigns her an unhappy life as a governess whose smallpox scars prevent her from marrying the man she loves; thus the charming picture of the beautiful little girl Mary serves as a sad preliminary to her empty life as a spinster in a society that offers little opportunity beyond the domestic expectations for women as mothers and wives.

In contrast, "The Mountain Child" (1842 *Keepsake*) features a barefooted peasant girl leading a goat through a mountain path, her fingers carefully gripping a bowl of milk as her dress threatens to fall to the waist. She looks directly at the viewer, as if offering the milk to the viewer rather than the goat. Marguerite Power's accompanying poem fondly remembers joyful days of childhood as enlightened times of simple country pleasures that wealthy city dwellers cannot imagine. As in Wordsworth, the innocent child of nature is the teacher of good moral values.

Figure 5.3 "Mary Danvers." *The Keepsake* for 1839. Engraving by Robinson after a design by Dyce

In spite of their textual diversity, both images—"Mary Danvers" and "The Mountain Child"—are visually seductive portrayals of young girls; Casteras explains the nineteenth-century viewer's attraction to little girls:

The lines of sexuality, both in real life and art, blurred between the child-woman and the woman-child. What was womanly about the girl thus had visual and sexual appeal, and conversely, what was girlish about the woman was both socially encouraged and enticing . . . The underlying double-edged attitude . . . is understandable especially since females were legally considered adults when they were twelve, the legal age of consent (i.e., to wed) for much of the Victorian era.[31]

The *Keepsake* woman reader might relate such images to the sensual little girl within herself, acknowledging her existence as a sexual being. As Deborah Gorham writes, society expected women to be sexual as well as childlike; they resolved the obvious contradiction "by focusing on the femininity of the daughter rather than on the adult woman . . . Unlike an adult woman, a girl could be perceived as a wholly unambiguous model of feminine dependence, childlike simplicity and sexual purity."[32] Thus the woman reader could safely identify her own sexuality in pictures of the young girls without fearing moral transgression or judgment, and without impolitely suggesting any social change.

The potential of a similar dynamic often occurs when the pictures feature adult peasant women, such as the 1829 *Keepsake*'s "The Country Girl." Here a gleaner gazes casually at the viewer from beneath a pretty bonnet, her hand holding an apron full of wheat, and the opposite elbow leaning against the gatepost. Distant workers waiting for the water jug at her feet continue without her in the field behind. Linda Nochlin explains how the presence of peasant women in art signifies a deviance from propriety: "At the same time that the peasant woman is represented as naturally nurturing and pious, her very naturalness, her proximity to instinct and animality, could make the image of the female peasant serve as the very embodiment of untrammeled, unartificed sexuality."[33] Women readers of the *Keepsake* could idealize the simple country life depicted in the engraving (an important public-relations motif during a period of urbanization and industrialization), while obscuring from their own view the social relations that governed their own lives, no less than actual peasants', preferring—in the way of repressive desublimation—the sensuous possibilities of the (nonexistent) peasant girl. Wordsworth's accompanying poem engages Romantic notions of rural pleasures, discussing how the peasant girl's face causes him to think about "scenes Arcadian."[34] His treatment of the engraving idealizes the country, but the picture suggests more than the simplicity of rural life; the sensual implications of the scene threaten the construct of female respectability, for middle-class ideals of propriety discouraged the female sexual impulse represented in stereotypes of peasant women. Peter Manning comments about "The Country Girl" and literary annuals that "the poem and plate exude a sensuality the more insinuating the more it is denied . . . the active role taken by women in their production, the class antagonisms visible beneath the lexicon of taste, or in the recurrent appetitive tropes, the annuals show what they would suppress."[35]

The women in these images appear sexual, healthy, and independent, while, as Lynda Nead explains, "The notion of respectability was defined for woman in terms of dependency, delicacy and fragility; independence was unnatural, it signified boldness and sexual deviancy."[36] Martha Vicinus outlines the ideal:

> Before marriage a young girl was brought up to be perfectly innocent and sexually ignorant. The predominant ideology of the age insisted that she have little sexual feeling at all, although family affection and the desire for

motherhood were considered innate . . . In her most perfect form, the lady combined total sexual innocence, conspicuous consumption and the worship of the family hearth.[37]

Falling in love with the appropriate man was the most important goal a young woman could attain; as Sarah Stickney Ellis wrote, "[Love] is woman's all—her wealth, her power, her very being."[38] Everything in a woman's education focused on preparing her for the ultimate goal of marriage. Advice manuals discussed elaborate courtship rituals designed to protect a girl's reputation; her conduct at a social event could ruin her chances at obtaining security in marriage.

The model in "Isabel" (1850 *Keepsake*) displays one of the worst behaviors for women, according to advice manuals; she is a coquette, according to the textual conversion of the picture by its accompanying tale. As she glances back to the side, out of our vision, holding to a chair, her ruffled neckline threatens to fall below the breast line and her sideway position invites the viewer to wonder how much the dress actually reveals. Isabel's smile opens to show her teeth, something the elegant *Keepsake* frontispieces of more sophisticated women would never allow. Her hair falls out of its restraint onto her shoulder and one can almost imagine her deftly working the fan she holds in flirtatious movement. The coquettish portrayal implies licentiousness, according to Deborah Gorham:

> The nineteenth-century image of the unchaste girl is frequently linked with those of the idle girl and the husband-hunter. Critics of the husband-hunter often imply that such girls could easily become sexually loose, and fall prey to seduction, or themselves seduce the men they hoped to ensnare in matrimony.[39]

Isabel's flirtations (in Mrs. Wadham Wyndham's story "The Tournament") indirectly cause the death of one man and nearly ruin her chances of happiness with another. A reader admiring such a beauty would be indulging in dangerous fantasies that could damage her position in society. Moralists feared that women who flirt disturbed the appearance of harmony in the domestic circle; yet the presence of this attractive model in the *Keepsake* engraving suggests a tolerance for such behavior, countering the advice of moralists.

Ellis specifically warned young women against transgressions of morality, explaining:

> The restrictions of society may probably appear to her both harsh, and uncalled for; but, I must repeat—society has good reasons for the rules it lays down for the regulation of female conduct, and she ought never to forget that points of etiquette ought scrupulously to be observed by those who have principle, for the sake of those who have not.[40]

Courtesy books instructed women to be careful about not attracting too much attention or showing too much of their feelings. As Ellis says, "No woman ever gained, but many, very many have been losers, by displaying all at first" (333). Casteras adds:

> Above all, a woman was never to yield to emotions or sexual promptings, lest she succumb to temptations which were viewed by some authors as downright satanic in their implications. Accordingly, ladies were never to be left alone with a man or to be subjected to any hint of conversational familiarity, and it was their role to monitor the range of suitable topics for discussion.[41]

Yet the *Keepsake* challenges these rules in many narrative illustrations depicting women who have illicit late-night trysts with Byronic lovers, exploring the forbidden territory outside the proper conduct defined for ladies, even while the factories of their fantasies exploit their subjective response in ways that solidify the social power of the very structures against which the faux sexuality appears to be an internal rebellion.

The *Keepsake*'s romantic love scenes usually take place in private, secluded environments far away from chaperones. "Carolina," from the 1835 *Keepsake*, illustrates a woman whose guitar playing is quickly giving way to seduction by a male friend in her isolated boudoir. His hand delicately touches her shoulder as he whispers in her ear, inches away from her parted lips. The accompanying story by Catherine Gore, "The Wife and the Widow," says the man is an enemy to Carolina's husband, planting seeds of jealousy in her ear about the husband's affairs with another woman; however, Gore's tale is not convincing when placed beside the image. The man's physical intimacy in the close confines of Carolina's private room and the exposure of her nearly naked breasts cast shadows of impropriety over the scene. A sleeping dog and pet goldfish on the window ledge echo the woman's domestic entrapment and boredom in the house, and a river outside the window leads to worlds Carolina will have few opportunities to know; an exciting encounter with the Byronic visitor would provide temporary diversion from the girl's surroundings.

"Elena and Gianni" (figure 5.4), from the 1848 *Keepsake*, illustrates a balcony love scene reminiscent of Romeo and Juliet. The man's hand reaches toward the woman's breast as the woman softly caresses her neck, her face taking on a significantly sweet emotional expression. Yet Albert Smith's tale, "Regnier's Vengeance," harshly expands the context, describing Elena as a widowed woman, a deceiver, and a coquette. Gianni is her forbidden lover, passing as a cousin. The narrator of Smith's tale comments, "You could hardly have thought that her sweet, mild face, expressing such love and confidence, could have been otherwise than the mirror of her mind. Alack! if all calm confiding eyes meant what they conveyed, Paradise would be at a discount!"[42] The engraving offers little visual evidence for such deceit. Smith's strange tale plots Elena against a rejected suitor named Regnier who tricks her into performing a mystical love ritual naked and then leaves her stranded in a lonely tower for days without clothes or water as punishment for her flirtations. Such a plot is an aberration in *Keepsake* style because of the narrator's sadistic tone that colludes with Regnier, who has reasons for

Figure 5.4 "Elena and Gianni." *The Keepsake* for 1848. Engraving by Mote after a design by Wright

revenge but feels little remorse for the severity of his actions. Such examples are reminders of the way text can change meaning. What begins with a visually pleasing love scene gets transformed, if one reads the accompanying story, into a misogynistic attack on women.

In "The Elopement" (1841 *Keepsake*), a couple is running away late at night to elope. A man leads his lover down an ancient stairway into a garden as they look back fearfully over their shoulders for pursuers. A woman who took such risks endangered her security in many ways. Her father may disown her, leaving her at the mercy of the impulsive young man who may or may not take responsibility for her welfare. If the father is forgiving, the woman still surrenders her inheritance to the husband upon marriage, trusting him to use it well and provide for her. Henry F. Chorley's contextual story, "The Sisters of the Silver Palace," adds another dangerous element to the situation, explaining that the father owed many people when he died, leaving his two daughters destitute. The woman is escaping the poverty of her family, trusting the man to be her main source of security. These random concerns make the midnight marriage portrayed in "The Elopement" a particularly frightening proposal.

Another clandestine departure takes place as servants watch out for intruders in "The Last Farewell" (1845 *Keepsake*). A passionate kiss in a candlelit doorway, with the dawn breaking just over the hill outside the window suggests a secretive sexual tryst. The story accompanying the engraving describes the lovers as caught between warring families in Naples, Italy. Countless *Keepsake* stories, poems, and engravings exploit middle-class fascination with Italy and other foreign influences, partly inspired by the romantic adventures of Byron. Italian love affairs in *Keepsake* literature and illustrations invite women to take Byron's example of living freely to heart, implicating his sexual deviance and rejection of accepted moral values. Images and stories such as "The Last Farewell" provide a merely imaginative opportunity for women to participate in foreign adventures with exciting new (frequently Byronic) types of merely imaginary men.

Keepsake art reflects the sorts of exotic foreign scenes and stereotypical characters aptly defined by Rana Kabbani in her study, *Imperial Fictions*.[43] In "The Persian Lovers" (1828 *Keepsake*), a couple sits closely entwined on a rock's surface, surrounded by rich jungle fauna. The accompanying poem describes the sensuous colors and sounds of the jungle surrounding them. As the man waits for his Persian maid, "the breezes round him waved their fans," and she runs through the grove toward him, "panting, weeping, smiling, sighing," for "Thus Persian maidens fall in love."[44] A proper English woman could never show such enthusiasm and eagerness to meet her man; the Persian maid's passionate response transgresses middle-class codes of propriety, but because she is a foreign woman, displaced from evangelical restrictions, she can act out her excitement in a way the *Keepsake* reader might wish to do. As Kabbani notes, "Europe was charmed by an Orient that shimmered with possibilities, that promised a sexual space, a voyage away from the self, an escape from the dictates of the bourgeois morality of the metropolis."[45] While such escapes generally apply to male fantasy, women might also wish for the maid's total abandonment to delirious pleasures, running counter to everything proscribed by the warnings of Ellis in her conduct manuals. Unlike depictions described in Richard Burton's Victorian edition of the *Arabian Nights*, where women tend to be "demonesses, procuresses, sorceresses, witches . . . fickle, faithless and lewd . . . [and] irrepressively malign," *Keepsake* stereotypes of foreign women tend to be Oriental versions of the English woman, freed (in contrast to women in the imperialized East, and in contrast to the customers of the *Keepsake*) from sexual codes (48–49).

The scene in "Azim and Shireen" (figure 5.5, 1841 *Keepsake*), implies many of the same elements of exoticism and sensuality. Here the couple reclines on a large sofa in a rich eastern garden, with flowering vines blooming at their heads, signaling sexual fertility. In the accompanying story, Meadows Taylor describes the flaming crimson carpet and velvet cushions beneath the couple, noting the hookah, which comforts Shireen and suggests erotic pleasures. Their intimate position on the couch indicates sexual familiarity as Azim plays with Shireen's seductive long hair; the scene evokes visions of a love made in paradise, without the restrictions or faults of British

Figure 5.5 "Azim and Shireen." *The Keepsake* for 1841. Engraving by Staines after a design by Maclise

society. Foreign women in the *Keepsake*'s art and literature enabled British women to explore variations on middle-class notions of feminine propriety. Taylor's text diverts the romantic image into a class-based critique on Azim's growing greed for his king's powerful magic armband. The engraving demonstrates a high degree of sensuality while providing a moral lesson on greed and the innocent Shireen's sad fate as a woman experiencing the misfortunes of love.

Keepsake images of romantic foreign scenes often display interesting reversals of conventional class constructs. In "The Faithful Servant" (figure 5.6, 1830 *Keepsake*), a woman's rescuer is a dark, Moorish servant saving her

Figure 5.6 "The Faithful Servant." *The Keepsake* for 1830. Engraving by Goodyear after a design by Cooper

from a terrifying lion attack; the horse, the lion, and the servant are going down with the woman as she looks up toward the heavens, her clothing torn away from her naked breast. John and Michael Banim's Arabian tale of the same name ennobles the servant, Mustapha, for the loyalty he displays for his undeserving master, whose favorite love is the woman in the picture. Mustapha also admires the woman, wishing he could have her for himself; however, he dies fighting the lion, his bravery causing the master to reform his selfish ways. The visual scene evokes a powerful female fantasy of a white woman being taken by the "noble savage," whose personal qualities far surpass the master's weak, selfish nature. The servant's racial status implicates stereotypes of a heightened sensuality in the dark-skinned servant, and invites a deviant curiosity in the erotic possibilities of interracial sexual pairings. Mustapha's death distances his socially unacceptable attraction for the woman in the illustration, while answering secret fantasies of women wishing for such a wild, exotic rescue from the staid social environment of England, and thus, through furnishing women's emotional experience, containing them all the more safely and totally within that social structure.

Breast exposure becomes a motif in such scenes, indicating the victim's sexual vulnerability; a woman in "The Fatal Error" (1850 *Keepsake*) also has a bloody stab wound in her breast. Curiously, the accompanying story offers few clues to the picture's meaning, hinting at rapid composition of *Keepsake* volumes that frequently contributed to similar disjunctions. As discussed in later chapters of "*Colour'd Shadows*," editors often reluctantly overlooked details such as unity in their rush to meet deadlines, especially as good contributors became increasingly more difficult to procure. In the engraved illustration for the 1850 volume, the positioning of the woman's fingers and the placement of her arm above the dagger on the floor point to the wound as being self-inflicted. As the dagger falls to the ground, the woman's rescuer grasps the fainting woman, gaping at the wound on her naked breast. The possibility of suicide suggests a woman abused or abandoned by a lover, or a desperate attempt to end a life of domestic disfunction. The dagger becomes a phallic symbol in this case, emphasizing her fatal victimization, and the stone barrier behind her becomes a symbol of patriarchal enclosure. The rescuer's facial expression indicates honest motives, but the woman's position in the arms of a male protector is, nevertheless, precarious. The illustration works as a frightening display on its own, without a literary text to clarify, inform, or transfer meaning.

Many men are much less honest and worthy of a woman's trust in *Keepsake* pictures which depict violent plots such as the shocking scene in "Theresa in Her Dungeon" (figure 5.7, 1840 *Keepsake*). The story meant to accompany this image, J. W. Donaldson's "Count Rudiger of Hengstenberg," is a dense, complicated tale of two warring German aristocrats. Theresa is a victim of the dispute, imprisoned for being a daughter of the enemy, according to Donaldson. The man who holds her is supposedly her rescuer in Donaldson's account, and she is standing up to embrace him. However, the position of Theresa's body in the illustration indicates she is actually trying

Figure 5.7   "Theresa in Her Dungeon." *The Keepsake* for 1840. Engraving by Robinson after a design by Stephanoff

to get away from an intruder, and the man is grabbing her in a way that leaves no doubt about his intentions. A realistic alternative to Donaldson's story is that the man is there to terrorize and rape or kill Theresa, as the cocky jailer watches at the door with vicarious pleasure, perhaps hoping to have his turn with her. The woman's isolated surroundings offer little protection as she tries to defend herself against the wild man in her cell. The possibilities for two such widely varying interpretations exemplifies the potential problems with using the written *Keepsake* texts to define meanings in the engravings; the images often offer distinct impressions quite separately from the text until the writer inscribes his or her meaning onto the image. Of course, the textual inscription may or may not be the one that holds the reader's imagination, if it is read at all. Yet this dungeon scene, with or without the literary text, could strike at fears of *Keepsake* women readers familiar with the power of male sexuality—in this image, a terrifying potential.

As in *Keepsake* literature, many images examine the results of a disturbed patriarchal society; rejected lovers and women imprisoned, abused, or threatened by men abound in story pictures demonstrating the pain and grief of such victims. In the 1829 *Keepsake* engraving "Lucy on the Rock," a woman stands at the edge of a dangerous cliff facing tumultuous seas and strong winds, gripping to the rock as she looks desperately out to the infinite darkness. The woman looks to be at the edge of an angry universe, driven there as an outcast of society. The accompanying story by John and Michael Banim, "The Half-Brothers," locates her on the rock in search of her son who has jumped into the stormy seas to save a drowning sailor. However, the illustration also suggests a suicidal woman at the end of her wits, outcast and alone. The Banim brothers write her as a fallen woman with a bastard child, but they provide her with a happy ending that seems comical compared to the engraving, which shows little room for such a lucky fate. Few women who found themselves pregnant outside marriage lived to see happy endings, and Victorian literature is replete with examples of such doomed unfortunates; the infinite ocean depths often become the only home the *Keepsake*'s fallen women ever know. The Banim brothers' tale is either a demonstration of male ignorance about women's lives or a utopian fantasy, a proposition the engraving clearly refutes. Without the silly story, the woman becomes a metaphor for isolation and female angst. The ocean in *Keepsake* art conveys the image of an overwhelming power that threatens to destroy everything in the natural world, paralleling woman's physical and emotional vulnerability in patriarchal society.

In a similar portrayal, the woman convicted of stealing food for her bastard child in Lady Blessington's 1834 *Keepsake* poem "The Storm" clings to the wreckage of a sinking ship in the story's accompanying engraving. Whipped about by the waves, the woman's final end parallels her stormy life of destitution; the terrifying, infinite ocean depths will soon relieve the poor woman from her agonizing life. And again, in "The Last Moment" (1848 *Keepsake*), a woman reaches to the heavens in final surrender as she holds to a ship's sinking remains. Camilla Toulmin's accompanying poem, "A Tale That Was Told to Me," portrays the woman as a poor teacher traveling to work with children in India. When the ship wrecks in a storm, she gives her seat on the rescue boat to a married couple, becoming a martyr for the dominant family structure for, as she clings to the mast of the sinking ship, the man and his wife row to safety and the family remains intact. The underlying message in Toulmin's tale is that there is no place for a single woman in society, and the married couple becomes the priority in any sinking ship, although the spinster later receives the status of a saint as she floats ashore in her white garments, her hair "dank from the ocean baptism," looking younger "than when swayed by the hopes and the fears and the passions of life."[46] Casteras notes that such emigrants frequently became objects of interest for artists in the early Victorian period:

> Unmarried and invariably unqualified for real employment outside the home, she was often viewed as "superfluous" or "redundant" being due to the demographic reality in mid-century and beyond of surplus numbers of Englishwomen. In the late 1850s and 1860s the stirrings of feminism, severe signs of economic crisis, and other factors stimulated public interest in encouraging distressed middle-class females to emigrate.[47]

The 1848 engraving examined above shows an early awareness of such issues. For this woman the ocean becomes a welcome sanctuary compared to the emptiness of her own life as a social outcast.

Yet, the acceptable life as a married woman did not guarantee happiness; an ivy-covered doorway and a caged blackbird signify domestic imprisonment for a woman pictured in "Annot" (1849 *Keepsake*). In Anna Maria Hall's companion story, "A Sketch," Annot pities the bird fluttering against the cage: "The prisoner ran round and round the bars with ruffled feathers; he shook them with his bill,—he wanted to escape."[48] She realizes he wants to be free, in spite of the risk of losing her comfort, care, and security. Annot consents to marry a man she does not love, under pressure from relatives, breaking an engagement with a man she loves. Now the pet bird represents her own feelings about the situation: "Never was well-dressed slavery more complete than mine. I must not think my own thoughts or go my own ways" (40). As a dependent, Annot sees few choices except to surrender to her aunt's request, yet she is angry at herself for choosing security over freedom.

Countless *Keepsake* engravings market the roles of wife and mother, depicting "Good Angels" saving a child from a field of dragons in the 1832 *Keepsake*. Here women and motherhood become God's defense against a vicious, animalistic world full of flesh-eating dragons, images traditionally troped male. Hungry gape-mouthed dragons outnumber a group of angels as they snake around them with firm long bodies, becoming phallic symbols threatening to suffocate the angelic women. In spite of the angel's perfect performance in her role as mother/savior to humanity, she faces death in the clutches of the demons gnashing at her skirts.

As social concerns about women became more prominent in the mid-Victorian years, *Keepsake* illustrations from later volumes correspondingly examine the plight of single women forced to accept bleak opportunities as a seamstress, governess, or domestic servant, especially in later *Keepsake* volumes. "The Orphan" (1852 *Keepsake*) portrays the painful reality of women without the protection of family who must go out into the world seeking employment. The woman's companion is a servant sent by an uncaring uncle to accompany her to the carriage station. He waits impatiently, unconcerned with her future as she sits grieving, her only companion the caged bird that symbolizes her entrapment. The fence separates her forever from her innocent past and marks her transition to an uncertain future alone and without opportunity. The lonely road beyond the fence leads off into the distance, promising little hope except the spiritual solace offered by a church spire on the horizon.

Richard Redgrave's "The Daily Teacher," engraved for the 1844 *Keepsake* (figure 5.8), creates sympathy for single women desperately trying to survive on little pay and hard work as governesses or teachers. Women who pursued such occupations often faced discrimination and hardship because of their odd position as single women in the household, an unpredictable sexual element that supposedly invited trouble for the male of the house, and Victorian literature is replete with examples. One need only recall the most obvious, Jane Eyre, memorialized in Charlotte Brontë's novel three years after the *Keepsake* published this engraving.[49] The woman in Redgrave's painting sits in a dark room surrounded by books and papers, her eyes sadly

Figure 5.8 "The Daily Teacher." *The Keepsake* for 1844. Engraving by C. Heath after a design by Redgrave

staring at the wood floor. A small window in another room is a remote source of fresh air, but the spindly potted plant offers little hope of nourishment. Anna Maria Hall's accompanying story amplifies the desolation in the woman's life, describing her arduous tasks and the harsh treatment she receives from her employer. The woman is a victim of the narrow definitions assigned to women as wife and mother in marriage, leaving little room for her survival outside the confines of the home.

A later engraving in the 1856 *Keepsake* further explores the plight of working women. Its title, "Je travaillais la nuit, le jour avec courage, mais ne gagnais assez," explains the overworked woman's story: "I work diligently night and day, but I cannot earn enough." The dingy room where the woman spins cloth is a prison for her as she stares wearily out the window from her wooden bench. The image portrays angelic suffering while providing a harsh commentary on economic realities of the industrial society. *Keepsake* readers might enjoy a comfortable middle- class living, but images of working women such as those portrayed in *Keepsake* engravings ask readers to consider the need for social change.

"The Gleaner" in the 1854 *Keepsake* is a visual image much like earlier descriptions of the peasant woman, but the accompanying text tells a quite different story, offering a success story that encourages female independence. In a tale by Mrs. Ward (not the Victorian novelist Mrs. Humphrey Ward) about the illustration, "Letty Bloomfield," the gleaner works in the field after her father dies, only because, "like a brave-hearted English girl as she was, she preferred gleaning to a life of dependence."[50] Letty eventually gets her proper inheritance and buys back the property she formerly worked on as a gleaner. Rather than portraying a simple country girl, Ward subverts the illustration to make her into a respectable, hardworking, middle-class woman.

Many *Keepsake* images depict women who have the courage and opportunity to flee their oppressive environment. The 1829 *Keepsake*'s "Adelinda" illustrates a young woman dressed as a boy resting alone in the mountain wilderness; having succeeded with her escape, she now considers the next step. Mary Shelley's story "Ferdinando Eboli" describes Adelinda's daring escape from imprisonment in her own home, and her subsequent adventures living with a band of robbers who help rescue her lover, Ferdinando. The engraving shows a reluctant hero, worried and alone, as she languishes in her repose. The image portrays the courage a woman must have to face the world in battle alone. Adelinda is short in provisions, but her formidable weapons of revenge include more than the sword lying on the rock by her side; she can choose the life of an outcast bandit, gathering her forces for an attack on the man who abused her. While this fictional solution was more possible than legal justice for abused women in 1829, few women would be willing to risk such action themselves.

The "Island Bride" in figure 5.9 (1845 *Keepsake*), is a Greek woman escaping marriage to a relative's son, but her alternatives appear only slightly improved after her successful run to freedom. Her mother is trying to force her to marry "a happy compound of idleness and ruffianism" whose father is a "cunning, avaricious, and unprincipled man," according to William H. Harrison, writer of the accompanying tale.[51] The woman (Eliodore) is unhappy with her inferior position, but she knows that "the law has given this man a power over me which it would be madness to provoke" (23). Eliodore must surrender to the force of family wishes, no matter how corrupt, or take advantage of the escape offered by Harrison's English hero Forester; yet the woman will not be free from the laws of patriarchy in England either. Forester guides Eliodore to "safety," but he stops short of marrying her, feeling "A pang of doubt . . . to trust her little argosy of happiness to the uncertain sea of man's love—uncertain alike in its depth and its purity"(28). Although she eventually marries another British soldier, even Forester knows that Eliodore's future holds little chance for happiness if it depends on the approval and devotion of a man. The illustration shows Eliodore as she makes her way through the mountain rocks with her servant, looking hopefully to a rendezvous with her rescuer; after reading Harrison's tale, we see the island bride's fortuitous escape as ambiguous and uncertain as she leaves the protection of one male tyrant for another.

The best escape a nineteenth-century woman could realistically hope for was the imaginative fantasies provided by literature. The conservative and repressive force of even the erotic images is not a conspiratorial propaganda, but a side effect of the commercial relations. Mimetic images of reading women become a frequent feature of *Keepsake* art throughout the years, in a

Figure 5.9 "The Island Bride." *The Keepsake* for 1845. Engraving by A. Heath after a design by Corbould

thinly disguised and conventional advertisement for itself. An engraving titled "The Novel" from the 1835 *Keepsake*, features a woman sitting dreamily at the edge of her bed, her dress falling carelessly off her breast, as she holds what appears to be a part-issue novel. The bedroom scene surrounding the reader provides a suitable setting for the romantic impulses such material encourages. The woman seems lost in her imagination, perhaps creating romantic plots of her own from the suggestions given her in the novel. The viewer of the engraving can in turn create her own dreamy fantasy by imagining the engraved woman's thoughts. References to reading in fiction usually question reading practices, according to Kate Flint:

> Polemic against the common expectation that women automatically and unreflectingly identified with central women characters, or that they would be unfailingly corrupted by reading about matters concerning sexuality, was met head on within the pages of those very books which caused conservative commentators the greatest anxiety.[52]

Indeed, Lord Viscount Morpeth's poem, "The Lady and the Novel," satirizes the responses of women readers to romantic fiction. Enumerating popular plots and characters from contemporary novels, Morpeth warns *Keepsake* readers to "Calm the wild tumult, probe the vain desire,/And—more than all—don't set the bed on fire."[53] Yet the lifeblood of *Keepsake* literature was the romantic fiction Morpeth attacks, and the woman featured in the engraving demonstrates the imaginative escape the *Keepsake* could provide, and the consequent mystification of real conditions.

An illustrated book in the hands of "Rosina" (1833 *Keepsake*) is a folio romance, according to Mary Shelley's tale "The Invisible Girl." However, the figures on the book's pages indicate romance of an educational variety. The reader, settled snugly in her well-appointed boudoir, browses through the folio pages with interest as a large exotic bird perches upon the mirror against the wall. Significantly, this bird is free to fly, suggesting Rosina's unfettered intellectual freedom. Women occupied with reading were challenging domestic ideology. Martha Vicinus explains:

> The cornerstone of Victorian society was the family; the perfect lady's sole function was marriage and procreation . . . All her education was to bring out her 'natural' submission to authority and innate maternal instincts. Young ladies were trained to have no opinions lest they seem too formed and too definite for a young man's taste, and thereby unmarketable as a commodity.[54]

Reading books enlarges a woman's perspective, giving her opinions about the world that questions her inferior position; thus the image of a woman reading provides a clear example of an activity that ran counter to her purpose in society.

Later *Keepsake* title-pages often feature self-reflective motifs of women reading, emphasizing the book's role in this private activity. The 1852 *Keepsake* title page shows a woman reading in her garden as her pet dog looks on. The woman is oblivious to the dog while she reads an illustrated book such as the *Keepsake,* and the domestic enclosure of the archway that nearly pulls her back into the darkness of the home has little power. The woman's intensive concentration allows her to shut out the external world inside, accepting only the text lying in her lap.

The 1855 *Keepsake* shows a woman completely enclosed with books in a laboratory of thick volumes carelessly jumbled around on the floor beside the table. A telescope looks to the sky outside the window and a large bottle, perhaps filled with chemicals, takes up space on the crowded table as the woman fills a large flower vase with a bouquet. The laboratory may belong to the woman's father, brother, or husband, but she looks intently at the telescope as if planning to explore the heavens at her first opportunity; because the picture's placement on the title-page suggests a special relationship to the readership, the laboratory could also be the woman's private study. Nineteenth-century British society offered few opportunities for women to become scientists or scholars, but these *Keepsake* images invite the viewer to imagine such a life for themselves, opening the door for future change. Admiring these images, a woman exposed herself to important ideas about her own self-determination and intellectual independence.

The woman reader is often positioned outdoors in *Keepsake* engravings, among the vines and flora of the garden, as if the natural world is the only place she can go for complete freedom to indulge her creative mind. The woman in "Florine" (1840 *Keepsake*) looks up from reading a quarto-sized book as if interrupted by an unwelcome intruder. She sits in a corner of the garden where lilies and morning glories compete for attention. Her bonnet hanging loosely from her arm suggests her temporary relief from propriety. Yet Florine can find a release from domestic enclosure through the new ideas literature provides about her world in books. Florine holds her hands gracefully on the pages as if it were a precious personal possession to which she can always return for comfort.

In the 1854 *Keepsake* illustration "Ora May" (figure 5.10), the woman's reading activity takes place at the farthest edge of the domestic enclosure, the home. As she turns the protective tissue over what is possibly another *Keepsake* engraving, Ora May's world is much larger, as if reading provides her with the entire valley below at the touch of her fingertips on the page. *Keepsake* images such as these provided models for womanhood that promoted reading as a tool for escape as well as intellectual development. Sally Mitchell's still-vital conclusions about women's novel reading of the nineteenth century point to an important element of the *Keepsake*'s success with its fiction, poetry, and illustrations: readers choose recreational reading material to inspire daydreaming, a type of "mental story-telling":

> Daydreaming is itself a synthetic or even literary activity. Forbidden feelings can be pleasurably experienced because they are not directly expressed: the literary faculty has found analogues or substitutes which are in the realm of the permissible, or at least the privately permissible. But the literary ability of ordinary individuals is not great. That is why fiction, or the mass media, influences the content of our daydreams.[55]

According to Mitchell, literature provides readers with "the codes to express existing emotional tensions, which are either formless because of decorum—because no one has ever talked about the subject or admitted that it

Figure 5.10   "Ora May." *The Keepsake* for 1854. Engraving by A. Heath after a design by Corbould

exists—or severely repressed because of social context" (32). The *Keepsake* cooperates with such desires and works within the paratexts of its engraved and literary product, as well as its physical presentation as a beautiful book, to weave a web that invites much speculation about nineteenth-century women's intellectual imagination.

"The Fate of Woman at Its Root": Elizabeth Barrett's *A Drama of Exile* and Jean Ingelow's *A Story of Doom*

From the moment she began writing *A Drama of Exile*, Elizabeth Barrett planned for her two-volume *Poems* to begin with that long dramatic poem. With the poem barely completed, she wrote to R. H. Horne on 20 December 1843: "it must take a first place in the book.... The object is the development of the peculiar anguish of Eve—the fate of woman at its root." Eight months later, the book was in print and winning her praise in letters from Thomas Carlyle and Harriet Martineau. Clear evidence shows, however, that she knew the poem would not be liked widely, and its daunting presence as the first poem in the two-volume *Poems*—a placement on which she insisted—had nothing to do with calculations of popular success. On 1 October 1844, three months after the book appeared, she writes to Cornelius Matthews: "I am glad that I gave the name of 'Poems' to the work instead of admitting the 'Drama of Exile' into the title-page and increasing its responsibility; for one person who likes the Drama, ten like the other poems."[1]

To judge from the relative amount of published commentary on her poems, Barrett was not mistaken about the lack of interest that *A Drama of Exile* would inspire, but she persisted in placing it first in subsequent collections (1850, 1853, 1856). Though she lived near the publisher of *Poems*, Edward Moxon, and though he was not reluctant about allowing and accepting authors' corrections, the book—by far her most widely and well-received publication at the time, and for a long time afterward—escaped her control in many ways. In the same year, an American edition appeared, to which Barrett added a paragraph in the front matter, saying "this edition precedes the English one by a step."[2] Though dated 1845, the two-volume American edition appeared two months after the London edition titled (against her wishes) *A Drama of Exile: and Other Poems*.

The two-volume *Poems* signals its meta-poetic theme. Title after title indicates that these poems are about art, and most often poetry: for example, "The Seraph and the Poet," "Of a Portrait of Wordsworth, by R. B. Haydon [*sic*]," "To George Sand: A Desire," "To George Sand: A Recognition," "A Vision of Poets," "The Poet and the Bird," "L.E.L.'s last Question," "Catarina to Camoëns," "A Portrait," and "The Dead Pan" ("O brave poets, keep back nothing"). This profound and extensive thematic preoccupation appears in *A Drama of Exile*, too; Barrett's ambivalence about the prominence and appeal of the poem and her determined but half-way unsuccessful attempt to control its public appearance involves a conflict of purposes and meanings outside the poem.

Like earlier long poems in biblical symbolism by British women (e.g., Elizabeth Smith's *The Brethren: A Poem in Four Books* of 1787 and Barrett's own *The Seraphim* of 1838),[3] Elizabeth Barrett's *A Drama of Exile* tells a contemporary story in mythological form.[4] In contrast to later writings by Christina Rossetti (*e.g., Face of the Deep,*),[5] or Alice Meynell ("Christ in the Universe"),[6] but in this respect like Jean Ingelow's epic retelling of the episode of Noah in *A Story of Doom*,[7] Elizabeth Barrett's poem has nothing to do with religion as understood by a literal believer. Meanings of the work do not involve belief in the actual existence of its supernatural characters. Instead, its meanings involve two very real sorts of things, both of them quite historical.[8] The more obvious meaning is its critical treatment of gender, using the story of Eve to deny the patriarchal myth of female inferiority;[9] this gender theme is the core of the social meanings of the poem. A more complex frame of meanings concerns hermeneutics, or the philosophy of interpretation. Elizabeth Barrett writes consistently with the biblical criticism that spread from France in the eighteenth century to England and Germany, becoming the Higher Criticism. The topics and contentions in her poem include the mental and cultural acts of interpretation—*A Drama of Exile* and *A Story of Doom* are about the interpretative acts that they (and their genres) perform in social and personal frames of reference and not only in the domain of literary simulations.

In 1842, just two years before the first publication of *A Drama of Exile*, Barrett published in *The Athenaeum* a series of essays on the patristic writers,[10] dismissing their theology and their authority, but arguing learnedly about their poetry, principally from a philological point of view: Barrett is determined "by no means to recognize a *hierarchy*, whether in the Church or in literature"; "To these 'Fathers,' as we call them filially, with heads turned away, we owe more reverence for the grayness of their beards than theological gratitude. . . . the fact *is* . . . remarkable—how any body of Christian men can profess to derive their opinions from 'the opinions of the Fathers.'"[11] Barrett writes that she is interested in their theme of "*love*, and love is much"; but "we rather distrust them as commentators, and utterly refuse them the reverence of our souls" (514). Patristic exegesis (what she calls "fatherly opinions") is important to both of the main themes of *A Drama of Exile*. In terms of gender, the love of the Mother transcends the law of the Father; and in terms of the hermeneutic theme, the historical relativity and multiplicity of interpretations (rather than the dogma of the Church Fathers) calls all doctrines into question. Belief-systems are ephemeral human products and not eternal truths.

In its rewriting of the story of the exile from Eden, Barrett's poem goes further than earlier poems by women on this topic. In *Salve Deus Rex Judaeorum* (1611),[12] Aemilia Lanyer gives to the wife of Pontius Pilate a speech denying the exclusive guilt of Eve for the crime that brought exile from paradise. Superimposing the Edenic myth over the story of the trial of Jesus Christ, Lanyer makes it clear that her theme is the moral and social problem encoded in the Genesis myth and its male exegetical history. But in *A Drama of Exile*, Barrett suggests more. Here, Eve positively embraces the mortal life of the body *outside* the walls of the garden, outside the fatherly law.[13] Here, motherhood, incarnation, and the physical beauty of art all represent a positive preference for the tragically brief but embodied life, heavy with mortality ("the thought of death being always imminent,/Immovable and dreadful in your life" [ll. 1451–52]);[14] but that embodied life becomes beautiful in its momentary fusions of bodily sense, and feeling, and mind—more beautiful far, according to Barrett's Eve, than the dualizing patristic myths that beggared the body to imperialize and legislate the soul. When Adam says, of his postlapsarian love for Eve, that this love "crown[s] my discrowned brow," Eve says, "I am renewed.... Because I comprehend/This human love" (ll. 493–504). Eve's ascendancy emerges: Adam says "I follow thee" (l. 550). Whereas Byron's *Cain* (1821) had offered principally the integrity of an independent human mind as the compensation for the loss of Eden,[15] Barrett's poem offers three different values, each an advantage of the anti-patriarchal, anti-hierarchical, and post-Edenic life on the physical earth—mortal motherhood and its love, the incarnation, and the tangible beauties of art. Though Lucifer seeks to torment her with her mortality, infants sing to Eve: "O we live, O we live—/ And this life that we receive/Is a warm thing and a new" (ll. 1582–84). Eve says, "I hear a sound of life—of life like ours—/ Of laughter and of wailing, of grave speech" (ll. 1642–43), and she embraces mortal motherhood as a blessing rather than a curse: "Shall I be mother of the coming life?" (l. 1652). A vision of Christ appears, and he speaks in praise of fallen humanity, after humanity refused subordination to supposedly higher powers: "This regent and sublime Humanity, / Though fallen" (1780–81).[16] Adam accordingly honors Eve: "Mother of the world, / . . . arise, aspire . . . First woman, wife, and mother! . . . Rise with thy daughters!" (ll. 1824–37). Christ's transfiguration occurs, in *A Drama of Exile*, precisely as his transformation from spirit to physical body (see the stage direction at l. 1922), and amongst his praises of the mortal Eve, Christ says "I, wrapping round me your humanity, . . . set a holy passion to work clear/Absolute consecration" (l. 1969, 1977–78), not for immortal souls but for "The whole creation" (l. 1986);[17] and his prescription, like Freud's, is to "Live and love . . . Live and work" (ll. 1995–97). This materializing of the values of the Edenic fable is extreme: a chorus of invisible angels sings praise of earthly "desire" (l. 2110), and advises, rather than looking upward toward heaven, "Listen down the heart of things" (2068, and again 2189).[18]

Among the sensual delights praised by Christ, the beauties of art are important examples. He tells Eve that mankind will be "Servants in pleasure, singers of delight . . . And praise you when he sings his own songs/For the clear song-note he has learnt in you" (ll. 1803–10). Like the incarnation of Christ in bodily form, art (and not doctrine, not hierarchy) glorifies human beings: "his golden fantasies/ . . . glorify you into soul from sense" (ll. 1812–13). Clearly, Barrett here inverts the patriarchal theologies she studied since childhood and repudiated in her essay of 1842.[19] She rejects the abstract eternity of patristic exegesis for a bodily love of material earth, gendered female.

Cyprian, for example, wrote that "the whole foundation of religion and faith proceeds from obedience and fear";[20] Barrett writes that instead the truth of human goodness is "love, their own divine" (l. 893). Eve's praises of physical and specifically bodily nature—and the praises of sensual nature which she gives to Christ—are repudiations of Cyprian's teachings that "whatever things are earthly, and have been received in this world, and will remain here with the world, ought so to be contemned even as the world itself is contemned" (par. 7). Barrett's conclusive advice, from the chorus of spirits, "Listen down the heart of things" (2068, and again 2189), repudiates very directly Cyprian's adjuration that innocent eyes should "look towards God and heaven, and not lower to the lust of the flesh and of the world, the eyes uplifted to things above" (par. 22). Cyprian writes, "cutting away the desires of the flesh, you obtain the reward of a greater grace in the heavenly home" (par. 23); Barrett's chorus sings hymns in praise of "desire" (l. 2110).

The conflict of views is not metaphysical or abstract, but, instead, *A Drama of Exile* replaces religion with social meanings, denying the inferiority of women in an England that was still twenty-three years away from the first parliamentary proposal of women's enfranchisement in 1867 (the proposal failed even then, of course) and thirty-eight years before the Married Women's Property Act ended the legal definition of a wife as property of the man (the doctrine of coverture).

The personal meanings of this story for Elizabeth Barrett are easy to identify. Her father prohibited any of his children's marrying, and her own medical quarantine at home apparently amounted sometimes to a grotesque incarceration. Elizabeth Barrett's intellect produced this liberatory transformation and not Robert Browning's supposedly swashbuckling rescue of her. The book in which *A Drama of Exile* first appeared was the book in which Browning read a reference to himself, in response to which he first wrote to her. But there is nothing sentimental or small about the social meanings of *A Drama of Exile*. As I shall be illustrating in some detail, the themes of the poem are the removal of an oppressive religious illusion and the embrace of a merely but marvelously bodily and mortal life, and the capability and equality of women in love and in work. Eve's demand of Adam—"let me speak" (l. 1274)—is clear enough; and by the end of the verse drama, Adam learns that male tyranny is one among the sufferings of Eve: "Something thou hast to bear through womanhood,/Peculiar suffering answering to the sin,—/Some pang paid down for each new human life,/Some weariness in guarding such a life . . . .And pressures of an alien tyranny/With its dynastic reasons of larger bones/And stronger sinews" (ll.1857–67).[21]

The gender politics of the poem are also exegetical politics. Among the Church Fathers, Tertullian wrote that womanhood must "expiate that which she derives from Eve,—the ignominy, I mean, of the first sin, and the odium (attaching to her as the cause) of human perdition."[22] Barrett's hermeneutical inventions carry a polemical burden. As the frequency of the language-theme in the verse drama would suggest (see, e.g., ll. 769, 1053–54, 1076–79), Barrett writes partly about language as a material force.

The poems that accompany *A Drama of Exile* in the two-volume *Poems* in 1844 make evident the linguistic character of Barrett's concerns—that is, the extent to which linguisticality is itself a dominant theme. "The Soul's Expression" begins with "stammering lips" and reflects upon the relationship between a "song of soul" and the "portals of the sense" (ll. 1, 9–10). In "The Seraph and Poet" she writes, "The poet sings upon the earth grave-riven,/Before the naughty world" (ll. 6–7). The institution of literature is clearly one of her subjects: she includes a sonnet "On a Portrait of Wordsworth." In "Comfort," the "divinest voice" speaks "In humanest affection" (ll. 8–9). She indicates that the stakes are high: the subject of a meditation on poetic "voices" concerns "Futurity," not this or that particular project (l. 1). Her sociopolitical theme is evident: "Work and Contemplation" concludes that "our work" is "better for the sweetness of our song" (ll. 13–14). "The Romaunt of the Page" is an exercise in feminist literary revisionism.[23]

Two poems addressed to George Sand relate writing to gender. "Lady Geraldine's Courtship" is, of course, about professional writing and its relation to "wealth, position" and "tradition" (stanza LXIV). In a letter to Hugh Stuart Boyd (1 August 1844), she writes that, in negotiations with her publisher, Moxon, she was determined to end the two-volume set with "The Dead Pan," which in turn ends, "O brave poets, keep back nothing,/Nor mix falsehood with the whole!" (stanza XXXIX).[24] Barrett's hermeneutical concerns include the properties of language as a medium which is a product of human work, precursor texts and Barrett's revisionary treatment of them, and the social function of writing as a profession and a political act. These are her themes, and not just the heritage of dogma encrusting ancient fables.[25]

In the letter to R. H. Horne in which she says that *A Drama of Exile* is about "the fate of woman at its root," she also writes that "the principal interest is set on Eve; the 'first in the transgression.' 'First in the transgression' has been said over and over again, because of the tradition—but first and deepest in the sorrow, nobody seems to have said."[26] "The tradition" to which she refers obviously involves the misogyny of patristic exegesis. Again, the gender theme is obvious enough, but the hermeneutic theme is more difficult, in part because it involves an historical understanding that Barrett's intellectual contemporaries shared. This theme concerns ideas and not only bodies, acts, and laws. Reflexively, the poem is *about* its own temporary appropriation of ancient myth for temporary (and con-temporary) meanings.[27] This is a second-order meaning indebted to (and consistent with) the Higher Criticism that came to see exegetical history and historical scripture canonization with a materialistic confidence but a philosophicalskepticism.

A Victorian account of the historical development of the Higher Criticism is Mark Pattison's essay, "Tendencies of Religious Thought in England," which appeared in *Essays and Reviews* in 1860.[28] Though George Eliot's translation of David Friedrich Strauss's *Life of Jesus* did not appear until 1846,[29] the mythological school of biblical criticism was already available to Elizabeth Barrett and her English contemporaries in the 1830s and 1840s in two forms. One is an essentially negative critique in the terms of French enlightenment philosophy, concerned with the exploitative fictions of religious dogma,[30] and the other is an essentially positive interest in the terms of German myth criticism associated with Friedrich Schleiermacher and concerned with literary and cultural–historical projects rather than doctrine *per se*.[31]

In 1770, Paul Henri Thiry, Baron d'Holbach, wrote in *The System of Nature* that "the elements of nature were . . . the first divinities of man" and that "the elements were deified." "Thus began Priesthood," says Holbach; "subsequent speculators no longer recollected the source from whence their predecessors had drawn their Gods," that is, material objects.[32] In that view, brutal rulers exploited these primitive fictions of supernatural characters to enslave the multitudes. In Germany, in 1781, and in a philological context rather than a political argument, Eichhorn argued that older materials in the second century after Christ composed the gospels. Friedrich Schleiermacher showed that earlier and independent narratives of folk origin composed the Book of Luke. Four years before Elizabeth Barrett wrote *A Drama of Exile*, Strauss observed that statements by the writers of the biblical books contain "an admixture of the mythical."[33] Despite the negative force of this line of humanistic interpretation, in terms of discrediting the supposed veracity of scripture, the positive implications concerning the historical and literary imagination were quite explicit as well. In Germany, Friedrich Schlegel is perhaps the writer most frequently associated with "Romantic irony," whereby, as Janice L. Haney says, "mythoi can be used, but never believed."[34] In *The Spirit of Hebrew Poetry*, Herder defended the value of biblical poetry on the grounds that the Bible embodied imagination (not truth), and an imaginative reading allows modern people a grasp of the historical context that gave that biblical poetry meaning.[35] In England, in *The Marriage of Heaven and Hell* William Blake also uses the notion that "the ancient Poets animated all sensible objects with Gods," and he launched a celebration of imaginative freedom from the idea that "All deities reside in the human breast."[36]

Sixteen years after *A Drama of Exile* appeared, but seven years before Ingelow's *A Story of Doom*, Benjamin Jowett writes (as Elizabeth Barrett had done in her essays on the Church Fathers) not of the Bible but rather interpretations *of* the Bible when he observes that "modes of interpreting vary as time goes on; they partake of the general state of literature or knowledge."[37] In contrast to what Barrett achieves in *A Drama of Exile*, Jowett's conclusions are negative in their skeptical force: "the sense of Scripture has become confused, by the help of tradition, in the course of ages, under a load of commentators" (337). With some wit, he invites his readers to imagine the works of Plato or Sophocles being subject (as the Bible has been subject) to such a variety of interpretations over time, according to the ideas of an interpreter's age or country, or an allegory of the history of modern Europe (335–36). On the matter of Bible assembly by later editors, clerics, and priests out of folk materials, Jowett observes that the biblical books "are fragmentary, and [a good interpreter] would suspect himself, if out of fragments he were able to create a well-rounded system" (341). What hermeneutics achieves, then—in Schleiermacher's works, or Jowett's—is a liberation from superstitious beliefs and an insight into human work, including the human fabrication of doctrines: "These interpretations would destroy one another if they were all placed side by side . . . . He who notices the circumstance that the explanations of the first chapter of Genesis have slowly changed, and, as it were, retreated before the advance of geology, will be unwilling to add another to the spurious reconcilements of science and revelation," and "a history of the Interpretation of Scripture . . . would clear away the remains of dogmas, systems, controversies, which are encrusted upon them. It would show us the 'erring fancy' of interpreters . . . unable to pass beyond the limits of their own age" (339).

Both Elizabeth Barrett and Jean Ingelow shared much with this line of hermeneutical thinkers, including the recognition that (whatever the biblical books and their constituent elements originally meant) generations appropriate the scriptures to allegorize their own concerns in their own temporary contexts of actual human and social strife. However, in contrast to the negative line of thought concerned primarily with debunking the authority of superstition (which was Holbach's project, e.g., in *Christianity Unveiled*), these poets share with Blake, Byron (whose own verse dramas on biblical themes obviously influence Barrett's), Herder, and Schlegel an appreciation for the possibilities of this symbol-system.[38] Where Jowett ridicules the use of scripture to allegorize the temporary concerns of one's own historical moment, Barrett and Ingelow (without regard to the kind of doctrinal credulity that Blake calls "vulgar") vigorously do exactly that, allegorizing Victorian conflicts with biblical and Miltonic symbols, and in Miltonic form, simultaneously lifting into thematic clarity the historical variability of the interpretations themselves.

When Barrett first published *A Drama of Exile* in 1844, in the two-volume set entitled *Poems*, she made obvious the kind of reference that this poem and this set of poems have. As the first poem in the collection, it begins with an

epigraph from Victor Hugo which in turn begins "Of the nation [*patrie*] . . . ."
But the political meanings are one part of a more total materialism. In an
opening dialogue between Gabriel and Lucifer (who, Gabriel says, is an Idea)
the bodily Adam is, in contrast to such an Idea, "red-clay and a breath—who
must . . . Live in a new apocalypse of sense,/With beauty and music wav-
ing in his trees" (ll. 160–62). In a second scene, outside the closed gate of
paradise, Eve says to Adam, "Have I not strength to look up to thy face?"
(l. 394). Not only does she hereby assert her own strength, but she also
affirms the immediate and the human (here and now) in contrast to that
which is already a myth, a memory, an idea.

Adam refers to the concept of property, and whether a woman has any,
saying that God gave the world to *both* Adam *and* Eve. The meaning of that
remark would not have been lost in an England undergoing agitation for
women's right to own property [and much later Emily Pfeiffer's important
book *Women and Work* (1888) is perhaps the best Victorian statement of
that struggle and its reasons[39]]. Eve refers to her "human love" in fallen
earth as another kind of garden (l. 504). Eve understands "Eden" as a
metaphor for "human love." Eve pardons Lucifer, and the poem gives that
character a line that voices a critique of patristic religion, much as Barrett
herself did in her own voice in the 1842 essay on the Greek Christian poets,
where she discusses patristic exegesis: Lucifer complains that the humanism
just expressed by Adam and Eve will be distorted in history, mistaken "For a
new doctrine suited to thine heirs,/And [subsequent generations will] class
these present dogmas with the rest/Of the old-world traditions" (l. 735–37).
That statement recalls an earlier one by Percy Bysshe Shelley, a favorite poet
and important source for Barrett, who said of Dante and Milton that "The
Divine Commedia and *Paradise Lost* have conferred upon modern mythology a systematic form; and when change and time shall have added one more
superstition to the mass of those which have arisen and decayed upon the
earth, commentators will be learnedly employed in elucidating the religion
of ancestral Europe, only not utterly forgotten because it will have been
stamped with the eternity of genius."[40]

A denial of dualism (soul/body, thought/thing) follows: "What is this
thought or thing/Which I call beauty? Is it thought, or thing?/Is it a
thought accepted for a thing?/Or both? or neither?—a pretext—a word?"
(ll. 769–72). The incarnation of thought and thing in the condition of
beauty is art, obviously, but here it is also human love: "The essence of all
beauty I call love . . . . The consummation to the inward sense/Of beauty
apprehended from without/I still call love" (ll. 777–81). The morning star
sings: "Henceforward, human eyes of lovers be/The only sweetest sight" (ll.
882–83). Again, Eve repudiates dualism: "leave us not/To doubt betwixt
our senses and our souls" (ll. 960–61).

Eve thinks of children ("small humanities/Which draw me tenderly across
my fear . . . with strange innocence" [ll. 1026–27]). She says "I hear a sound
of life," and asks, "Shall I be the mother of the coming life?" (ll. 1641, 1652).
A vision of Christ appears and says to "Spirits of the earth,"

"Humanity,/Though fallen, exceeds you!" (ll. 1780–81). When Adam calls Eve "Mother of the world"(l. 1824), therefore, in dramatic and poetic context that title takes on a philosophical weight: the incarnation of life and beauty in motherhood and in art disproves the dualism of soul and body. Further, Barrett feminizes the three forms of beauty—art, mortal mother-love, and incarnation—in a distinctly social, economic, and political frame of reference. Just one year before, Carlyle's *Past and Present* (1843) responded to the economic depression of 1842 and the massive unrest among workers in England, with an appeal to work. "Rise with thy daughters" (l. 1848), Adam says in *A Drama of Exile*, and Eve then says "I accept/For me and for my daughters this high part/ . . . Noble work/Shall hold me in the place of garden rest" (ll. 1897–1900). Just before he vanishes, the vision of Christ says that his "wrapping round me your humanity" opens "a new Eden-gate" (l. 1969). Pages later, an imaginary chorus of angels celebrates the new vision of incarnated good within mortal life: "Live, work on, O Earthy!" (l. 2207). And the poem closes when, wise enough to "Listen down the heart of things" (l. 2068 and again l. 2189), the woman and the poet (the woman who is the poet) hears, right here in the "prison" of the "Actual" (l. 2245), a "sound of life" coming through the silence (l. 1642)—the sound of human beauty and love, that which is "Earthy" being animated and made good by human "thought" and "desire" (ll. 2109–10).

This self-conscious treatment of historically varied interpretations is clear. Barrett's version refuses the gendered polarity of guilt and the total subordination of women encoded in patristic exegesis and then differently in *Paradise Lost*. Her poem discusses explicitly how generations distort and invent spurious doctrines from ancient fables, and she freely helps herself to symbolic myths for contemporary social themes. Beyond its topical references to 1840s England and to the struggle for sexual equality, the poem makes the historical and human acts of meaning-formations into a hermeneutic theme by suggesting that this making up of meanings is something that people do, and that meanings (as of scripture) are temporary, constructed by mortals in their varying times.

Jean Ingelow's *A Story of Doom* also knowingly makes the mediations of text and tale and meaning into a hermeneutic theme in its retelling of the story of Noah (from Genesis 6–9).[41] *A Story of Doom* also appropriates the myth and its symbols to represent contemporary social conflicts—foremost among them the politics of sex, but also Chartism and the conflicts over the franchise that resulted in the passage of the Second Reform Bill in 1867, the year in which *A Story of Doom* first appeared. More than Barrett's earlier poem, *A Story of Doom* makes a theme of the Bible's being an assemblage of fragmentary scriptures, and of the mediations through retellings and translations and differing versions affecting the ancient tales. *A Story of Doom* does not develop the theme of beauty in art or the metaphor of the incarnation, but it does import into the story of Noah concerns with contemporary science (including eugenics) as the earlier poem did not.

A Story of Doom recalls *A Drama of Exile*, however, when, in Book I, Niloiya, the wife of Noah, says of Eve that "She fell by great desire to rise"

(I, 156) and that "the mother sits/Higher than Adam." The sexual politics are troubling, however: Book IV includes a condemnation of the practice of arranged marriages and women are metaphoric slaves. Book V dramatizes and condemns the beating of women, and throughout the poem, the Niloiya's viewpoint is quite as central as Noah's, as the poem cuts and crosscuts between them and their locales and conflicts.

The command, from a Voice of whose nature or existence he is not sure, troubles Noah: the Voice tells him that he "go forth to warn his kind" (I, 208). His mission becomes a political one, in a context of class conflict. He goes to the palace of the mighty, to whom (while they are on their thrones) he speaks of the injustices suffered by the weak, the small, and the slaves in chains. As in the nineteenth century, the mighty have (in Book VII) already crushed rebellion, and intend to assert again the power of their ancient regime. The threatened flood is a commonplace metaphor for revolutionary change in the nineteenth century, as when (in Book VII) Noah imagines the destruction of the palaces of the mighty. He condemns the master rule, and Noah's mission (and its lack of success) recalls (for example) the unsuccessful presentations of the Peoples' Charter to parliament in 1839 and again in 1848—the mighty will not hear, let alone redress the sufferings of the poor. The eloquently blunt ending, "The door is shut" (IX, 128), spoken while the sky blackens and the flood waters impend, counts as the warning that Noah, like this poem, seeks to deliver. Without redress of the wrongs, which the mighty inflict on the weak and the poor, destruction of the ancient regimes impends.

Some, but not all, of the science in the poem reads strangely like a parody of mythographic writings in the early stages of anthropology and geology. For example, Noah's tribe believes that giant elephants are "a cunning folk," and they avoid territories of the elephants' crafty civilization (Book I). Methuselah is angry because God supposedly sent angels to kill the wicked lizards that drove his chariot (Book II). However, the treatment of eugenics is not parodic, but rather quite serious. In an obvious anticipation of H. G. Wells's cruelly class-conflicted society in *The Time Machine*, Niloiya's mothers used eugenics to breed pygmies for slaves, "Inferior in their wits, and in their size,/And well content to serve" (I, 300–01). Francis Galton first founded the eugenics movement, arguing for the selective breeding of people for desirable traits, in 1865, two years before the first publication of *A Story of Doom*.[42] Angels rebuke the mothers for breeding men like animals, but, in the women's view, the wisdom of the mothers is higher than the wisdom of the obedient angels.

The topical references (to the enfranchisement of women, wife-beating, Chartists, and the fear of revolution) together with the polemical treatment of nineteenth-century science make up only one dimension of the meanings of the poem. Even its representation of the history of religious myths (as in the putative belief in the civilization of elephants) furnishes a first-order frame of reference, in which the poem represents historical or contemporary issues and ideas narratively and allegorically. But in a second-order frame of meaning, the poem dramatizes its own textuality, staging the sorts of difficulty afflicting documentary evidence which contributed to calling the ancient faiths and dogmas into doubt and even obsolescence by the time that Ingelow wrote her poem. Quotations within quotations within quotations appear often, as when Noah quotes what his wife told him her mother had said about breeding pygmies, or when black angels with fettered feet, who crack out of a giant egg in the cave of Satan the dragon, report to the dragon what they had heard Noah say that the mysterious Voice said to him. A messenger-angel comes to the dragon, but the dragon then tells him that a previous message informed him that the master of heaven said that a message to him said that the lord's tongue lets fall "A lovely song, whose meaning was unknown" (III, 242). The poem dramatizes thus the problem of hermeneutic difficulty. Doubts include the angel's doubts that the lord expressed doubts about the meaning of the reported message; Niloiya expresses doubts about Noah's mission; Noah expresses doubts about the reality of the voice he heard; and the text of the poem crosscuts between Noah's wandering and Niloiya's regime at home, without transitions.

Even in its first edition (1867), Book II presents without explanation two alternative versions of a soliloquy by Noah, one of them in square brackets followed immediately by the alternative version (II, 12–35 and 36–73). In the first version, Noah says to himself (in square brackets) that those who have been recommending that he give up his prophetic mission do not counsel him well; in the second version, outside the square brackets, he says to himself that those who recommended that he give up his prophetic mission do counsel him well. I emphasize that Ingelow did not replace the one soliloquy with the other which contradicts it—she left both standing, preventing outright the illusion of a certainty or the stability of a fixed meaning, let alone a truth.

In both *A Drama of Exile* and *A Story of Doom*, the free appropriation of biblical symbols for contemporary references rests on an emptying of the obsolete credulities largely dispelled from the literary culture, first by the skepticism of the enlightenment and then the Higher Criticism. In both, textual layering of the new poem occurs upon their Miltonic antecedents (Ingelow's poem includes a council of the fallen angels in Book III, recalling *Paradise Lost* quite specifically), not to reproduce the Miltonic poem but to illustrate their own differences in meaning. Both layer the modern poems atop their biblical antecedents. In Book III Ingelow writes a scene in the cave of the dragon that incorporates narrative materials from Genesis (the tale of Noah), the Book of Revelation (the chaining of the dragon), and the Miltonic council of the fallen angels. In contrast to Barrett's poem, a lyrical drama modeled on Milton's *Samson Agonistes*, the documentary form in *A Story of Doom*—including quotations within quotations within quotations of rumors, and including broken fragments of epic books that crosscut between one another without transition, and including the unexplained presence of alternative versions of key speeches—imitates the documentary arguments of the Higher Criticism. It is not *only* the handling of the legends, but also these documentary features of the work, that make a theme of hermeneutics and its uncertainties, simultaneously recording the doubts to which hermeneutics gave rise and a delight in the imaginative freedom that followed.

C H A P T E R 7

"VARIED FORMS PASS GLITT'RING": VIOLET FANE'S *DENZIL PLACE: A STORY IN VERSE*

Three salient characteristics of Violet Fane's poetic work appear with clarity and brevity in "Lancelot and Guinevere," and the first is a contrast of male and female points of view:

"Oh! read to me some other lay," a woman says to her husband, explaining to him her preference for "some simple rhyme" or a "tender ballad," rather than Tennyson's *Idylls of the King*; but "Her husband did not seem to hear,/Or, if he heard, he heeded not." After her husband reads aloud most of Tennyson's poem—and it is not "Guinevere," but rather "Elaine"that he reads—and after the poem reveals the woman listener's emotional responses, episode by episode, the woman tells him to stop reading. She throws his book on the grass and says to her husband:

> "Alas, for lawless love!" she sigh'd,
> > "I share the cross of Guinevere;
> Like her my guilty secret hide,
> > Like her I earn the doom I fear.
>
> "To see one day his passion fade,
>   Or hear him say *mine* pales beside
> The love of some such lily main
>   As she who floated down the tide."[1]

The poem suggests the severance of husband and wife in mind, heart, and body, not only in the husband's refusal to heed his wife's request and in her adulterous confession, but also in her husband's wordless response: "Her lord stepp'd down upon the grass,/And vanish'd in the twilight dim" (146).

The intertextual relationship that Fane foregrounds as the poem's principal subject matter repeats the conflict between man and woman. She does not want to hear Tennyson's poem, she throws it to the ground, and even when responding to the portions that she hears against her will, she identifies with Guinevere, not Elaine. That relationship appears again in the form of the art/life relationship portrayed within the poem's fiction. During the reading, the woman internalizes emotions named in the poem, identifying with the fictitious character, and, after her husband has left, "Reader and book alike forgot;/She trembles, hearing on the stair/The coming step of Lancelot" (146).

In the much more substantial and complex form of *Denzil Place: A Story in Verse* (1875), which is Fane's twelve-book verse novel in the tradition of Elizabeth Barrett Browning's *Aurora Leigh*, Fane develops those three forms of relationship again, with more complex artistry and with more explicit treatment of larger, social, and historical issues, including the democratic revolutions of the eighteenth and nineteenth centuries, the conflict of religious tradition and progressive thought, and a belletristic theme with explicit Pre-Raphaelite allegiances. *Denzil Place* has an unusually citational style, quoting and alluding to dozens of literary works, densely, including often her own earlier poems. Fane museumizes poetry, puts it in a glass case for self-conscious inspection under the sign of artifice. This feature of the poem thematically relates to its narrator's reflections on fiction, and to the physical features of the printed book.[2]

The printer's colophon on the verso of the title page identifies Harrison and Sons, printers in St. Martin's Lane, and Fane's book gave them a more than normally complicated set of tasks. Most of the book pages consist of the blank-verse narrative set in the same modern-face Caslon typography as William Morris's *The Defence of Guenevere and Other Poems* (1858).[3] However, for each of the twelve books of the poem, an untitled lyric, alone on the recto of an unpaginated leaf, and set in much smaller font, precedes the narrative. Atop the first page of each of the twelve books, two epigraphs are set, in the same small font as the intercalary lyrics. Typographically, these verses in small font set off the large roman numeral capitals, the ornamentally enlarged initial capital of the narrative verse, and the two different sizes of capital letters used for the epigraphic attributions. A verse Epilogue ends immediately above an ornamental tailpiece (252) which is, like the font of the paratextual poetry, the same as that which appears in her earlier book, *From Dawn to Noon*. *From Dawn to Noon* is an important paratext for *Denzil Place* in more ways than one.[4] From those bibliographical facts alone (although I will turn to others), some important interpretative issues arise: paratextual matter includes epigraphs to the poem's two Parts, intercalary verses (without title or label), epigraphs to the poem's twelve books, the non-narrative Conclusion that follows the twelve narrative books, and the non-narrative Epilogue that comments on the non-narrative Conclusion. At the same time that social polemics engage the poem in real-world issues (e.g., naming Mazzini and Garibaldi), and at the same time that the narrative uses a variety of rhetorical devices to achieve a reality-effect (including the narrator's explicit statement that she personally visited the estate, Denzil Place, and that the characters are not fictitious), nonetheless the poem consistently distances materials and meanings behind museum glass: devices curtail reality-effects, in the interest of insisting upon the reality of textual condition. *Denzil Place* uses typographical codes to encase the plain narrative in the alienating environment of artifice and exegesis, just as its rhetoric uses topics (politics, including sexual politics) and tropes (narrative appeals) to reproduce the conventional realism of nineteenth-century fictions.

At this point, an issue in interpretation theory warrants explicit attention. During the last twenty years of nineteenth-century studies, no one has done more to integrate bibliographical codes with interpretation of their meanings than Jerome McGann.[5] What we have said here about the citational style of the museum-glass of poetry is a point that McGann makes in relation to other works, specifically to their use of typographical and bibliographical resources. McGann's great essay, " 'Thing to Mind': The Materialist Aesthetic of William Morris," is germane to a theoretical crux on which our argument here (and in fact throughout this book) depends, and we summarize here some of that essay's contentions to identify some of the theoretical principles upon which those contentions seem to rest.

The relationship between literary meanings and authorial intentions has of course afflicted interpretation theory for centuries, and it does not cease to afflict it even when the material production of a book (which is corporate) and the historical reception of a work (which escapes all individual control) affect interpretations. "In a social environment dominated by typographical media and publishing institutions, poets no longer stand in the same immediate relation to their work"; instead, in the nineteenth century, "poets had increasingly to accommodate the production and distribution of their work to persons and institutions whose interests were primarily commercial" (45). Cogently and even brilliantly, McGann shows how, in the relatively conventional typography of *The Oxford and Cambridge Magazine* and *The Defence of Guenevere and Other Poems* (1858) but nowhere more completely than in Morris's manuscript book, *A Book of Verse*, "the fundamental subject is the craft and the art of the making" (46)—the physical making of the book no less than the imagination and sensation that the poetical book embodies and represents. The stakes are high: "living under the rule of the commercial and managing men of that world" of industrialized countries overhung with smoke, workers "might, according to Morris, find their lives again by regaining contact with that fuller and more humanly material condition" of craft and art, each with his own two hands (54).[6]

McGann infers (correctly, in my view) that physical features of the book, typography as well as calligraphy and graphic ornamentation, express that polemical intention. He shows that "Morris's financial investment in *The Oxford and Cambridge Magazine* would have given him and his friends authority to name their printer.... Morris was involved in a deliberate effort to see that Chiswick Press would print these early works" (47). His investment gave him power to affect press decisions about the visible presentation of the poems. The claim that the typographical features of those early books express Morris's intentions requires evidence that Morris had control or at least influence over the visible features of that typography.

Solid evidence indicates that Violet Fane did not have similar control over the appearance of *Denzil Place*. The verse Epilogue begins with a missing capital, whose physical space is clear from the composition of all of the lines of the poem:

EPILOGUE

> lay aside my pen,—my story ends,
> "Of some few years in some few English lives;"
> Warning of evils wrought by bosom friends
> To some few English husbands and their wives,—
> A simple story—unimprov'd by rhymes,
> And unembellish'd with that mystic glow
> Which hovers o'er the tales of olden times,
> The chivalresque romaunts of long ago.

All four pages of the Epilogue are set in that way: lines flush with the left margin alternate with indented lines. The single exception is the ungrammatical first line, "lay aside my pen," evidently a printer's error for "I lay aside my pen." Remembering A. E. Housman's important principle that the lost original intention might have been less conventional than a scribe's emendation would have been, we might consider that the intended wording might have been an imperative—"Lay my pen aside." However, in an autographed presentation copy, Fane entered the capital, "I," in the empty space in that line, in her own hand.[7] According to most, but not all, theories of scholarly editing, one should simply correct the printer's error (as Fane did, manually), and read, reproduce, and interpret the sentence which is not, in typographical fact, there: "I lay aside my pen."

However, the issue in which I am interested here is not a matter of editing, but a matter of interpretation: to infer artistic intent (as McGann does, from the typography of *The Defence of Guenevere*) requires evidence of the artist's control. Here, in the instance of the missing "I," we have evidence of the opposite: Fane's hand indicates that "she meant" to write, and did, manually, write something other than what the typographical page says. According to the form of reasoning governing McGann's interpretation, then, no inference of literary meaning from strictly typographical evidence is possible here. That is the matter on which I want to suggest a different view. McGann rightly emphasizes the alienation and attentuation of authorial control during the industrialization and mechanization of literature. At the very least, the missing "I" in *Denzil Place* furnishes an example of that attenuation of poetic control by corporate and industrial production, in contrast, for example, to Morris's handmade pages in *A Book of Verse*. Authorship functions as a mirage of personality and individuality even under the material conditions of their antitheses, which are corporate institutions and mass production. Further, however, in Morris's poems (to which Fane's poem alludes more than once) and in Fane's, this issue and the conflicts and discontents to which it gives rise are among the rhetorical and typographical meanings of the poems.

The rhetorical structures include multiple narrative points of view. Most often, an anonymous narrator tells of the viewpoint of Constance Leigh, humanitarian but lonely young wife whose marriage to an elderly "ultra-Tory" (7) was arranged when she was an impoverished orphan. Rarely, but crucially, the poem narrates the viewpoint of Geoffrey Denzil, a long-absent neighbor who becomes her desperate lover, and this narration always highlights its difference from Constance's point of view. The anonymous woman narrator whose voice mediates Constance and Geoffrey sometimes emerges as a separate voice and, at last, a distinct character, whose viewpoint always expresses emotional and intellectual distance from those of Constance and Geoffrey.

Further outside those points of view, each of the intercalary lyrics thematically fits the book it precedes, but none shows any sign of having been composed for this occasion, or for this "story in verse." None of the lyrics shares characters, action, or setting with the narrative books of the poem, but instead the lyrics ornament the book from without. Each lyric offers itself as *other* work by the same poet who wrote the narrative in twelve books. Further outside the narrated viewpoints, the epigraphic verses, all by other writers, establish and multiply even more distant vantages on both the narrative and the viewpoints internal to it. The structure wraps alienating curtains around each level of articulation as character, narrator, poet, or other poets encases the other, while internally at each level the differences multiply. Throughout *Denzil Place*, these interactions among viewpoints alienate the poetic materials and simultaneously foreground the themes of artifice and interpretation, sometimes by overt intertextuality and sometimes by explicit narrative reflection on those themes.

After the epigraph to Part I (two lines from Shelley on "love" being a "blight and snare"), the original text (but not its narrative) begins with a lyric in small type, alone and unlabelled on its own leaf, signed [B2] but not numbered. In a voice that has no parallel in the tale itself, this lyric complains of a life that is "not living," anticipating the unfulfilled life of Constance which is to be narrated in the book that this lyric precedes. The lyric associates that condition of non-living with delusion: "I seem to dream a mad unmeaning dream/About some fairy thing I have not known," but the lyric closes with a reference to a feeling that the speaker is "drifting . . . To meet some unknown, unexpected thing." In that generic way, the lyric presents an analogy to Constance's upcoming and catastrophic meeting with Geoffrey Denzil, soon to be narrated in the book, but not in Constance's voice, with reference to Constance, nor in the narrator's voice. The lyric shares the emotional theme only by analogy. Like its isolation on the leaf, this difference in voice and specific subject calls attention chiefly to the portability of the theme among discrete verbal embodiments.

Very quickly after the narration of Constance's marriage to old Sir John, Book I politicizes the conflict: to him, "The Hydra-headed monster call'd 'Reform'" threatens him and his class with "defiance" (7). Neighbors who "all led dreary lives/Yet did not know it" characterize the social context of their lives (7). The narrator's tone is unmistakable: the country gentry of Sir John's neighborhood in Sussex are "human vegetables" (8). A "meddling man" from London "made" Sir John rebuild some cottages in which the poor on his land lived, "desolate and damp," often ill and often dead from fevers caused by drainage problems—the poor "drank the water of polluted wells." The parson advised leaving the drainage alone and accepting the afflictions "Sent down by God upon our sinful race" (8–9).

Constance knows first everything that we learn of the other characters. She plays with her little stepson Roland, gathering flowers in the fields, while, as she knows, Sir John corresponds with "those in London who were then in power" and who consider him "A useful county man" (12). Among the squalor of the poor and the "human vegetables" of the neighborhood, Constance lifts her head like a rose (8). Numerous binaries disjoin Sir John and Constance: age, class, and his inclination toward political dragons (7) as opposed to her "cowslips in the dewy field" (11). Much of Book I is satire of Sir John and his class, busy in "The war against the liberty of man,—/The war against the poor the rich have made" (13). Constance's "passionate love/Of Nature" distinguishes her vague Christianity from her profound "Pantheism," wishing to worship among the trees as the ancient Druids did rather than "Here, in the mouldy church" (13–14). Constance's first sighting of Geoffrey, young master of Denzil Place, riding his chestnut horse to his house, introduces another opposition, between her ultra-Tory husband and gallant Geoffrey, gifted with a reformer's zeal. Viewpoint again closes Book I: Constance hides in the shadows of foliage to watch Geoffrey trot past in the sunlight.

Like the intercalary lyric that precedes Book I, the poem (again, alone on its leaf, without title or label or numeration) emphasizes artifice and delusion. Though it sounds in advance an emotion of which the following book also speaks, it does so in a voice so alien to the narrator and characters of *Denzil Place* as to suggest the *bricolage* of a literary annual rather than narrative coherence. Further, short lines (trimeter varied with dimeter) rhyme heavily ("dreaming" is used as a rhyme word seven times in the poem's thirty lines). "Seeming" and "streaming" repeat often, and a refrain repeats four times. That much versification, in contrast to the blank verse of *Denzil Place*, makes the versification doubly conspicuous; like its small typography, its formal artifice sets it apart as a thematic wrapper for the tale of which it is not a part. Then, atop the first page of Book II, an epigraph from Wordsworth comments on both the pantheism from Book I and the coming impetuosity of the lovers in Book II:

> . . . A youth to whom was given
> So much of earth, so much of heaven,
> And such impetuous blood. (25)

The narrative of Book II provides plentiful allusions to *Aurora Leigh*, deepened by simultaneous allusion to precursor works to which Barrett

Browning alludes in *Aurora Leigh*: English and European works by women writers, using the binary of warm Italy and cold England to represent at once the political antitheses of revolution and reaction, the sexual binary, and the dialectic of freedom and constraint.[8] These works include Madame de Staël's novel *Corinne, ou l'Italie* and Letitia Elizabeth Landon's *The Improvisatrice* and *The Venetian Bracelet*, both of them long narrative poems and both of them using the image-cluster of sun, south, and flower to characterize Italy, sexual awakening and indulgence, and political revolution.

Book II of *Denzil Place* opens in England, narrating Geoffrey Denzil's ennui. In his view, England is a stern, cold, and gray mother, in comparison with the violet-scented lands recently toured. He has returned, however, weary of "perpetual change/And exile" (26), and when he visits his neighbor Sir John, he sees Constance, whom he sees as a bud or flower, out of place in the prosaic and worm-eaten setting of Sussex. Alluding to Dante's sonnet-sequence, the narrator says that "Then there began for Constance a new life" (31). Again the sexual theme relates to the political theme:

> Love had always turn'd another way
> When he met Pleasure....
> And Pleasure seem'd a ghastly haggard shape
> When sad Experience had untied her mask,
> But still, if Love were not an empty name
> How sweet to love! (35)

Constance tells him of the peasants' suffering on his lands—dying in childbirth, living without shelter—and he responds philanthropically. He also engages in political argument with Sir John, who fears "the mob/Under their bloody flags of liberty" (38). Sir John suspects Geoffrey of association with Mazzini's Young Italy movement, and he mentions the guillotine: Mazzini had fled a death sentence, arriving in London in 1837, fighting with Garibaldi in 1848 and returning to London in 1850; in 1857 he was again sentenced to death and again he fled to England. The publisher of *Denzil Place*, Chapman and Hall, published Mazzini's *The Duties of Man* in 1862. Subsequently (42), the verse novel reveals that Geoffrey is personally involved in Mazzini's expatriated Italian revolutionary movement. What Geoffrey tells Sir John, however, is that the masses groan, and the only cure is the spirit of reform, which is far from Sussex, and more generally the rural reaches of England, and more generally England as a whole. To John's frightened statements about revolutionary bloodshed, Geoffrey replies as Romantic-period poets had replied to reactionary condemnations of the French Revolutionary Terror:

> When men arise, long smarting under ills,
> They do not always act with self-control
> And dignity; they only feel their wrongs,
> And have not leisure for those tender tears
> The fortunate at home can shed at ease
> Over the ills of others! (39)

Geoffrey's explanation of 1848 revolutionary violence recalls Shelley's explanation of the Reign of Terror:

> [A] nation of men who had been dupes and slaves for centuries were incapable of conducting themselves with the wisdom and tranquillity of freemen so soon as some of their fetters were partially loosened. That their conduct could not have been marked by any other characters than ferocity and thoughtlessness is the historical fact from which liberty derives all its recommendations . . . . Can he who the day before was a trampled slave suddenly become liberal-minded, forbearing, and independent? This is the consequence of the habits of a state of society . . . .[9]

Coleridge wrote to the same effect: "the mind is predisposed by its situation"; and "why should the lower Orders attack us but because they are brutalized by Ignorance and rendered desperate by Want?"[10] As Coleridge did not, but as Shelley, de Staël, Landon, and Barrett Browning emphatically did, and (see chapter 4) as the *Keepsake* artists sometimes did as well, *Denzil Place* engages the sexual liberation of its heroine with the political liberation of nations, and specifically (as in *Aurora Leigh*) of Italy and England.

Among these political disputations, and much more explicitly than Barrett Browning had done in *Aurora Leigh*, Fane includes arguments about religion that recall the same Romantic-period writers and conflicts: Geoffrey says that religion is "a superstitious creed of terrorism" (42). As I show elsewhere, an argument of Baron d'Holbach and other eighteenth-century French philosophers about "creeds" influenced French Revolutionary writers and leaders and, subsequently, British writers of the Romantic period, most clearly Thomas Paine and then Shelley. This is the argument that religion was invented as a device to enslave the masses by way of superstition, and that it continues to function in that way in the nineteenth century.[11]

After another intercalary lyric in a different voice, and after two epigraphs in two other voices (one from Lawrence Sterne on undiscerned forces that govern life, and another from Adah Isaacs Menken about saving a beloved person from death), the narrator of Book III alludes to Holbach again, in relation to a different idea:

> To those who own the kindling blood of youth,
> In would say, "Watch and ward!—beware, beware!—
> Look from the topmost tow'r, like 'Sister Anne,'
> But unlike her, 'tis not for coming friend
> That In would have you search with shaded eyes
> Along the far horizon; 'tis the foe—
> The moral whirlwind In would have you fear!" (52)

Holbach had written of that moral whirlwind:

> In those terrible convulsions that sometimes agitate political societies, shake their foundations and frequently produce the overthrow of an empire—there

is not a single action, a single word, a single thought, a single will, a single passion in the agents, whether they act as destroyers or victims, that is not the necessary result of the causes operating; that does not act as of necessity it must act from the peculiar situation these agents occupy in the moral whirlwind.[12]

Like other Enlightenment materialists, Holbach here overlays the physical, political, and moral orders of human life, suggesting that they embody a single structure. The alignment of liberations in *Denzil Place*—sexual and political—recalls the philosophical monism of Holbach, to which Fane here alludes. Like the overt allusions to the metaphorical geographies of *Corinne*, *The Improvisatrice*, and *Aurora Leigh*, this allusion to layered levels of meaning replicates rhetorically the multiplied wrappers of citation that signal its poetic pastiche and which foreground the textual materials of which the poem is built.

In fulfillment of the epigraph's thematic forecast, Book III narrates a feared death of the beloved and his recovery. Geoffrey rescues little Roland from a fire in Fairleigh Court, and is himself carried out, unconscious. Satirical comedy characterizes the action sequence when Sir John's sister, Jane L'Estrange, screams in the house-fire, "save all you can . . . my dressing-case—/My keys, my purse" (55) while instead Geoffrey saves little Roland. When unconscious Geoffrey is carried away, the moon emblematizes a calm, still viewpoint on the sublunary turmoil, while Constance fears "The dim vast desert of an empty world" (61), and later alone with his unconscious body, she prays:

> She did not pause to think
> If this, her love, was sinful, or against
> The laws that God or man has made for man—
>
> . . .
>
> "Oh, if you die," she said, "you break my heart, . . .
> In love you more than life—come back to me." (63–64)

At this point, the plot exploits a trope of understanding and misunderstanding: Geoffrey is secretly awake while she weeps over him, and when he recovers, he absents himself for the sake of protecting Constance from their guilty love. He relocates to Germany, and the narrator's voice adds verbal irony to the theme of misunderstanding: "I feel assured/He had not heard the tender words she said/When she believed him dying" (70).

The intercalary lyric between Books III and IV reiterates the Guinevere-theme in affected archaisms that insist on the literariness of the presentation:

> Oh, love! thou who shelt'rest some
> 'Neath thy wings so white and warm,
>
> . . .
>
> Had this wrong thing been the right,
> Thou had'st seem'd as worth the winning
> And with will as firm and strong
> In had lov'd with all my might!

The derivativeness of that defense of Guinevere is its most literal (and literary) subject matter, and it is less a matter of Tennyson's *Idylls of the King* than Morris's "Defense of Guenevere." As McGann says, "her defense lies . . . like Sheharazade's, in her words, in the text she spins out as she seeks to hold off the impending doom of an arbitrary and self-serving moral code" (*Black Riders*, 55). Fane's soliloquy is not in the voice of the character, but detached from any specified voice and affixed between books like a cut-out in a collage, another signifier of the textual condition of itself and of the book as a whole.

The fittingness of that poetic preface to Book IV is its hermeneutic theme. As Constance languishes in her guilty and lovelorn "desolation" (73), she also thinks, "Ah, what a history in ev'rything!" (75), and she thinks of "tatt'ling neighbors" (75) in terms of literary history:

> Ah, then those books! a language in themselves!
> Accomplices in crime! The subtle mark
> Beneath those passages that breathe of love!—
> The Lancelots and guilty Guineveres—
> All their forbidden converse underlined—
> The Fausts and Marguerites, and Hèloise
> And Abelard, Francesca—all the throng
> Of wicked lovers and illicit loves! (76)

Like Barrett's "Catarina to Camoëns," and then her *Sonnets from the Portuguese*, and like the later allusiveness of Christina Rossetti's *Monna Innominata*, which is a sonnet sequence *about* Barrett's, that literary list in Fane's poem dissolves the narrative fiction into its textual history. The relationship among the palimpsestic precursor poems replicates their collective relationship to this new poem, *Denzil Place*. Further, the relationship between the intercalary lyrics in their fine print and the narrative books that they introduce is itself a replica of the literary relationships in Fane's list. The voices, settings, persons, and plot differ, and the merely thematic continuity among the parts serves to highlight the fragmentary assemblage of the actual book.

Each of the twelve books of *Denzil Place* illustrates that structure and that auto-hermeneutic meaning equally well, but one set of examples is so complex and so crucial to the poem's narrative strategies that it warrants separate analysis. As the narrative approaches its end (or pretends to do so, while actually staging its ongoing construction), the narrator returns to the foreground to dramatize her own reality-effect. After the guilty consummation of the adultery, after the idyllic sequence in the flowers, color, and sun of Italy, after Constance's ambivalence between convent and carnality, and after the death of old Sir John, the happy ending (which is not an ending) is joyful marriage in Edenic Italy, for half-a-year of whose "blissful nights" the narrator would exchange "The future years of loveless solitude" which she (the narrator) anticipates for herself (221). This is new: the narrator identifies herself as a character, with a dramatic problem, only in Book XI, and she does so to distinguish herself and her dramatic problem from her characters. A passage on the nuptial sleep of Constance and Geoffrey imitates Dante Gabriel Rossetti's "Nuptial Sleep," but only to deny it in the antithetical characterization of the anonymous narrator herself: she wishes for what she narrates for Constance:

> For days which darken into blissful nights
> When, heart to heart, in one another's arms
> We sink not into blank forgetfulness,
> Since e'en in sleep the senses realize
> The sacred presence of our best belov'd!
> For nights that fade into the happy dawn
> When, after this sweet half-unconsciousness,
> We wake to know we were not duped by dreams,
> But that we hold against our grateful heart
> Our dearest treasure! oh, for days and nights
> Such as In sometimes dream of, give me grief
> And after-pangs of bitter suffering,
> But let me glory in the unknown joy
> Of some such days and nights before In die! (221)

Unlike the earlier and most explicitly Pre-Raphaelite passage in *Denzil Place*, that revisionary treatment of "Nuptial Sleep" internalizes the narrator and her conflicts into the poem. The earlier reference, in Book VIII, characterizes her voice, concretizes the meanings of the artistry by aligning it with the state-of-the-nation, and shows a contemporary understanding of the social polemic that is over-painted in Rossetti's art,[13] but it does not make her a character in the story she narrates. When Constance fell ill, in Italy but before Geoffrey's arrival, she awoke in a convent:

> She saw a bending form, and recognised
> Sister Theresa's pallid pensive face—
> Beside the open window at her work
> She sat, her busy needle up and down
> Plied without ceasing, whilst a moted beam
> Of golden sunshine falling on her head,
> Liken's her to those pale prë-Rafaelite
> Pictures of suff'ring saints, which seem to waft
> A faint, sad, odour of ascetiscism
> Down to these striving, money-making days
> In which we live. (155)

The binary opposition of convent and guilty love, asceticism and sensation, is of course not new here, but its rhetorical force in relation to the meanings of art in 1875 are newly specific. Still, the narrator in that passage stands outside the narrative reference, like an intercalary poem, until the nuptial-sleep moment in Book XI: from that point onward she identifies herself more and more specifically as she dismantles the literary illusion just constructed.

The happy ending comes to fulfillment in Constance's marriage to Geoffrey, and then her pregnancy—"Incomprehensible and beautiful,—/ That inexplicable, sweet incarnation/Of two-fold love" (223–24), which ends Book XI. Suddenly, however, the intercalary lyric between Books XI and XII undoes the happy ending. It is an elegy for a beloved woman. The opening lines of Book XII mark this dark change in part by the most sustained and explicit statement yet of the narrator's own attitude:

> Alas, I would in this uncertain world
> All prosper'd where it seem'd that all went well!
> I would that never without urgent cause,
> Those who are bless'd and loving, wronging none,
> Should, as it were, be cheated of their dues
> And robb'd by Fate of their hard-earn'd content. (227)

Thus the narrator introduces her change of mind about old Sir John, now seen as "an honest, red-faced kind old man" (228) rather than the monster of cruel domination that he was in Book I. After her marriage to Geoffrey in Italy, and after two years of "fleeting days" of love and joy, the prayed-for birth of Constance's first child comes, and she dies in childbirth. Like *Aurora Leigh* and unlike *Corinne*, then, this tale narrates the fulfillment of sexual love at its end (or apparent end); but like *Corinne* and unlike *Aurora Leigh*, the end darkens with the death of the heroine. Six years later, Geoffrey inherits wealth and returns to England, and at this point the poem introduces another and more strange reality-effect: The daughter of Constance and Geoffrey is named Violet.

This use of the poet's pseudonym for the name of the poem's character coincides with the emergence of the narrator as a character, first as a personal voice in Books XI and XII, and then as a bodily presence in the four-page Conclusion that follows the conclusion of the story-in-verse:

> The other day, in somewhat pensive mood,
> I saunter'd down a dusty Sussex lane
> Late in the afternoon; the sun was hot,
> And tho' the road was shaded by the oaks . . .
> Yet still I long'd for those intenser shades
> I saw afar, between the iron gates
> Of Denzil Place, (for I had sought the scene
> Of this sad simple story, and could see
> The woods of Denzil Place and Fairleigh Court) . . . . (245)

Nowhere in the entire novel-in-verse has the narrator represented herself as a character in the setting of the tale; like the intercalary verses between the books of the poem, the narrator has been an unidentified voice from without the time and space of the action, but here, in the Conclusion, she emerges on the road in Sussex that borders the woods of Denzil Place. This frame around the tale is of course one among many frames, including the epigraphic, intercalary, and allusive packaging of the contents of the tale.

At the conclusion of the four-page Conclusion, the narrator sees "a youth and maiden" ride past Denzil Place—Violet, of course, and Roland, who (as the narrator learns from "An agèd woman" who walks by) are deeply in love and expected to marry in the fullness of time. And then, the Conclusion concludes finally with a passage that, contrary to the reality-effect that the Conclusion has contrived, returns to imaginariness, and closes with an image not of a woman, but of art:

> ...should these two, who like some glowing dream
> Of Prince and Princess in a fairy-tale,
> So gaily gallopp'd past me, on the road
> To Life and Love; then should these two be bless'd
> With ev'ry earthly good; —around their knees
> May happy children laugh and sport in glee,
> And children's children, in the after years—
> Good little Geoffreys and fair Constances,
> Who must not sin like naughty grandpapa,
> Or pretty grandmama, who died so young,
> And whose sweet picture, in a muslin dress
> "With coral-color's sash and shady hat,
> And looking like an angel," they will see
> Hanging within the walls of Denzil Place. (248)

The sort of immortality that Geoffrey imagines and which the narrator articulates for him is an *apologia* for art. The persistence of Constance in the painted portrait, in the image of art, is apparently reminiscent of the Victorian theme that Thomas McFarland has pointed out most cogently, the substitution of psychology for the literal immortality of the personal soul.[14] In *Denzil Place* the emphasis on the object, on the image-as-object, makes this *topos* less personal, or at least adds a more materialistic dimension of meaning. The emotional phenomenon persists in Geoffrey, and implicitly in the wondering and dreaming of Violet: in contrast to the classical elegiac trope in which the dead beloved survives in the movements of nature (the trope that Fane repeats in the intercalary lyric between Books XI and XII), here the visible, physical record stimulates a persisting presence in the mind, but it also retains its now-impersonal materiality on the wall. As the poet Maureen Smith has said, elegantly, "you raise them from their dreaming every time you unearth their works from the archives and take them into your head."[15] Smith's binary opposition of the archive and the dream puts both the inanimate matter of the object and the animated flux of dream and imagination persistently in view, persistently different, persistently intimate in the productive contradiction of life (or its illusions) and the inertness of the object *per se*. That contradiction, represented as the condition and meaning of art, including poetry, is the reflexive theme of *Denzil Place*.

If the death of Constance in Book XII wraps the narrative, then the Conclusion wraps *that* package in a twofold reminder of the fictitious status of its materials. The allusion to fairytales ("like some glowing dream/Of Prince and Princess in a fairy-tale") is one instance, and another is the imagined future of multiplied Constances and Geoffreys. Then, the ultimate image, the last word, is not an image of children, lovers, or Sussex, but an image of an artifact.

Of course that is and is not the last image. A four-page Epilogue follows the four-page Conclusion. The Epilogue is about art: it reflects on the contradictory illusionism and reality-effect that the poem, and literature generally, achieves:

> my story ends,
> "Of some few years in some few English lives;"
> Warning of evils wrought by bosom friends
> To some few English husbands and their wives,—
> A simple story—unimprov'd by rhymes,
> And unembellish'd with that mystic glow
> Which hovers o'er the tales of olden times,
> The chivalresque romaunts of long ago. (249)

The story is and is not an artificial ornament. Her characters "liv'd and mov'd/And had their being outside the gilded rim/Of this poor book"; "in truth I knew both her and him"; not literally, of course, but "as, may be,/A sculptor recognises, blent in one/From many models borrow'd, arm or knee" (248).

The Epilogue says that the poem as a whole does and does not contain a "moral or advice." The reader is expected to think that it does not; but the narrator thinks that she does see a moral, though she suspects that it may not be there: if Constance's heart had been harder, she would have been blameless. "She was the eager champion of the poor,/And Denzil was her helper in the cause,/High were their motives. . . ." Though Denzil repudiated the religiosity of the church, he would have formed a new religion better than the present one (250). Like the false happy-ending of the tale, and like the merely imaginary happy ending of the Conclusion, the Epilogue undermines the artificial light of supposedly moral progress: "E'en as they sagely planned/The reformation of the human kind,/They saw their boasted bulwarks blown as sand/At the remorseless mercy of the wind!" (251). Finally, then (or almost finally) the Epilogue also ends on an image of an image. The moon rises, and the dew glistens on statuary as the narrator says farewell to her old home, Denzil Place, and "Farewell sad witness of her shame and woe" (252).

Beneath the last line of the Epilogue, a floral ornament appears, very like the floral ornaments that follow each poem in Fane's *From Dawn to Noon* three years earlier. Longmans published *From Dawn to Noon*, whereas Chapman and Hall published *Denzil Place*, and the different printing arrangements evidently led to the simulation of the floral ornament (rather than simply using the same one). Spottiswoode and Co., New Street Square, printed the first edition of *From Dawn to Noon*; Harrison and Sons, St. Martin's Lane, printed *Denzil Place*. In *Denzil Place*, this is the *only* floral ornament in the volume, and its appearance on the Epilogue page helps to connect this volume with the earlier one. The typography of the Epilogue also reproduces the typography of *From Dawn to Noon*, and not the typography of the twelve books of *Denzil Place*. Further, the language, the imagery, the allusiveness, the metapoetic theme, and the play of the personal reality-effect in the Epilogue appear in the earlier book as well. The poem that introduces "Noon" in *From Dawn to Noon* is a precursor or prototype of the beginning of the Epilogue to *Denzil Place*:

> I take my pen, and almost weep to find
> That I can only write of what I know—
> Athwart the shrunken mirror of my mind
> No varied forms pass glitt'ring to and fro.
>
> No clanking forms of gallant knights and squires
> Whose glories once my childish voice would praise,
> No feudal castles, from whose turret spires
> The captive maid her ev'ning song would raise.
>   . . .
> I am my own unworthy heroine now . . . . (59)

A bibliographical fact about that passage in *From Dawn to Noon* also helps to explain the mysterious omission of the initial capital in the Epilogue to *Denzil Place*. Here again is the line from the Epilogue, and here is the line from *From Dawn to Noon* that Fane and her publishers and printers recycle, as they recycle motifs from works by Barrett Browning, de Stael, Morris, and scores of others. The visual presentation represents alike the artistry of typography and verse, illustrating both the verity and the fiction that Fane asserts and questions when she says "I am my own unworthy heroine now," and when the real absence of that supplement of personal feeling is made a visible absence on the material page:

EPILOGUE

———

lay aside my pen,—my story ends,
"Of some few years in some few English lives;"

TAKE my pen, and almost weep to find
That I can only write of what I know—
Athwart the shrunken mirror of my mind
No varied forms pass glitt'ring to and
fro.

No clanking forms of gallant knights and
squires
Whose glories once my childish voice would
praise,
No feudal castles, from whose turret spires
The captive maid her ev'ning song would raise.

Notes

Introduction

1. M.H. Abrams, *The Mirror and the Lamp: Romantic Theory and the Critical Tradition* (New York: Oxford University Press, 1953); Abrams, *Natural Supernaturalism: Tradition and Revolution in Romantic Literature* (New York: Norton, 1971); Anne K. Mellor, *Romanticism and Gender* (New York: Routledge, 1993). The phrase, "art of disillusion," is the title of the chapter on Landon's work in Jerome McGann, *The Poetics of Sensibility* (Oxford: Clarendon Press, 1996), 143. Coleridge's famous formulation states, "What is poetry? is so nearly the same question with, what is a poet? that the answer to the one is involved in the solution of the other," *Biographia Literaria*, ed. James Engell and Walter Jackson Bate (two vols. published as "Volume 7" in *The Collected Works of Samuel Taylor Coleridge*, gen. ed. Kathleen Coburn (Princeton: Princeton University Press, 1983)).
2. On the poems about commodities, see Daniel Riess, "Letitia Landon and the Dawn of English Post-Romanticism," *SEL: Studies in English Literature 1500–1900* 36, no. 4 (Autumn 1996): 807–27. For the quoted verse, see Landon, *The Troubadour* [1825], in *The Poetical Works of Letitia Elizabeth Landon: A New Edition* (London: Longman, Orme, Brown, Green, and Longman, 1839), 2:10. An excellent study of a related set of issues—the relationship of industrialized publication to literary form—is Lee Erickson, *The Economy of Literary Form* (Baltimore: Johns Hopkins University Press, 1996).
3. William Maginn, "Regina's Maids of Honour. List the First," *Fraser's Magazine for Town and Country* (January 1836): 80.
4. For outstanding and influential examples of the sort of criticism that demonstrates the interpretative power of textual criticism, see Donald H. Reiman, *Romantic Texts and Contexts* (Columbia: University of Missouri Press, 1987); Jack Stillinger, *Multiple Authorship and the Myth of Solitary Genius* (New York: Oxford University Press, 1991); Stillinger, *Coleridge and Textual Instability: The Multiple Versions of the Major Poems* (New York: Oxford University Press, 1994); Jerome J. McGann, *The Textual Condition* (Princeton: Princeton University Press, 1991).
5. Ian Balfour, *The Rhetoric of Romantic Prophecy* (Stanford: Stanford University Press, 2002), 115–16.
6. Margaret J.M. Ezell, *Writing Women's Literary History* (Baltimore and London: The Johns Hopkins University Press, 1993), 7.
7. For discussion of the literary pose, see Tricia Lootens, "Receiving the Legend, Rethinking the Writer: Letitia Landon and the Poetess Tradition," in *Romanticism and Women Poets: Opening the Doors of Reception*, ed. Harriet Kramer Linkin and Stephen C. Behrendt (Lexington: The University Press of Kentucky, 1999), 242–84; Linda Peterson, "Rewriting *A History of the Lyre*: Letitia Landon,

Elizabeth Barrett Browning and the (Re) Construction of the Nineteenth-Century Woman Poet," *Women's Poetry, Late Romantic to Late Victorian. Gender and Genre, 1830–1900*, ed. Isobel Armstrong and Virginia Blain (London: Macmillan, 1999), 115–32; Yopie Prins, *Victorian Sappho* (Princeton: Princeton University Press, 1997), 209–25; and Glennis Stephenson, "Letitia Landon and The Victorian Improvisatrice: The Construction of L. E. L.," *Victorian Poetry* 30, no. 1 (Spring 1992): 1–17.

8. Hartley Coleridge, Rev. of *The Dream and Other Poems*, by the Hon. Mrs. Norton, *The Quarterly Review* 66 (September 1840): 376, 378; Rev. of *The Undying One and Other Poems*, *The Edinburgh Review* (June 1831), 366.

9. Theodor Adorno, "Culture Industry Reconsidered," in *The Culture Industry*, ed. J.M. Bernstein (London: Routledge 1991), 99.

10. Guy DeBord, *The Society of the Spectacle*, tr. Donald Nicholson-Smith of the 3rd French ed. (New York: Zone Books, 1994), 17, 33.

11. For reproductions of this and other political engravings by Gillray, and for useful glosses, see *The Satirical Etchings of James Gillray*, ed. Draper Hill (New York: Dover, 1976). For accounts of the paper-money controversy, see Terence Allan Hoagwood, *Skepticism and Ideology: Shelley's Political Prose and Its Philosophical Contexts from Bacon to Marx* (Iowa City: University of Iowa Press, 1988), 187–93; and Hoagwood, "Keats, Fictionality, and Finance," in *Keats and History*, ed. Nicholas Roe (Cambridge: Cambridge University Press, 1995), 127–42.

12. Three works of Victorian culture-criticism that we have in mind here—Carlyle's *Past and Present* (1843), Matthew Arnold's *Culture and Anarchy* (1869), and John Ruskin's *Unto This Last* (1860)—record both the ascendancy of money as the mode of social existence and a critique of the drift toward a reference-free way of life to which that mode of existence was tending. For DeBord's statement, see DeBord, *The Society of the Spectacle*, 43.

13. Aileen Dawson, *Masterpieces of Wedgewood in the British Museum* (Bloomington: Indiana University Press, 1984), 117.

14. George Herbert, *The Temple: Sacred Poems and Private Ejaculations* (Cambridge: Printed by Thomas Buck and Roger Daniel, printers to the Universitie, 1633).

15. This advertisement for Quaker Oats is reproduced (without comment on the iconography) by Ann Hulbert and Judith Rich Harris, "Raising the American Child," *The Wilson Quarterly* 23, no. 1 (Winter 1999): 19.

16. *Golden Thoughts on Mother, Home and Heaven. From Poetic and Prose Literature of All Ages and All Lands*, ed. The Reverend Theo. L. Cuyler, D.D. (New York: E.B. Treat, 1878).

17. Baudrillard, *The System of Objects* (1968), tr. Mark Poster, in *Jean Baudrillard: Selected Writings* (Stanford: Stanford University Press, 1988), 22. A photograph of this vase appears in Antoinette Faÿ-Hallé and Barbara Mundt, *Porcelain of the Nineteenth Century* (New York: Rizzoli, 1983), fig. 355, with commentary, 203.

18. A photograph of this plate, with a brief commentary, appears in Faÿ-Hallé and Mundt, *Porcelain of the Nineteenth Century*, pls. 82 and 63.

19. See Faÿ-Hallé and Mundt, *Porcelain of the Nineteenth Century*, 86 and fig. 128.

20. Altick, *The English Common Reader: A Social History of the Mass Reading Public, 1800–1900*, 2nd ed. (Columbus: Ohio State University Press, 1998), 139.

21. Faÿ-Hallé and Mundt, *Porcelain of the Nineteenth Century*, 92 and fig. 140.
22. Whitman, "Song of the Exposition," in *Leaves of Grass: A Textual Variorum of the Printed Poems*, ed. Sculley Bradley et al. (New York: New York University Press, 1980), 3: 618; Philip B. Meggs, *A History of Graphic Design*, 3rd ed. (New York: John Wiley, 1998), 151.
23. D.F. McKenzie, "The Book as an Expressive Form," *The Book History Reader*, ed. David Finkelstein and Alistair McCleery (London: Routledge, 2002), 29.
24. T.S. Eliot, "Tradition and the Individual Talent" (1919), in *Selected Essays of T.S. Eliot*, New ed. (New York: Harcourt, Brace and World, 1964), 7.
25. I.A. Richards. *Practical Criticism, A Study of Literary Judgment* (London: Kegan Paul, Trench, Trubner, 1929); and *Principles of Literary Criticism* (London: Kegan Paul, Trench, Trubner; New York: Harcourt, Brace, 1925).
26. Cleanth Brooks and Robert Penn Warren, *Understanding Poetry* (New York: H. Holt, 1938).
27. Lukacs, *Studies in European Realism*, tr. Edith Bone (New York: Grosset and Dunlap), 1964.
28. de Man, *Allegories of Reading: Figural Language in Rousseau, Nietzsche, Rilke, and Proust*, (New Haven: Yale University Press, 1979). On "New Historicism," see *New Historical Literary Study: Essays on Reproducing Texts, Representing History*, ed. Jeffrey N. Cox and Larry J. Reynolds (Princeton: Princeton University Press, 1993).
29. Dara Rossman Regaignon, "Instructive Sufficiency: Re-Reading the Governess through *Agnes Grey*," *Victorian Literature and Culture* 29 (2001):102; Bruce Boehrer, "'Lycidas': The Pastoral Elegy as Same-Sex Epithalamium," *PMLA* 117 (2002): 222; Ted Underwood, "Romantic Historicism and the Afterlife," *PMLA* 117 (2002): 238; Terrell Scott Herring, "Frank O'Hara's Open Closet," *PMLA* 117 (2002): 414; Michael Lackey, "'God's Grandeur': Gerard Manley Hopkins' Reply to the Speculative Atheist," *Victorian Poetry* 39, no. 1 (Spring 2001): 83–90; James Finn Cotter, "Hopkins and Augustine," *Victorian Poetry* 39, no. 1 (Spring 2001): 73, 75.
30. Henry F. Chorley, *Memorials of Mrs. Hemans, With Illustrations of Her Literary Character From Her Correspondence*, 2 vols. (London and New York: Saunders and Otley, 1836), 1: 103–04.
31. Wallace Stevens, "The Snow Man," in *Harmonium* (New York: Knopf, 1923), 24.
32. Prins, *Victorian Sappho*, 174.
33. Roger Chartier, "Labourers and Voyagers: From the Text to the Reader," in *The Book History Reader*, ed. David Finkelstein and Alistair McCleery (London: Routledge, 2002), 48.

CHAPTER 1 MARY ROBINSON

1. Roland Barthes, "From Work to Text," in *Image-Music-Text*, ed. and tr. Stephen Heath (New York: Hill and Wang, 1977), 157.
2. Fredric Jameson, "The Ideology of the Text," in *The Ideologies of Theory: Essays 1971–1986. Volume I: Situations of Theory* (Minneapolis: University of Minnesota Press, 1988), 19.

3. An outstanding and authoritative expression of the traditional view is G. Thomas Tanselle, *A Rationale of Textual Criticism* (Philadelphia: University of Pennsylvania Press, 1989). The most eloquent and influential challenge to the traditional view is McGann, *A Critique of Modern Textual Criticism* (Chicago: University of Chicago Press, 1983), against which Tanselle's book reaffirms traditional values. Recent editions for scholarly use which honor the physical character of books that actually exist include the Scholars' Facsimiles series [hundreds of books, including Mary Robinson's *Sappho and Phaon*, intro. Rebecca Jackson and Terence Hoagwood (Delmar, NY: Scholars' Facsimiles, 1994) and *The Keepsake* (1829), intro. Terence Hoagwood and Kathryn Ledbetter (Delmar, NY: Scholars' Facsimiles, 1999)], Jonathan Wordsworth's series, Revolution and Romanticism 1789–1836 [dozens of books, including Mary Robinson's *Lyrical Tales*, intro. Jonathan Wordsworth (Oxford: Woodstock Books, 1989)], and the Cornell Wordsworth volumes, under the general editorship of Stephen Maxfield Parrish, including *The Thirteen-Book Prelude*, ed. Mark L. Reed (Cornell University Press, 1991), and—despite the total transposition of medium—electronic facsimiles including the Rossetti Archive, ed. Jerome McGann <http://jefferson.village.virginia.edu/rossetti/index.html>, the scholarly website *Romantic Circles* (e.g., Mary Darby Robinson, *A Letter to the Women of England, on the Injustice of Mental Subordination*, ed. Adriana Craciun and others <http://www.rc.umd.edu/editions/contemps/robinson/cover.htm>) and The *Lyrical Ballads* Bicentenary Project, ed. Ronald Tetreault <http://www.dal.ca/~etc/lballads/welcome.htm>.

4. Outstanding examples of literary criticism that is informed by cognizance and analysis of such meanings include Jerome J. McGann, *The Textual Condition* (Princeton: Princeton University Press, 1991), and *Literature in the Marketplace*, ed. John O. Jordan and Robert L. Patten (Cambridge: Cambridge University Press, 1995). A collection of essays devoted to the interpretative significance of material media is *Materialism and Textuality*, ed. Terence Allan Hoagwood, published as an issue of *Studies in the Literary Imagination* 30, no. 1 (Spring 1997). Often, excellent work on the physical media of literary texts is informative but not self-consciously devoted to critical and interpretative argument: for obvious reasons the works of William Morris have attracted much productive scholarly attention to their media [e.g., William S. Peterson, *The Kelmscott Press: A History of William Morris's Typographical Adventure* (Berkeley: University of California Press, 1991)], and likewise studies of William Blake's illuminated works [e.g., Joseph Viscomi, *Blake and the Idea of the Book* (Princeton: Princeton University Press, 1993)].

5. For an outstanding and permanently important example of scholarly work that is explicitly devoted to the principles to which I refer, including the notion of a "work" as existing in an author's mind, see *Opus Maximum*, volume 15 in *The Collected Works of Samuel Taylor Coleridge*, ed. Thomas McFarland with the assistance of Nicholas Halmi (Princeton: Princeton University Press, 2002).

6. The word "legitimate" refers conventionally to the Petrarchan form, and it is also important in terms of the polemical context of writings by women: Charlotte Smith's *Elegiac Sonnets* of 1784 were widely received as if they had no other meaning or importance than private excess of feeling—i.e., sentimentality and weakness, which are treated in terms of femininity in the language of

every published review. At the same time, Smith's sonnets were disparaged as not "legitimate"—i.e., not composed in the Petrarchan form. In her preface to *Sappho and Phaon*, Robinson cites Smith as an exemplary writer of sonnets, and, with that praise of Smith in the preface, the claim represented by the word "legitimate" on Robinson's title-page puts her sonnets in contentious dialogue. Robinson makes a claim for the legitimacy of her work in the critical context in which Smith's sonnets were disparaged. On the contemporary reception of Smith's sonnets, see Florence Hilbish, *Charlotte Smith: Poet and Novelist* (Philadelphia: University of Pennsylvania Press, 1941), and Loraine Fletcher, *Charlotte Smith: A Critical Biography* (New York: St. Martin's Press, 1998).

7. Pascoe, introduction to *Mary Robinson: Selected Poems* (Peterborough, Ontario: Broadview, 2000); Robinson, *Memoirs of the Late Mrs. Robinson, Written by Herself*, 4 vols. (1801; rpt. London: Hunt and Clarke, 1826), 32; Shteir, "Mary Robinson," in *A Dictionary of British and American Women Writers 1660–1800*, ed. Janet Todd (Totowa, NJ: Rowman and Littlefield, 1987).

8. Principal sources of information about Mary Robinson include her posthumously published *Memoirs*, the anonymous and independently written biographical essay prefixed to *Poetical Works of the Late Mrs. Mary Robinson* (London: Richard Phillips, 1806), and Pascoe's splendidly researched biographical essay cited above.

9. For the text of this work and a textual introduction, see Robinson, *A Letter to the Women of England*.

10. On Bell, see Stanley Morison, *John Bell, 1745–1831: Bookseller, Printer, Publisher, Typefounder, Journalist* (Cambridge: Cambridge University Press, 1930); Charles H. Timperley, *A Dictionary of Printers and Printing, with the Progress of Literature, Ancient and Modern* (London, 1839); Timperley, *Encyclopedia of Literary and Typographical Anecdote* (London, 1842); and Frank Arthur Mumby, *Publishing and Bookselling: A History from the Earliest Times to the Present Day*, 3rd ed. (London: Jonathan Cape, 1954), 193.

11. Blakey, *The Minerva Press 1790–1820* [London: Printed for the Bibliographical Society at the University Press, Oxford, 1939 "(for 1935)"], 3.

12. Coleridge, *Table Talk and Omniana*, quoted by Blakey, *The Minerva Press*, 1–2.

13. Blakey, *The Minerva Press*, 2.

14. Lamb, "Sanity of True Genius," in *Last Essays of Elia*; qtd in Blakey, *The Minerva Press*, 3.

15. Blakey is the best source of information on Lane. See also Timperley, *Encyclopedia of Literary Anecdote*, 853.

16. Fox, preface to *Santa Maria* (London: Kearsley, 1797).

17. On the social and political significance of Bage's novels, see Mary Wollstonecraft's review of *Man as He Is* in the *Analytical Review* 24 (October 1796): 398–99; and Gary Kelly, *The English Jacobin Novel 1780–1805* (Oxford: Clarendon Press, 1976).

18. On Johnson, see Gerald P. Tyson, *Joseph Johnson: A Liberal Publisher* (Iowa City: University of Iowa Press, 1979).

19. Wollstonecraft, *A Vindication of the Rights of Woman* (1792), ed. Carol H. Poston (New York: Norton, 1975), 22.

20. Peterson, "Becoming an Author: Mary Robinson's *Memoirs*," in *Revisioning Romanticism: British Women Writers, 1776–1837*, ed. Carol Shiner Wilson and Joel Haefner (Philadelphia: University of Pennsylvania Press, 1994), 40, 43. Curiously, the mail-ordered copy of this book that I am using arrived with some of its pages printed upside-down, and is thus a palpable reminder that books are still manufactured things.

21. Curran, "Mary Robinson's *Lyrical Tales* in Context," in *Re-Visioning Romanticism*, ed. Wilson and Haefner, 21.

22. McGann, *The Poetics of Sensibility* (Oxford: Oxford University Press, 1996), 111–12.

Chapter 2 Felicia Hemans

1. Henry F. Chorley, *Memorials of Mrs. Hemans, With Illustrations of Her Literary Character From Her Correspondence*, 2 vols. (London and New York: Saunders and Otley, 1836), 1: 103–04.

2. Francis Jeffrey, review of *Records of Woman* and *The Forest Sanctuary*, *Edinburgh Review*, 50 (October 1829): 47 and *passim*; Lydia Sigourney, prefatory essay in [Harriet Hughes], *The Works of Mrs. Hemans; With a Memoir of Her Life, by Her Sister. In Six Volumes* (Edinburgh: William Blackwood and Sons; London: Thomas Cadell, 1839), e.g., xv; Chorley, *Memorials*, 1:104.

3. Joanna Baillie, "Introductory Discourse" to *A Series of Plays* (1798), in *The Complete Poetical Works of Joanna Baillie. First American Edition* (Philadelphia: Carey and Lea, 1832), 11, 15. Baillie mentions the spectacle of public executions among her examples of pleasurable excitements.

4. Wordsworth, preface to second edition of *Lyrical Ballads* (1800; rev. 1802, 1836, and rpt. 1850), in *William Wordsworth: Selected Prose*, ed. John O. Hayden (Harmondsworth: Penguin, 1988), 279–80.

5. Among many examples of critical work which has moved discussion beyond the illusion of personal feeling, I will mention Jerome McGann's *The Romantic Ideology* (Chicago: University of Chicago Press, 1983), which influentially called into question the traditional (and personalistic) illusions of Romanticism.

6. One valuable account of Hemans's business practices and sales success is Paula Feldman, "The Poet and the Profits: Felicia Hemans and the Literary Marketplace," *Keats-Shelley Journal* 46 (1997): 148–76.

7. Susan Wolfson, " 'Domestic Affections' and 'the spear of Minerva': Felicia Hemans and the Dilemma of Gender," in *Re-Visioning Romanticism: British Women Writers, 1776–1837*, ed. Carol Shiner Wilson and Joel Haefner (Philadelphia: University of Pennsylvania Press, 1994), 144.

8. Sweet and Melnyk, "Introduction: Why Hemans Now?" in *Felicia Hemans: Reimagining Poetry in the Nineteenth Century*, ed. Sweet and Melnyk (Houndmills and New York: Palgrave [St. Martins], 2001), 6; Armstrong, "Natural and National Monuments—Felicia Hemans's 'The Image in Lava': A Note," in *Felicia Hemans*, ed. Sweet and Melnyk, 219.

9. [Hughes], *The Works of Mrs. Hemans; With a Memoir of Her Life, by Her Sister*, vol. 1.

10. Feldman, introduction to *Records of Woman With Other Poems* (Lexington: University of Kentucky, 1999), xv–xvi.

11. McGann, "Literary History, Romanticism, and Felicia Hemans," in *Re-Visioning Romanticism*, ed. Wilson and Haefner, 210–27.

12. Stuart Curran, "Romantic Poetry: The 'I' Altered," in *Romanticism and Feminism*, ed. Anne K. Mellor (Bloomington: Indiana University Press, 1988), 189.

13. An excellent account of commodity-poems in the period is Daniel Riess, "Letitia Landon and the Dawn of English Post-Romanticism," *Studies in English Literature 1500–1900* 36 (1996): 807–27.

14. Alaric Alfred Watts, *Alaric Watts: A Narrative of His Life. By His Son*, 2 vols. (London: Richard Bentley and Son, 1884), 1:250.

15. Mrs. Hemans, "A Spanish Lady," in *The Literary Souvenir; Or, Cabinet of Poetry and Romance*, ed. Alaric A. Watts (London: Longman, Rees, Orme, Brown, and Green; and John Andres, 1827), 120.

16. On Heman's and de Stael's *Corinne*, see Nanora Sweet, "Corinne and the Woman as Poet in England: Hemans, Jewsbury, and Barrett Browning," in *The Novel's Seductions: Stael's Corinne in Critical Inquiry* (Lewisburg, PA: Bucknell University Press, 1999), 204–20.

17. Wolfson, note to "Juana" in *Felicia Hemans: Selected Poems, Letters, Reception Materials* (Princeton: Princeton University Press, 2000), 388.

18. Charlotte Smith, *The Emigrants* (1793), in *The Poems of Charlotte Smith*, ed. Stuart Curran (New York: Oxford University Press, 1993), Book 1, ll. 280–81, 145.

19. For a different development of the originally Hegelian metaphor of the "enemy within," see Tricia Lootens, "Hemans and Home: Victorianism, 'Internal Enemies,' and the Domestication of National Identity," *PMLA* 109 (1994): 238–53.

20. Mary Hays, *The Victim of Prejudice* (London: Joseph Johnson, 1799), 2: 215. This work is available in a facsimile of the first edition, intro. by Terence Allan Hoagwood (Delmar, NY: Scholars' Facsimiles and Reprints, 1990).

21. On Hays's *The Victim of Prejudice*, see Hoagwood, *Politics, Philosophy, and the Production of Romantic Texts* (DeKalb: Northern Illinois University Press, 1996), 122–39.

22. Giorgio Vasari, *The Lives of the Artists* (1568), tr. Julia Conaway Bondanella and Peter Bondanella (1991; rpt. Oxford: Oxford University Press, 1998), 439–44; and Laura Marie Roberts Ragg, *The Women Artists of Bologna* (London: Methuen, 1907), 167–87. See also Feldman, *Records of Woman With Other Poems*, 171.

23. Note to "Juana." *Felicia Hemans: Selected Poems, Letters, Reception Materials* (Princeton University Press, 2000), 351n.

24. Feldman, *Records of Women With Other Poems*, xxiv.

CHAPTER 3 *FRASER'S*

1. William Maginn, "Regina's Maids of Honour. List the First," *Fraser's Magazine for Town and Country* (January 1836): 80.

2. Dorothy Mermin, *Godiva's Ride: Women of Letters in England, 1830–1880* (Bloomington, IN: Indiana University Press, 1993), xiv.

3. Linda Peterson, "Rewriting *A History of the Lyre*: Letitia Landon, Elizabeth Barrett Browning and the (Re)Construction of the Nineteenth-Century Woman Poet," *Women's Poetry, Late Romantic to Late Victorian: Gender and Genre, 1830–1900*, ed. Isobel Armstrong and Virginia Blain (New York: St. Martin's Press, 1999), 116.

4. Alice Acland, *Caroline Norton* (London: Constable, 1948), 44.

5. Patricia Marks, "Harriet Martineau: *Fraser's* "Maid of [Dis]Honour," *Victorian Periodicals Review* 19, no. 1 (Spring 1986): 28, 33.

6. Harriet Devine Jump and I discussed our perspectives on literary annuals and their women editors at the 18th and 19th Century British Women Writers Conference in Lawrence, Kansas in March, 2001, where she presented an excellent paper, " 'The False Prudery of Public Taste': Scandalous Women and the Annuals, 1820–1850," recently published in *Feminist Readings of Victorian Popular Texts: Divergent Femininities*, ed. Emma Liggins and Daniel Duffy (Aldershot: Ashgate, 2001), 1–17. Although our views differ on the textual revelations of literary annuals, we share an amused appreciation for the ironies of these women's scandalous lives in context with books purported to be morally restrictive and regulated for middle-class domestic consumption. We coincidentally discuss some of the same works in our essays.

7. William Maginn, "Gallery of Literary Characters. Lady Morgan," *Fraser's Magazine for Town and Country* 11 (May 1835): 529.

8. Miriam M.H. Thrall, *Rebellious Fraser's: Nol Yorke's Magazine in the Days of Maginn, Thackeray, and Carlyle* (New York: Columbia University Press), 20.

9. Maginn, "Morgan," 529.

10. Rev. of *Lady Morgan's Memoirs: Autobiography, Diaries, and Correspondence, The Westminster Review* 23 ns (April 1863): 490.

11. Ibid., 501.

12. Ibid., 501–02.

13. G.H. Lewes, "Our Survey of Literature and Science," *The Cornhill Magazine* 5 (January 1863): 132.

14. Harriet Martineau, Rev. of "A Letter to the Queen on the State of the Monarchy" by a Friend of the People, *The London and Westminster Review* 32 (April 1839): 466.

15. John Wilson Croker, Rev. of *France* by Lady Morgan, *Quarterly Review* 32 (April 1817): 264, 286.

16. Lady Morgan, *Lady Morgan's Memoirs: Autobiography, Diaries and Correspondence*, ed. Geraldine Jewsbury and Hepworth Dixon (London: William H. Allen, 1862), 2:280–81.

17. Henry Stewart Cunningham, Rev. of *Lady Morgan's Memoirs: Autobiography, Diaries and Correspondence, National Review* 16 (April 1863): 444.

18. Harriet Martineau, *Harriet Martineau on Women*, ed. Gayle Graham Yates (New Brunswick, NJ: Rutgers University Press, 1985), 214.

19. John Wilson Croker, Rev. of *Illustrations of Political Economy* by Harriet Martineau, *Quarterly Review* 44 (April 1833): 151.

20. Maginn, "Regina's," 80.

21. Thrall, *Rebellious Fraser's*, 86.

22. Martineau, Rev. of "Letter," 458.

23. Marguerite Blessington, *The Blessington Papers*, ed. Alfred Morrison (Printed for Private Circulation, 1895), 169.

24. Benjamin Robert Haydon, *The Diary of Benjamin Robert Haydon*, 5 vols., ed. Willard Bissell Pope (Cambridge, MA: Harvard University Press, 1963), 4:271.

25. Thomas Moore, *The Journal of Thomas Moore*, ed. Wilfred S. Dowden (Newark: University of Delaware Press, 1983), 3:1219.

26. Samuel Carter Hall, *Retrospect of a Long Life: From 1815 to 1883* (New York: Appleton, 1883), 369.

27. Jane Wilde, "The Countess of Blessington," *Dublin University Magazine* 45 (1855): 333.

28. "Literary 'Lions': Countess of Blessington," *Hunt's London Journal* 19 (November 9, 1844): 235.

29. Marguerite Blessington, "A Tale of the Baptistry of St. Marks," *The Keepsake* for 1847, ed. The Countess of Blessington (London: Longman, 1846), 13.

30. Marguerite Blessington, "The Storm," *The Keepsake* for 1834, ed. Frederic Mansel Reynolds (London: Longman, 1833), 189.

31. Maginn, "Regina's," 80.

32. Hall, *Retrospect*, 397.

33. See Jerome McGann and Daniel Riess, *Letitia Elizabeth Landon: Selected Writings* (Peterborough, Ontario: Broadview, 1997), for a comprehensive listing of Landon's work.

34. Glennis Stephenson, "Letitia Landon and the Victorian Improvisatrice: The Construction of L. E. L.," *Victorian Poetry* 30, no. 1 (Spring 1992): 2.

35. William Charles Macready, *Diaries of William Charles Macready, 1833–1851*, ed. William Toynbee (London, 1912), 1:262.

36. Letitia Elizabeth Landon, "The Lily of the Valley," *Fisher's Drawing Room Scrap-Book* for 1836 (London: Fisher, 1835), 9.

37. In Germaine Greer's "The Tulsa Center for the Study of Women's Literature: What We Are Doing and Why We Are Doing It," *Tulsa Studies in Women's Literature* 1, no. 1 (1982):19, she discusses a "most compromising poem" by L. E. L. in this volume and makes an argument, similar to mine, about L. E. L. and Maginn's affair; however, I do not find the poem she discusses in either of my copies of the 1836 *Drawing Room Scrap-Book*. She cites page 83 for the poem, but my volume has 57 pages.

38. Jacqueline Labbé, *The Romantic Paradox: Love, Violence and the Uses of Romance, 1760–1830* (New York: St. Martin's Press, 2000), 160.

39. Qtd. in Anne Katherine Elwood, *Memoirs of Literary Ladies of England*, 2 vols. (London: Henry Colburn, 1843), 2:322–23.

40. Emma Roberts, "Memoir of L. E. L.," in *The Zenana and Minor Poems of L. E. L.* (London: Fisher, 1839), 10.

41. Elwood, *Memoirs*, 2:324.

42. Labbé, *Romantic Paradox*, 159.

43. Untitled, *The Age*, 19 July 1836, 196.

44. Micael M. Clarke, *Thackeray and Women* (DeKalb, IL: Northern Illinois University Press, 1995), 8.

45. Catherine J. Hamilton, *Women Writers: Their Works and Ways* (London: Ward, Lock & Bowden, 1893), 131.

46. Caroline Norton, "Marriage and Love," *The Sorrows of Rosalie and Other Poems* (1829), *Selected Writings of Caroline Norton*, facsimile reproduction, ed. James O. Hoge and Jane Marcus (Delmar, NY: Scholars' Facsimiles & Reprints, 1978), 119.

47. Neal Gabler, *Life: The Movie* (New York: Random House, 1998), 198, 162–63, 165.

48. Caroline Norton, "The Haunted Wood of Amesoy," *Katie Bouverie, and Other Tales and Sketches, in Prose and Verse*, 2 vols. (Philadelphia: Carey & Hart, 1836), 1:171–84.

49. Caroline Norton, "The Dream," *The Dream and Other Poems* (London: Henry Colburn, 1841), 35.

50. Caroline Norton, "The Future," *The Undying One and Other Poems* (1830), *Selected Writings of Caroline Norton*, facsimile reproduction, ed. James O. Hoge and Jane Marcus (Delmar, NY: Scholars' Facsimiles & Reprints, 1978), 202.

51. Rev. of *The Undying One and Other Poems* by the Hon. Mrs. Norton, *Edinburgh Review* 53 (June 1831): 365.

52. Hartley Coleridge, Rev. of *The Dream and Other Poems* by the Hon. Mrs. Norton, *Quarterly Review* 66 (1840): 382.

53. Yopie Prins, "Personifying the Poetess: Caroline Norton, 'The Picture of Sappho,' " *Women's Poetry, Late Romantic to Late Victorian: Gender and Genre, 1830–1900*, ed. Isobel Armstrong and Virginia Blain (New York: St. Martin's Press, 1999), 61.

54. Hamilton, *Women Writers*, 133.

55. James Hamilton Fyfe, "Mrs. Norton," *Temple Bar* 52 (January 1878): 109.

56. Caroline Norton, "Lawrence Bayley's Temptation," *The Keepsake* for 1834, ed. Frederic Mansel Reynolds (London: Longman, 1833), 147.

57. Eric Trudgill, *Madonnas and Magdalens: The Origins and Development of Victorian Sexual Attitudes* (New York: Holmes, 1976), 270.

58. Deborah Gorham, *The Victorian Girl and the Feminine Ideal* (Bloomington: Indiana University Press, 1982), 4–5.

59. Norton, *The Dream*, xii.

60. Charles and Frances Brookfield, *Mrs. Brookfield and Her Circle* (New York: Scribner's, 1906), 209.

61. Henry Crabb Robinson, *Diary, Reminiscences, and Correspondence of Henry Crabb Robinson*, 2 vols., ed. Thomas Sadler (Boston: Houghton, Mifflin, 1877), 2:335–36.

62. Frances Ann Kemble, *Records of a Girlhood* (New York: Henry Holt, 1879), 175.

63. Qtd. in Clarke, *Thackeray and Women*, 35–36.

64. Coleridge, Rev. of *The Dream*, 376–78.

65. John Murray, *A Publisher and His Friends: Memoir and Correspondence of the Late John Murray*, 2 vols., ed. Samuel Smiles (London: John Murray, 1891), 2:415.

66. William Bates, *The Maclise Portrait-Gallery of Illustrious Literary Characters* (London: Chatto and Windus, 1883), 55.

67. Anne Hector, "Mrs. Norton," *Women Novelists of Queen Victoria's Reign* (London: Hurst & Blackett, 1897), 289.

68. Mermin, *Godiva's Ride*, 12.

69. Jerome Christensen, *Lord Byron's Strength: Romantic Writing and Commercial Society* (Baltimore and London: The Johns Hopkins University Press, 1993), xx.

70. Andrew Elfenbein, *Byron and the Victorians* (Cambridge: Cambridge University Press, 1995), 59, 60.

71. Mermin, *Godiva's Ride*, 8, 11.

72. Angela Leighton, *Victorian Women Poets: Writing Against the Heart* (Charlottesville: University Press of Virginia, 1992), 82, 81.

73. Yopie Prins, *Victorian Sappho* (Princeton: Princeton University Press, 1999), 213.

74. Hall, *Retrospect*, 386.

75. Qtd. in Jane Perkins, *The Life of Mrs. Norton* (London: John Murray, 1909), 155.

76. Acland, *Caroline Norton*, 156–57.

77. Caroline Norton, *Some Unrecorded Letters of Caroline Norton in the Altschul Collection of the Yale University Library*, ed. Bertha Coolidge (Privately printed by Yale University Library, 1934), 9.
78. Peterson, "Rewriting", 121–22.
79. Prins, "Personifying the Poetess," 53.
80. Tricia Lootens, *Lost Saints: Silence, Gender, and Victorian Literary Canonization* (Charlottesville: University Press of Virginia, 1996), 10.
81. Bates, *Maclise Portrait Gallery*, 356.

CHAPTER 4 WOMEN EDITORS

1. A small group of book history scholars formed in 1991 to create The Society for the History of Authorship, Reading & Publishing (SHARP), a professional organization that promotes the study of book history through their annual conference, a newsletter, and an annual hardcover scholarly journal, *Book History*. According to the SHARP Web site (www.sharpweb.org/intro.html), "book historians study the social, cultural, and economic history of authorship; the history of the book trade, copyright, censorship, and underground publishing; the publishing histories of particular literary works, authors, editors, imprints, and literary agents; the spread of literacy and book distribution; canon formation and the politics of literary criticism; libraries, reading habits, and reader response." The first annual conference in New York in 1993 registered 130 attendees. The organization's website now boasts 1,000 members.
2. Dorothy Mermin, *Godiva's Ride: Women of Letters in England, 1830–1880* (Bloomington and Indianapolis: Indiana University Press, 1993), 44.
3. Margaret Beetham, *A Magazine of Her Own? Domesticity and Desire in the Woman's Magazine, 1800–1914* (London and New York: Routledge, 1996), 42.
4. G.H. Lewes, "The Condition of Authors in England, Germany, and France," *Fraser's Magazine* 35 (1847), 285.
5. Julia Swindells, *Victorian Writing and Working Women: The Other Side of Silence* (Minneapolis: University of Minnesota Press, 1985), 40.
6. Barbara Onslow, *Women of the Press in Nineteenth-Century Britain* (Basingstoke, Hampshire and New York: Palgrave Macmillan, 2000), 116.
7. Judith Pascoe, "Mary Robinson and the Literary Marketplace," *Romantic Women Writers: Voices and Countervoices*, ed. Paula R. Feldman and Theresa M. Kelley (Hanover and London: University Press of New England, 1995), 258.
8. J.G. Lockhart, *The Life of Sir Walter Scott, Bart.* (Edinburgh: Black, 1879), 686.
9. Charles Lamb, *Letters of Charles Lamb*, 2 vols., ed. W. Carew Hazlitt (London: Bell, 1886), 2: 265.
10. Alfred, Lord Tennyson, *The Letters of Alfred Lord Tennyson*, ed. Cecil Y. Lang and Edgar F. Shannon, Jr. (Cambridge, MA: Harvard University Press, 1981), 1:63 and 146. For more information on relationships between authors and annuals editors, see Kathryn Ledbetter, "Lucrative Requests: British Authors and Gift Book Editors," *Papers of the Bibliographical Society of America* 88, no. 2 (June 1994): 207–16 and "'BeGemmed and BeAmuletted': Tennyson and Those 'Vapid' Gift Books," *Victorian Poetry* 34, no. 2 (Summer 1996): 235–45.

11. Camilla Toulmin (Mrs. Newton Crosland), qtd. in Alison Adburgham, *Women in Print: Writing Women and Women's Magazines from the Restoration to the Accession of Victoria* (London: George Allen and Unwin, 1972), 264.

12. S.C. Hall, *Retrospect of a Long Life: 1815 to 1883* (New York: D. Appleton and company, 1883), 176.

13. A. Bose, "The Verse of the English 'Annuals,'" *Review of English Studies*, 4th ser. 13 (January 1953), 38.

14. Nigel Cross, *The Common Writer: Life in Nineteenth-Century Grub Street* (Cambridge: Cambridge University Press, 1985), 165.

15. Thomas Moore, *The Journals of Thomas Moore*, ed. Wilfred S. Dowden (Newark: University of Delaware Press, 1983), 1:1530.

16. Frederick W. Faxon, *Literary Annuals and Gift Books: A Bibliography 1823–1903*. 1912. Repr. with supplementary essays by Eleanore Jamieson and Iain Bain (Middlesex: Private Libraries Association, 1973).

17. Moore, *The Journals of Thomas Moore*, 1579.

18. William Makepeace Thackeray, "A Word on the Annuals," *Fraser's Magazine* 16 (1837): 758.

19. Isobel Armstrong, "Misrepresentation: Codes of Affect and Politics in Nineteenth-Century Women's Poetry," in *Women's Poetry, Late Romantic to Late Victorian: Gender and Genre, 1830–1900*, ed. Isobel Armstrong and Virginia Blain (Basingstoke, Hampshire: Macmillan, 1999), 28.

20. Jane Wilde, "The Countess of Blessington," *Dublin University Magazine* 45 (1855): 344.

21. Marion Shaw, "Tennyson and his Public 1827–1859," in *Tennyson*, ed. D.J. Palmer (London: Bell, 1973), 53.

22. *The Letters of Alfred, Lord Tennyson*, 144.

23. R.R. Madden, *The Literary Life and Correspondence of The Countess of Blessington* (New York: Harper, 1855), 2: 351.

24. N.P. Willis, *Pencillings by the Way* (London: Bohn, 1846), 353.

25. Alison Adburgham, *Women in Print: Writing Women and Women's Magazines from the Restoration to the Accession of Victoria* (London: George Allen and Unwin, 1972), 258.

26. Charles Dickens, *The Letters of Charles Dickens*, eds. Kathleen Tillotson et al. (Oxford: Clarendon, 1969), 2: 58–59.

27. Qtd. in Willard Connely, *Count d'Orsay, the Dandy of Dandies* (London: Cassell, 1952), 349.

28. Qtd. in Madden, *The Literary Life*, 1: 235.

29. Benjamin Disraeli, *Letters: 1835–1837*, ed. J.A.W. Gunn et al. (Toronto: University of Toronto Press, 1982), 225.

30. Madden, *The Literary Life*, 2: 427.

31. Michael Sadleir, *The Strange Life of Lady Blessington* (Boston: Little, 1933), 193–94.

32. R.R. Madden, *The Literary Life*, 1: 175.

33. Robert L. Patten, *Charles Dickens and His Publishers* (Oxford: Clarendon Press, 1978), 18.

34. Moore, *The Journals of Thomas Moore*, 5: 2027.

35. William Jerdan, *The Autobiography of William Jerdan*, vol. 3 (London: Arthur Hall, Virtue & Co., 1852–53), 185.

36. Moore, *The Journals of Thomas Moore*, 1835.

37. See Jerome McGann and Daniel Riess, *Letitia Elizabeth Landon: Selected Writings* (Broadview, 1997), for a comprehensive listing of Landon's work, compiled by Cynthia Lawford.

38. Lamon Blanchard, *The Life and Literary Remains of L. E. L.*, (Philadelphia: Lea & Blanchard, 1841), 1: 70.

39. Angela Leighton, *Victorian Women Poets: Writing Against the Heart* (Charlottesville and London: University Press of Virginia, 1992).

40. Moore, *The Journals of Thomas Moore*, Vol. 3: 1826–1830, 1305.

41. Beetham, *A magazine of her own?*, 43.

42. Quotations from *The History of the Lyre* are taken from *The Poetical Works of Letitia Elizabeth Landon*, ed. William B. Scott (London: George Routledge and Sons, 1873), and refer to page numbers in this edition. This book has been reproduced in facsimile with an introduction and additional poems, ed. F. J. Sypher (Delmar, NY: Scholars' Facsimiles, 1990).

43. Terence Hoagwood and Kathryn Ledbetter, "Life of Letitia Landon," in "L. E. L.'s '*Verses*' and *The Keepsake* for 1829," in the *Romantic Circles* scholarly Web site,<http://http://www.rc.umd.edu/editions/contemps/lel/-keepcov.htm>.

44. An excellent study of this set of poetry and its meanings is Daniel Reiss, "Letitia Landon and the Dawn of English Post-Romanticism," *Studies in English Literature 1500–1900* 36 (Autumn 1996): 807–27.

45. W. Howitt, *Homes and Haunts of the Most Eminent British Poets* (London: Bentley, 1847), 2:133. This anecdote is also quoted by Glennis Stephenson, *Letitia Landon: The Woman Behind L. E. L.* (Manchester: Manchester University Press, 1995), 7; Stephenson's excellent study is one of the most valuable resources on the poet.

46. McGann and Riess, *Letitia Elizabeth Landon: Selected Writings* (Peterborough: Broadview Press, 1997), 31. McGann and Reiss cite Stephenson, *Letitia Landon*, 174.

47. Jerome McGann's short but important account of Landon's work, "Waking from Adam's Dream: L. E. L.'s Art of Disillusion", in *The Poetics of Sensibility* (Oxford: Clarendon Press, 1996) points out that Landon's work illustrates "imaginative writing as a commercial activity" (145); her poetry "comes inflected with a disturbing mood or tone of bad faith"; it "recreates a factitious world" (146); and some of her poetry offers a "debunking move on the superficialities of love and romance" (148) while nonetheless purveying those superficialities for money. This line of argument clearly influences our present chapter, but the argument differs in that we are suggesting that the critical reflexivity that we are pointing out in *A History of the Lyre* is a critique of the inhuman commercialization of poetic art, and not an instance of it.

48. Leighton, *Victorian Women Poets*, 75.

49. Mary Russell Mitford, *Letters of Mary Russell Mitford*, ed. Henry Chorley (London: Bentley, 1872), 1: 221.

50. Elizabeth Barrett Browning, *The Brownings' Correspondence*, ed. Philip Kelley and Ronald Hudson, 4: 290.

51. Mitford, *Letters*, 159.

52. Swindells, *Victorian Writing* 34–35.

53. Lewes, "The Condition of Authors" 285.

CHAPTER 5 *KEEPSAKE* ILLUSTRATIONS

1. Horkheimer and Adorno, *The Dialectic of Enlightenment*, tr. John Cumming (New York: Continuum, 1994), xiv.
2. Gerard Genette, *Paratexts: Thresholds of Interpretation*, tr. Jan E. Lewin (New York: Cambridge University Press, 1997), 1.
3. Lyotard, *The Postmodern Condition: A Report on Knowledge*, tr. Geoff Bennington and Brian Massumi (1979; rpt. Minneapolis: University of Minnesota Press, 1997), 72 and *passim*. Lyotard points out that Adorno expresses the same optimism about the insurrectionary power of art in Adorno's *Aesthetic Theory* (72).
4. A. Bose, "The Verse of the English 'Annuals,'" *The Review of English Studies* 4 no.13 (January 1953): 49.
5. For more on literary annuals, see Kathryn Ledbetter, "'BeGemmed and BeAmuletted': Tennyson and Those 'Vapid' Gift Books," *Victorian Poetry* 34, no. 2 (Summer 1996): 235–45; "'The Copper and Steel Manufactory' of Charles Heath," *Victorian Review*, Forthcoming, 2003; "Domesticity Betrayed: *The Keepsake* Literary Annual," *The Victorian Newsletter* 99 (Spring 2001): 16–24; L. E. L.'s "'Verses' and *The Keepsake* of 1829," hypertext edition of a *Keepsake* poem (and commentary), with Terence Hoagwood and Martin Matthew Jacobsen, *Romantic Circles* scholarly website (Fall 1998), <http://www.rc.umd.edu/editions/lel/keepcov.htm>; "Lucrative Requests: British Authors and Gift Book Editors," *Papers of the Bibliographical Society of America* 88, no. 2 (June 1994): 207–16; or "White Vellum and Gilt Edges: Imaging *The Keepsake, Studies in the Literary Imagination* 30, no. 1 (Spring 1997): 35–49.
6. Anne Renier, *Friendship's Offering: An Essay on the Annuals and Gift Books of the 19th Century.* (London: Private Libraries Association, 1964), 16.
7. Slavoj Žižek, *Welcome to the Desert of the Real* (London: Verso, 2002), 12.
8. Margaret Linley, "A Centre that Would Not Hold: Annuals and Cultural Democracy," in *Nineteenth-Century Media and the Construction of Identities*, ed. Laurel Brake, Bill Bell, and David Finkelstein (New York: Palgrave, 2000), 56.
9. Qtd. in William Bell Scott, *Autobiographical Notes of the Life of William Bell Scott*, ed. W. Minto, 2 vols. (New York: Harper, 1892), 1:114–15.
10. William Makepeace Thackeray, "A Word on the Annuals," *Fraser's Magazine* 16 (1837), 758–61.
11. Rev. of *The Keepsake* for 1850, *The Literary Gazette* 1713 (November 17, 1849), 842.
12. Richard D. Altick, *Paintings from Books: Art and Literature in Britain, 1760–1900* (Columbus, OH: Ohio State University Press, 1985), 86–87.
13. Luce Irigaray, *Speculum of the Other Woman* (1974), tr. Gilliam C. Gill (Ithaca, NY: Cornell University Press, 1985), 133.
14. Linda Nochlin, *Women, Art, and Power and Other Essays* (New York: Harper, 1988), 138–39.
15. Lynne Pearce, *Woman / Image / Text: Readings in Pre-Raphaelite Art and Literature* (Toronto and Buffalo: University of Toronto Press, 1991), 15.
16. Mary Ann Doane, "Film and the Masquerade—Theorising the Female Spectator," *Screen* 23 (September–October 1982): 77.
17. Edward Snow, "Theorizing the Male Gaze: Some Problems," *Representations* 25 (Winter 1989): 31.

18. Peter Brooks, *Body Work: Objects of Desire in Modern Narrative* (Cambridge: Harvard University Press, 1993), 283.

19. Pearce, *Woman/Image/Text*, 18.

20. Nochlin, *Women, Art, and Power*, 2.

21. J. Hillis Miller, *Illustration* (Cambridge: Harvard University Press, 1992), 150.

22. Ronald Pearsall, *Tell Me, Pretty Maiden: The Victorian and Edwardian Nude* (Exeter, England: Webb, 1981), 22.

23. Rozsika Parker and Griselda Pollock, *Old Mistresses: Women, Art and Ideology* (New York: Pantheon, 1981), 116.

24. Anonymous, "The Enchanted Stream; or, The Rider's Vision," *The Keepsake* for 1828 (London: Hurst, 1827), 284–86.

25. Rozsika Parker and Griselda Pollock, *Old Mistresses*, 116.

26. Stella Blum, ed., *Ackermann's Costume Plates: Women's Fashions in England 1818–1828* (New York: Dover, 1978), vi.

27. Susan P. Casteras, *Images of Victorian Womanhood in English Art* (Cranbury, NJ: Associated University Presses, 1987), 69.

28. Anna Maria Hall, "The Wild Rose of Rosstrevor," *The Keepsake* for 1850, ed. The Countess of Blessington (London: Bogue, 1849), 264.

29. Janice Radway, *Reading the Romance: Women, Patriarchy, and Popular Literature* (Chapel Hill: University of North Carolina Press, 1984).

30. See Jean-Christophe Agnew, "Coming Up for Air: Consumer Culture in Historical Perspective," in *Consumption and the World of Goods*, ed. John Brewer and Roy Porter (New York: Routledge, 1993), 21 [inclusive, for bibliography: 19–39]. See Laura Mandell's notes on this essay: <http://www.users.muohio.edu/mandellc/agnew.htm>.

31. Casteras, *Images of Victorian Womanhood*, 40–41.

32. Deborah Gorham, *The Victorian Girl and the Feminine Ideal* (Bloomington: Indiana University Press, 1982), 7.

33. Nochlin, *Women, Art, and Power*, 19.

34. William Wordsworth, "The Country Girl," *The Keepsake* for 1829, ed. Frederic Mansel Reynolds (London: Longman, 1828), 50–51.

35. Peter J. Manning, "Wordsworth in the *Keepsake*, 1829," *Literature in the Marketplace: Nineteenth-Century British Publishing and Reading Practices*, ed. John O. Jordan and Robert L. Patten (New York: Cambridge University Press, 1995), 65.

36. Lynda Nead, *Myths of Sexuality: Representations of Women in Victorian Britain* (Oxford: Blackwell, 1988), 28.

37. Martha Vicinus, "The Perfect Victorian Lady," *Suffer and Be Still: Women in the Victorian Age*, ed. Martha Vicinus (Bloomington: Indiana University Press, 1972), ix.

38. Sarah Stickney Ellis, *Daughters of England, Their Position in Society, Character & Responsibilities* (London: Fisher, n.d. [1842]), 315.

39. Gorham, *The Victorian Girl*, 54.

40. Ellis, *Daughters of England*, 317.

41. Casteras, *Images of Victorian Womanhood*, 86.

42. Albert Smith, "Regnier's Vengeance," *The Keepsake* for 1848, ed. The Countess of Blessington (London: Bogue, 1847), 239.

43. Rana Kabbani, *Imperial Fictions: Europe's Myths of Orient* (New York: Macmillan, 1986).

44. Anon., "The Persian Lovers," *The Keepsake* for 1828 (London: Hurst, 1827), 136–37.

45. Kabbani, *Imperial Fictions*, 67.

46. Camilla Toulmin (Mrs. Newton Crosland), "A Tale That Was Told to Me," *The Keepsake* for 1848, ed. The Countess of Blessington (London: Bogue, 1847), 36–37.

47. Casteras, *Images of Victorian Womanhood*, 66.

48. Anna Maria Hall, "A Sketch," *The Keepsake* for 1849, ed. The Countess of Blessington (London: Bogue, 1848), 36.

49. Winifred Gérin's *Charlotte Brontë: The Evolution of Genius* (Oxford: Clarendon, 1967) provides interesting examples of women readers for whom the *Keepsake*'s engravings became very important. According to Gérin, the Brontë children were *Keepsake* readers, and one of four *Keepsake* engravings of John Martin pictures hanging on the walls in the Brontë parsonage "accounts for a distinctive characteristic of the children's 'Glasstown' sequence of tales" (44). The images provided them with ideas about fashionable women who would later become models for their fictional characters, as demonstrated in Charlotte's reproduction of female portraits from the annuals in her sketchbook. Gérin also cites the annuals as a source for Jane Eyre's lover, Rochester (53), thus the present Redgrave illustration, along with Charlotte's own experience as governess, ostensibly provides context for Brontë's portrayal of Jane as governess of Thornfield and Anne's portrayal of Agnes Grey.

50. Mrs. Ward, "Letty Bloomfield," *The Keepsake* for 1854, ed. Marguerite Power (London: Bogue, 1854), 125.

51. William Henry Harrison, "The Island Bride," *The Keepsake* for 1845, ed. The Countess of Blessington (London: Longman, 1844), 22.

52. Kate Flint, *The Woman Reader 1837–1914* (Oxford: Clarendon, 1993), 255.

53. Lord Morpeth, George William Frederick Howard, "The Lady and the Novel," *The Keepsake* for 1835, ed. Frederic Mansel Reynolds (London: Longman, 1834), 28.

54. Vicinus, "The Perfect Victorian Lady" x.

55. Sally Mitchell, "Sentiment and Suffering: Women's Recreational Reading in the 1860s," *Victorian Studies* 21 (1977): 32.

Chapter 6 Elizabeth Barrett Browning

1. Thomas J. Wise, *A Bibliography of the Writings in Prose and Verse of Elizabeth Barrett Browning* (London: Printed for Private Circulation only, 1918), 51, 60–61.

2. Wise, *Bibliography*, 60.

3. Elizabeth Smith, *The Brethren: A Poem in Four Books* (Birmingham: Printed for the Author by Pearson and Rollason, 1787); rpt. with intro. by Terence Allan Hoagwood (Delmar, NY: Scholars' Facsimiles, 1991); Elizabeth Barrett, *The Seraphim and Other Poems* (London: Otley, 1838).

4. *A Drama of Exile* was first published in *Poems by Elizabeth Barrett*, 2 vols. (London: Moxon, 1844).

5. Christina Rossetti, *The Face of the Deep: A Devotional Commentary on the Apocalypse* (London: Society for the Promotion of Christian Knowledge, 1892).

6. Alice Meynell, "Christ in the Universe" [1901], in *Collected Poems* (London: Burns and Oates, 1913).

7. Jean Ingelow, *A Story of Doom and Other Poems* (London: Longmans, Green, 1867; Boston: Roberts, 1867).

8. Isobel Armstrong points out that "nearly a decade before the publication of *Aurora Leigh* (1856), Elizabeth Barrett Browning had pondered on the possibility of using Christianity in a way that would have been unthinkable to Christina Rossetti" [*Victorian Poetry: Poetry, Poetics and Politics* (London: Routledge, 1993), 368.] Armstrong's point is both correct and important, and I am suggesting that such use of Christian mythological imagery came to full flower even earlier, in 1844.

9. As usual, gender politics generate some conflicts among Barrett's friends as well as her foes. Henry Chorley, writing anonymously, pointed out in a review of the 1844 volumes that Barrett's poetry, including *A Drama of Exile*, has a seriousness of intellectual purpose beyond what Chorley allows other contemporary women poets: *Athenaeum* 878 (24 August 1844): 763–64. The personalizing, belittling, and misogynist assumption was of course widespread. A reviewer in *The Sun* writes that the subject-matter of *A Drama of Exile* exceeds Barrett's intellectual capacity, whereas in slighter poems her tender feeling is praiseworthy [*The Sun* (9 September 1844): 3]. In 1990, Antony H. Harrison renewed the argument that Barrett Browning was an example of the traditional ideology of sexual love, rather than a critic of it [*Victorian Poets and Romantic Poems* (Charlottesville: University Press of Virginia, 1990), 108–43]. The opposite view is one of Leighton's central contentions in *Victorian Women Poets* (Charlottesville: University Press of Virginia, 1992).

10. "Some Account of the Greek Christian Poets," *The Athenaeum* (February–August 1842); rpt. in *The Complete Poetical Works of Elizabeth Barrett Browning*, ed. Harriet Waters Preston (Boston: Houghton Mifflin, 1900), 513–42. In this essay, Barrett writes of Apolinarius (father and son), Amphilochius, Synesius, Eduocia [wife of Theodosius, and empress of the world, whose poems "perished with her beauty as being of one seed with it" (524)], Paul Silentatius, George Pisida, John Damascenus, Simeon Metaphrastes, John of Euchaita, Theodore Prodromus, John Tzetza, Clemens Alexandrinus, and Manuel Phile.

11. On Barrett's essay on the Church Fathers, see Dorothy Hewlett, *Elizabeth Barrett Browning: A Life* (New York: Knopf, 1952), 85–87.

12. For Lanyer's poem, see *Renaissance Women: The Plays of Elizabeth Cary and the Poems of Aemilia Lanyer*, ed. Diane Purkiss (London: Pickering and Chatto, 1994).

13. An anonymous reviewer in *Tait's Edinburgh Magazine* writes that *A Drama of Exile* is Barrett's best poem and that a comparison with *Paradise Lost* improves one's understanding of the excellence of Barrett's poem [*Tait's Edinburgh Magazine*, n.s. 23 (January 1856): 14–20)]. A dissenting voice, in the same year, argued that *A Drama of Exile* compares poorly with *Paradise Lost* in terms of its characterizations and its insufficiently lofty conceptions [*New Monthly Magazine* 107 (July 1856): 369–78].

14. *A Drama of Exile*, first published in *Poems by Elizabeth Barrett, In Two Volumes* (London: Edward Moxon,1844), reprinted in *Poems By Elizabeth*

Barrett Browning, 2 vols. (London: Chapman and Hall, 1850), where *Sonnets from the Portuguese* appears for the first time. For the sake of convenient usage, my quotations from *A Drama of Exile* will provide line numbers in the most readily available edition, *The Poetical Works of Elizabeth Barrett Browning*, ed. Ruth M. Adams (Boston: Houghton Mifflin, 1974), which reprints the text from Harriet Waters Preston's edition of 1900.

15. For an extended commentary on Byron's *Cain*, see Terence Allan Hoagwood, *Byron's Dialectic: Skepticism and the Critique of Culture* (Lewisburg, PA: Bucknell University Press, 1993), 100–51.

16. On the theme and language of motherhood in Barrett Browning's work, and on the relationship of that topic with the theme of artistic creation, see Nancy Huston, "A Tongue Called Mother," *Raritan* 9, no. 3 (1990): 99–108.

17. An anonymous reviewer in *New Quarterly Review* objected to the appearance of Christ as a speaking character in the poem [*New Quarterly Review* 5 (1845): 84–97; see also Gardner B. Taplin, *The Life of Elizabeth Barrett Browning* (New Haven: Yale University Press, 1957), 126]; but the poem represents the transfiguration of Christ precisely as a matter of Christ's becoming entirely human (l. 1922).

18. Dorothy Mermin's excellent study of Barrett Browning's poetry argues that *A Drama of Exile* "firmly disengages woman from the natural world with which Romanticism had identified her" [*Elizabeth Barrett Browning: The Origins of a New Poetry* (Chicago: University of Chicago Press, 1989), 89]. I would add that the poem's repeated and joyful praise of movements "down" toward "Earth" complicates the theme.

19. "As a mere girl, Miss Barrett had read the Greek Fathers in the original, under the guidance of the blind scholar, Hugh Stuart Boyd" (Harriet Waters Preston, in *The Poetical Works*, 513). See *Elizabeth Barrett to Mr. Boyd: Unpublished Letters of Elizabeth Barrett to Hugh Stuart Boyd*, ed. Barbara McCarthy (New Haven: Yale University Press, 1955).

20. Cyprian, *Treatise II.1: On the Dress of Virgins*, par. 2; in *Anti-Nicene Fathers*, vol. 5 <http://www.ccel.org/fathers>.

21. As Angela Leighton memorably observed, in Elizabeth Barrett Browning's poetry "the creed of feeling is constantly set against the 'hard and cold thing' of social reality" (*Victorian Women Poets: Writing Against the Heart*, 80).

22. Tertullian, *On the Apparel of Women*, in *The Anti-Nicene Fathers*, vol. 4 <http://www.ccel.org/fathers>. Even more influentially, St. Augustine wrote that morality is a "disease" that "was brought in through a woman's corrupted soul" (St. Augustine, *On Christian Doctrine*, book I, chapter 14, "How the Wisdom of God Healed Man," par. 13) <http://www.iclnet. org/pub/resources/text/ipb-e/epl-01/agdoc-02.txt>.

23. See Leighton, *Victorian Women Poets*, 82. Alice Falk has written cogently of Barrett's translations of *Prometheus Bound* in terms of her meta-textual revisionism, and specifically in the context of her learned and critical preoccupation with Greek texts ["Elizabeth Barrett Browning and Her Prometheuses: Self-Will and a Woman Poet," *Tulsa Studies in Women's Literature* 7 (1988): 69–85]. Published six years later than *A Drama of Exile*, *Sonnets from the Portuguese* is clearly another textual case-in-point, the sequence's meanings being primarily critical and hermeneutic with regard to the mediated status of all textuality: see Angela Leighton, "Stirring a Dust of Figures: Elizabeth

Barrett Browning and Love," *Browning Society Notes* 17 (1988): 11–24. The fact that these sonnets about textuality and its traditions have been misunderstood for a century-and-a-half as expressions of supposedly personal love is one of the bitter ironies of literary history: Mermin's influential book shows how *Sonnets from the Portuguese* is a knowing engagement and commentary on a historically male-dominated literary tradition (*Elizabeth Barrett Browning*, 103–05, 128–46).

24. Margaret M. Morlier points out that "The Dead Pan" is a critique of Christianity rather than a defense of it: " 'The Dead Pan': Elizabeth Barrett Browning and the Romantic Ego," *Browning Institute Studies* 18 (1990): 131–55.

25. There is a clear documentary record of at least a part of Barrett's personal history among these issues, including her emergence from an immersion in fatherly exegesis to a repudiation of it, founded on her rejection of Pauline doctrines (reaffirmed by the Church Fathers) asserting the evil of sexual love. Her diary of 1831–32 records her habit in June 1831 of reading seven chapters of Scripture each day. See *The Unpublished Diary of Elizabeth Barrett Barrett, 1831–1832*, ed. Philip Kelley and Ronald Hudson (Athens, Ohio: Ohio University Press, 1969), 19. She mentions critical works that she was reading as she thought over interpretative issues, including Thomas Hartwell Horne's *An Introduction to the Critical Study and Knowledge of the Holy Scriptures*, 3 vols. (London, 1818–21) and Adam Clarke's *The Holy Bible . . . with a Commentary and Critical Notes*, 8 vols. (London, 1810–25). However, on 17 September she writes against a hierarchical or class-stratified notion of salvation for an elect: "I *cannot* make up my mind from Scripture, to do otherwise than embrace the doctrine of general redemption" (130). Between 5 October and 6 November 1831 there is no reference to the Bible at all; then, she does not mention it again, after 6 November, until 18 March 1832, when she reads the Greek Testament as an alternative to attending church. She does so again on 1 April, recording her decision in terms of disputation: "Reading St. John's Gospel—& Nonnus's paraphrase upon it. I do *not* like Nonnus" (230). She often mentions her mentor, Boyd, in connection with her study of the Greek Bible and Greek poetry (e.g., 125, 238), and her correspondence with Boyd is often specific about her readings ("seven hundred and thirty-one lines of Gregory Nazianzen's poem *In laudem virginitatis*") and sometimes her thoughts about her readings (of Heterodorus, e.g., she writes to Boyd of "his secret of pure lies"): see *Elizabeth Barrett to Mr. Boyd*, 70, 69n. On Barrett's diary of 1831–32, see Judy Simons, "Behind the Scenes: The Early Diary of Elizabeth Barrett Browning", in *Diaries and Journals of Literary Women from Fanny Burney to Virginia Woolf* (Iowa City: University of Iowa Press, 1990), 83–105.

26. Wise, *Bibliography*, 54.

27. Widely in studies of Barrett Browning's works, de-personalizing the poetry has been a necessary critical preliminary for the direct treatment of its social and cultural polemics. See Anne Perry, "Sexual Exploitation and Freedom: Religion, Race, and Gender in Elizabeth Barrett Browning's 'The Runaway Slave at Pilgrim's Point,'" *Studies in Browning and His Circle* 16 (1988): 14–27; Glennis Stephenson, *Elizabeth Barrett Browning and the Poetry of Love* (Ann Arbor: UMI Research Press, 1989); Phyllis Elmore, "Elizabeth Barrett Browning: Argumentative Discourse in *Sonnets from the Portuguese*," Ph.D. dissertation, Texas Women's University, 1989, *DAI 51* (1990): 861; and,

perhaps most influentially, Mermin's *Elizabeth Barrett Browning: The Origins of a New Poetry.*

28. Benjamin Jowett et al., *Essays and Reviews* [containing essays by Frederick Temple, Roland Williams, Baden Powell, Henry Bristow Wilson, C.W. Goodwin, Mark Pattison, and Benjamin Jowett] (London: Parker and Son, 1860). Here, Pattison observes that in France in the later eighteenth century it was "well understood, by all enlightened men, that the whole sacerdotal brood were but a set of impostors, who lived by deceiving the people, and who had invented religion for their own benefit" (318). Pattison writes at some length of the rationalizing of theology in the late seventeenth and eighteenth centuries, mentioning John Locke (*The Reasonableness of Christianity*, 1695), John Toland (*Christianity Not Mysterious*, 1696), David Hume [*Treatise of Human Nature* (1739), but the posthumously published *Dialogues Concerning Natural Religion* (1779) are also germane], Kantian philosophy, deists, and an opposition to all revealed religion that was imported to England from Germany in the eighteenth and nineteenth centuries. Though he does not name names, he is probably referring obliquely to J.G. Eichhorn 1781 [Johann Gottfried Eichhorn, *Einleitung in das Alte Testament* (1781; Leipzig: Weidmann, 1803)] and Johann Gottfried von Herder's *The Spirit of Hebrew Poetry*, which appeared in an English translation in 1833 [*The Spirit of Hebrew Poetry*, tr. James Marsh (Burlington: E. Smith, 1833)].

29. David Friedrich Strauss, *The Life of Jesus, Critically Examined*, 4th ed. [tr. George Eliot] (London: Chapman, 1846.

30. On the French school of thought to which I refer here, see Voltaire's *Philosophical Dictionary*, tr. anon. (London: Leigh Hunt and John Hunt, 1824); and Paul Henri Thiry and Baron d'Holbach, *Christianity Unveiled* (London: R. Carlile, 1819).

31. On the German school of hermeneutics including Eichhorn and Schleiermacher, see two important studies by E.S. Shaffer: *"Kubla Khan" and "The Fall of Jerusalem": The Mythological School in Biblical Criticism and Secular Literature* (Cambridge: Cambridge University Press, 1975); and "The Hermeneutic Community: Coleridge and Schleiermacher," in *The Coleridge Connection: Essays for Thomas McFarland*, ed. Richard Gravil and Molly Lefebure (New York: St. Martin's, 1990). On Herder, Eichhorn, and their effect on English poetry of the nineteenth century, see Anthony John Harding, *Coleridge and the Inspired Word* (Kingston: McGill-Queen's University Press, 1985).

32. Paul Henri Thiry, Baron d'Holbach, *The System of Nature; or, Laws of the Moral and Physical World*, tr. H.D. Robinson (Boston: Mendum, 1853). The first English translation (anon.) was published in London in 1795.

33. David Friedrich Strauss, *The Life of Jesus, Critically Examined*, 1: ix–x. See Harding, *Coleridge and the Inspired Word*, 85.

34. Janice L. Haney, "'Shadow-Hunting': Romantic Irony, *Sartor Resartus*, and Victorian Romanticism," *Studies in Romanticism* 17 (1978): 313. See also Harding, *Coleridge and the Inspired Word*, 19.

35. Herder, *The Spirit of Hebrew Poetry*, tr. James Marsh (1833; rpt. Naperville, IL: Aleph Press, 1971), 2:51.

36. William Blake, *The Marriage of Heaven and Hell*, pl. 11, in *The Complete Poetry and Prose of William Blake*, rev. ed., ed. David V. Erdman (Garden City, NY: Doubleday, 1982).

37. Jowett, "On the Interpretation of Scripture," in *Essays and Reviews*, 331.

38. An anonymous reviewer in *Spectator* writes that Barrett's poem is based on Byron's *Cain*: *Spectator* 17, no. 843 (24 August 1844): 809–10.

39. Emily Pfeiffer, *Women and Work. An Essay* (London: Trübner & Co., 1888).

40. Shelley, *A Defence of Poetry*, in *The Complete Works of Percy Bysshe Shelley*, ed. Roger Ingpen and Walter E. Peck (London: Ernest Benn, 1926–30), 7: 125. Barrett's interest in Shelley's writing is everywhere evident: as I have suggested elsewhere [see my *Prophecy and the Philosophy of Mind: Traditions of Blake and Shelley* (Tuscaloosa: University of Alabama Press, 1985), 131–86], Shelley's *A Defence of Poetry* is closely related to his verse drama, *Prometheus Unbound* (1820), and, in turn, Barrett's earlier verse drama, *Prometheus Bound*, is deeply influenced by Shelley, and so is *A Drama of Exile*.

41. Studies of Ingelow's *A Story of Doom* are few, but one scholarly treatment of the poem's gender politics is Heidi Johnson, " 'Matters That a Woman Rules': Marginalized Maternity in Jean Ingelow's *A Story of Doom*," *Victorian Poetry* 33, no. 1 (Spring 1995):75–88. There are likewise few book-length studies of Ingelow: one is Maureen Peters, *Jean Ingelow, Victorian Poetess* (Totowa, NJ: Rowman and Littlefield, 1972).

42. On Galton and eugenics, see Daniel J. Kevles, *In the Name of Eugenics: Genetics and the Uses of Human Heredity* (New York: Knopf, 1985); H.G. Wells, "Comment on Francis Galton's Eugenics: Its Definition, Scope, and Aims," *American Journal of Sociology* 10, no. 1. (July, 1904): and Geoffrey Russell Searle, *Eugenics and Politics in Britain* (Leyden: Noordhoff, 1976).

Chapter 7 Violet Fane

1. Violet Fane, "Lancelot and Guinevere," in *From Dawn to Noon* (1872; London: Longmans and Co.; New York: G.W. Carlton & Co., 1881), 141. "Violet Fane" is a pseudonym that appears in books by Mary Montgomerie Lamb, granddaughter of the eleventh Earl of Eglinton. A biographical essay in her *Poems by Violet Fane*, 2 vols. (London: John C. Nimmo, 1892) says that her father "was himself a verse-writer" and that "her mother was a highly intellectual and accomplished woman" (1: vi). In 1864 she married Henry Sydenham Singleton, "an Irish landowner" (*DNB*). In 1872 her book *From Dawn to Noon* appeared, containing sixty-one poems, and in 1875 *Denzil Place: A Story in Verse*. She published altogether seven collections of poetry, three novels (three volumes each), one play, and a collection of essays. She was a correspondent of Matthew Arnold and Oscar Wilde, and in 1894, a year after Singleton's death, she married Sir Philip Henry Wodehouse Currie, who was appointed British Ambassador to Constantinople. She lived in Constantinople during the Armenian revolt, massacres in the city, and a revolt in Crete, after which Currie was transferred to Rome. She died in England in 1905. See the introductory essay by Terence Allan Hoagwood and Nicole Stewart in Fane, *Denzil Place* (Delmar, NY: Scholars' Facsimiles, 1996), 3–11.

2. Fane, *Denzil Place: A Story in Verse* (London: Chapman and Hall, 1875). This book is available in a facsimile edition with an introduction by Terence Hoagwood and Nicole Stewart (Delmar, NY: Scholars' Facsimiles and Reprints, 1996).

3. William Morris, *The Defense of Guenevere and Other Poems* (London: Bell & Daldy, 1858).

4. Fane, *From Dawn to Noon.*

5. See, e.g., McGann, *A Critique of Modern Textual Criticism* (Chicago: University of Chicago Press, 1983); *The Beauty of Inflections: Literary Investigations in Historical Method and Theory* (Oxford: Clarendon Press, 1985); *Social Values and Poetic Acts: The Historical Judgment of Literary Work* (Cambridge, MA: Harvard University Press, 1988); *Towards a Literature of Knowledge* (Chicago: University of Chicago Press, 1989); *The Textual Condition* (Princeton, NJ: Princeton University Press, 1991); *Black Riders: The Visible Language of Modernism* (Princeton, NJ: Princeton University Press, 1993).

6. McGann, " 'Thing to Mind': The Materialist Aesthetic of William Morris," *Black Riders,* 45–75.

7. This autographed presentation copy is located at the Humanities Research Center in the Harry Ransom Center at the University of Texas, Austin. For Housman's principles of textual criticism, see, e.g., *"The Name and Nature of Poetry" and Other Selected Prose,* ed. John Carter (1961; New York: New Amsterdam Books, 1989), 36. and Terence Allan Hoagwood, *A. E. Housman Revisited* (New York: Simon and Schuster Macmillan, 1995), 36–38.

8. On this feminist poetic tradition, see Nanora Sweet, "The Bowl of Liberty: Felicia Hemans and the Romantic Mediterranean," *DAI* 54, no. 7 (1994):2593A; Sweet, "History, Imperialism, and the Aesthetics of the Beautiful: Hemans and the Post-Napoleonic Moment," in *At the Limits of Romanticism: Essays in Cultural, Feminist, and Materialist Criticism,* ed. Mary Favret and Nicola Watson (Bloomington: Indiana University Press, 1994); and Sweet, "'Lorenzo's' Liverpool and 'Corinne's' Coppet: The Italianate Salon and Romantic Education," in *Lessons of Romanticism: A Critical Companion,* ed. Thomas Pfau (Durham, NC: Duke University Press, 1998), 244–60.

9. Shelley, preface to *Laon and Cythna: or, The Revolution of the Golden City. A Vision of the Nineteenth Century,* in *The Complete Works of Percy Bysshe Shelley,* ed. Roger Ingpen and Walter E. Peck (London: Ernest Benn, 1926), 1:240–41.

10. Coleridge, "On the Present War," in *Lectures 1795, On Politics and Religion,* ed. L. Patton and P. Mann, vol. 1 of *The Collected Works of Samuel Taylor Coleridge,* ed. Kathleen Coburn (Princeton: Princeton University Press, 1971), 52, 69.

11. Paul Henri Thiry, Baron d'Holbach, *The System of Nature; or, Laws of the Moral and Physical World,* tr. H.D. Robinson (1835; rpt [2 vols.] Kitchener: Batoche Books, 2001); and Thomas Paine, *The Age of Reason* (London: R. Carlile, 1819)—for publishing this edition, Carlile was tried for blasphemy. On the influence of Holbach's arguments about superstition, especially on Shelley and on William Blake, see Terence Allan Hoagwood, *Prophecy and the Philosophy of Mind: Traditions of Blake and Shelley* (Tuscaloosa: University of Alabama Press, 1985), 7–9; and Hoagwood, *Skepticism and Ideology: Shelley's Political Prose and Its Philosophical Context from Bacon to Marx* (Iowa City: University of Iowa Press, 1988), 163–65 and passim.

12. Holbach, *System of Nature,* 1: 33.

13. On Rossetti's polemical art and its relation to "the contemporary scene," see Jerome McGann, *Dante Gabriel Rossetti and the Game that Must Be Lost* (New Haven: Yale University Press, 2000): his work is best understood in the context of a critique of cultural forms that were (and are) attendant on an economy of exchange value—"consumerist, imperial, and spectacular" (9–11).

14. Thomas McFarland, *Originality and Imagination* (Baltimore: Johns Hopkins University Press, 1985).

15. Maureen Smith, private corr.

BIBLIOGRAPHY

Abrams, M.H. *The Mirror and the Lamp: Romantic Theory and the Critical Tradition*. New York: Oxford University Press, 1953.

———. *Natural Supernaturalism: Tradition and Revolution in Romantic Literature*. New York: Norton, 1971.

Acland, Alice. *Caroline Norton*. London: Constable, 1948.

Adburgham, Alison. *Women in Print: Writing Women and Women's Magazines from the Restoration to the Accession of Victoria*. London: George Allen and Unwin, 1972.

Adorno, Theodor W. "Culture Industry Reconsidered." In *The Culture Industry*. Ed. J.M. Bernstein. London: Routledge, 1991.

Agnew, Jean-Christophe. "Coming Up for Air: Consumer Culture in Historical Perspective." In *Consumption and the World of Goods*. Ed. John Brewer and Roy Porter. New York: Routledge, 1993.

Albright, Daniel. *Tennyson: The Muses' Tug of War*. Charlottesville: University Press of Virginia, 1986.

Aldis, Henry. *The Printed Book*. Cambridge: Cambridge University Press, 1916.

Altick, Richard D. *The English Common Reader: A Social History of the Mass Reading Public, 1800–1900*, 2nd ed. Columbus: Ohio State University Press, 1998.

———. *Paintings from Books: Art and Literature in Britain, 1760–1900*. Columbus, OH: Ohio State University Press, 1985.

Alexander, Mrs. (Anne Hector). "Mrs. Norton." *Women Novelists of Queen Victoria's Reign*. London: Hurst & Blackett, 1897, 277–90.

Anonymous. "The Enchanted Stream; or, The Rider's Vision." *The Keepsake* for 1828. London: Hurst, 1827, 284–86.

———. Introduction to *Poetical Works of the Late Mrs. Mary Robinson*. London: Richard Phillips, 1806.

———. "The Judges Are Going to Jail." *The Northern Star and Leeds General Advertiser* (8 February 1840).

———. "The Persian Lovers." *The Keepsake* for 1828. London: Hurst, 1827, 136–37.

———. Rev. of *Undying One and Other Poems*. *The Edinburgh Review* (June 1831): 366.

Armstrong, Isobel. "Msrepresentation: Codes of Affect and Politics in Nineteenth-Century Women's Poetry." In *Women's Poetry, Late Romantic to Late Victorian: Gender and Genre, 1830–1900*. Ed. Isobel Armstrong and Virginia Blain. Basingstoke, Hampshire: Macmillan, 1999, 3–32.

———. "Natural and National Monuments—Felicia Hemans's 'The Image in Lava': A Note." In *Felicia Hemans: Reimagining Poetry in the Nineteenth Century*. Ed. Nanora Sweet and Julie Melnyk. Houndmills and New York: Palgrave (St. Martin's), 2001, 212–30.

———. *Victorian Poetry: Poetry, Poetics, and Politics*. London: Routledge, 1993.

Arnold, Matthew. *Arnold: Poetical Works*. Ed. C.B. Tinker and H.F. Lowry. London: Oxford University Press, 1950.

Baillie, Joanna. "Introductory Discourse" to *A Series of Plays* (1798). *The Complete Poetical Works of Joanna Baillie. First American Edition*. Philadelphia: Carey and Lea, 1832.

Balfour, Ian. *The Rhetoric of Romantic Prophecy*. Stanford: Stanford University Press, 2002.

Barrett, Edward, ed. *The Society of Text: Hypertext, Hypermedia, and the Social Construction of Information*. Cambridge: MIT Press, 1989.

Barrett, Elizabeth Barrett. *Elizabeth Barrett to Mr. Boyd: Unpublished Letters of Elizabeth Barrett to Hugh Stuart Boyd*. Ed. Barbara McCarthy. New Haven: Yale University Press, 1955.

———. *Poems by Elizabeth Barrett*. 2 vols. London: Moxon, 1844.

———. *The Seraphim and Other Poems*. London: Otley, 1838.

———. *The Unpublished Diary of Elizabeth Barrett Barrett, 1831–1832*. Ed. Philip Kelley and Ronald Hudson. Athens, Ohio: Ohio University Press, 1969.

Barthes, Roland. "From Work to Text." *Image-Music-Text*. Ed. and tr. Stephen Heath. New York: Hill and Wang, 1977.

Bates, William. *The Maclise Portrait-Gallery of Illustrious Literary Characters*. London: Chatto and Windus, 1883.

Baudrillard, Jean. "The Precession of Simulacra." *Simulations*. Tr. Paul Foss, Paul Patton, and Philip Beitchman. New York: Semiotext(e), 1983.

———. *The System of Objects*. 1968. Tr. Mark Poster. *Jean Beaudrillard: Selected Writings*. Stanford: Stanford University Press, 1988.

Beetham, Margaret. *A Magazine of Her Own? Domesticity and Desire in the Woman's Magazine 1800–1914*. London: Routledge, 1996.

Blake, William. *The Marriage of Heaven and Hell. The Complete Poetry and Prose of William Blake*. Rev. ed. Ed. David V. Erdman. Garden City, NY: Doubleday, 1983.

Blakey, Dorothy. *The Minerva Press 1790–1820*. London: Printed for the Bibliographical Society at the University Press, Oxford, 1939 "(for 1935)."

Blanchard, Lamon. *The Life and Literary Remains of L. E. L.*. 2 vols.. Philadelphia: Lea & Blanchard, 1841.

Blessington (Lady), Marguerite. *The Blessington Papers*. Ed. Alfred Morrison. Printed for Private Circulation, 1895.

———. "The Storm." *The Keepsake* for 1834. Ed. Frederic Mansel Reynolds. London: Longman, 1833, 289–90.

———. "A Tale of the Baptistry of St. Marks." *The Keepsake* for 1847. Ed. the Countess of Blessington. London: Longman, 1846, 13–15.

Blum, Stella, ed. *Ackermann's Costume Plates: Women's Fashions in England 1818–1828*. New York: Dover, 1978.

Boehrer, Bruce. " 'Lycidas': The Pastoral Elegy as Same-Sex Epithalamium," *PMLA* 117, 2 (2002): 222–36.

Bolter, Jay David. *Writing Space: The Computer, Hypertext, and the History of Writing*. Hilsdale, NJ: Lawrence Erlbaum, 1991.

Bose, A.. "The Verse of the English 'Annuals.' " *The Review of English Studies* 4 ns, 13 (January 1953): 38–51.

Brookfield, Charles and Frances. *Mrs. Brookfield and Her Circle*. New York: Scribner's, 1906.

Brooks, Cleanth and Robert Penn Warren. *Understanding Poetry*. New York: H. Holt, 1938.

Brooks, Peter. *Body Work: Objects of Desire in Modern Narrative*. Cambridge, MA: Harvard University Press, 1993.

Browning, Elizabeth Barrett. *The Brownings' Correspondence*. 11 vols.. Ed. Philip Kelley and Ronald Hudson. Winfield, KS: Wedgestone, 1984.

———. *A Drama of Exile. The Poetical Works of Elizabeth Barrett Browning*. Ed. Ruth M. Adams. Boston: Houghton Mifflin, 1974, 67–98.

———. "Some Account of the Greek Christian Poets." *The Athenaeum* (February–August 1842); rept. In *The Complete Poetical Works of Elizabeth Barrett Browning*. Ed. Harriet Waters Preston. Boston: Houghton Mifflin, 1900, 513–42.

Casteras, Susan P. *Images of Victorian Womanhood in English Art*. Cranbury, NJ: Associated University Presses, 1987.

Chartier, Roger. "Labourers and Voyagers: From the Text to the Reader." In *The Book History Reader*. Ed. David Finkelstein and Alistair McCleery. London: Routledge, 2002, 47–58.

Chaucer. *The Book of the Duchess*. In *The Works of Geoffrey Chaucer*. Second Edition. Ed. F.N. Robinson. Boston: Houghton Mifflin, 1961, 266–79.

Chilcott, Tim. *A Publisher and His Circle: The Life and Work of John Taylor, Keats's Publisher*. London: Routledge and Kegan Paul, 1972.

Chorley, Henry F. *Memorials of Mrs. Hemans, With Illustrations of Her Literary Character From Her Correspondence*. 2 vols.. London and New York: Saunders and Otley, 1836.

———. Rev. of Elizabeth Barrett Browning's poetry. *Athenaeum 878* (24 August 1844): 763–64.

Christensen, Jerome. *Lord Byron's Strength: Romantic Writing and Commercial Society*. Baltimore and London: The Johns Hopkins University Press, 1993.

Clarke, Adam. *The Holy Bible . . . with a Commentary and Critical Notes*. 8 vols. London, 1810–25.

Clarke, Micael M. *Thackeray and Women*. DeKalb, IL: Northern Illinois University Press, 1995.

Coleridge, Hartley. Rev. of *The Dream and Other Poems* by the Hon. Mrs. Norton. *The Quarterly Review* 66 (September 1840): 374–82.

———. Rev. of *The Undying One and Other Poems* by the Hon. Mrs. Norton. *The Edinburgh Review* (June 1831): 366.

———. *Biographia Literaria*. Ed. James Engell and Walter Jackson Bate. Princeton: Princeton University Press [Bollingen Series], 1983.

Coleridge, Samuel Taylor. "On the Present War." *Lectures 1795, On Politics and Religion*. Ed. L. Patton and P. Mann. *The Collected Works of Samuel Taylor Coleridge*. Vol. 1. Ed. Kathleen Coburn. Princeton: Princeton University Press, 1971.

———. *Opus Maximum*. Vol. 15 in *The Collected Works of Samuel Taylor Coleridge*. Ed. Thomas McFarland with the assistance of Nicholas Halmi. Princeton: Princeton University Press, 2002.

Connely, Willard. *Count d'Orsay, the Dandy of Dandies*. London: Cassell, 1952.

Cotter, James Finn. "Hopkins and Augustine," *Victorian Poetry* 39, 1 (Spring 2001): 69–82.

Cox, Jeffrey N. *Poetry and Politics in the Cockney School: Keats, Shelley, Hunt and Their Circle*. Cambridge: Cambridge University Press, 1998.

Cox, Jeffrey N. and Larry J. Reynolds, eds. *New Historical Literary Study: Essays on Reproducing Texts, Representing History*. Princeton: Princeton University Press, 1993.

Croker, John Wilson. "Poems by Alfred Tennyson." *Quarterly Review* 49 (April 1833): 81–96.

———. Rev. of *France* by Lady Morgan. *Quarterly Review* 32 (April 1817): 260–86.

———. Rev. of *Illustrations of Political Economy* by Harriet Martineau. *Quarterly Review* 44 (April 1833): 136–52.

Cross, Nigel. *The Common Writer: Life in Nineteenth-Century Grub Street*. Cambridge: Cambridge University Press, 1985.

Cunningham, Henry Stewart. Rev. of *Lady Morgan's Memoirs: Autobiography, Diaries and Correspondence, National Review* 16 (April 1863): 443–66.

Curran, Stuart. "The 'I' Altered." *Romanticism and Feminism*. Ed. Anne K. Mellor. Bloomington: Indiana University Press, 1988.

———. "Mary Robinson's *Lyrical Tales* in Context." *Re-Visioning Romanticism*. Ed. Carol Shiner Wilson and Joel Haefner. Philadelphia: University of Pennsylvania Press, 1994.

Cuyler, The Reverend Theo. L., D. D., ed. *Golden Thoughts on Mother, Home and Heaven. From Poetic and Prose Literature of All Ages and All Lands*. New York: E.B. Treat, 1878.

Cyprian. *Treatise II.1: On the Dress of Virgins. Anti-Nicene Fathers*. Vol. 5. <http://www.ccel.org/fathers>.

Danzig, Allan. "The Contraries: A Central Concept in Tennyson's Poetry." In *British Victorian Literature: Recent Revaluations*. Ed. Shiv Kumar. New York: New York University Press, 1969.

Dawson, Aileen. *Masterpieces of Wedgewood in the British Museum*. Bloomington: Indiana University Press, 1984.

DeBord, Guy. *The Society of the Spectacle*. Tr. Donald Nicholson-Smith of the 3rd French ed. New York: Zone Books, 1994.

de Man, Paul. *Allegories of Reading: Figural Language in Rousseau, Nietzsche, Rilke, and Proust*. New Haven: Yale University Press, 1979.

Dibdin, Thomas. *Bibliophobia*. London: Henry Bohn, 1832.

Dick, Philip K. *Do Androids Dream of Electric Sheep?* Garden City, NY: Doubleday, 1968.

Dickens, Charles. *The Letters of Charles Dickens*. 7 vols. Ed. Kathleen Tillotson et al. Oxford: Clarendon, 1969.

Disraeli, Benjamin. *Letters: 1835–1837*. Ed. J.A.W. Gunn et al. Toronto: University of Toronto Press, 1982.

Doane, Mary Ann. "Film and the Masquerade—Theorising the Female Spectator." *Screen* 23, 3–4 (September–October 1982): 74–87.

Eichhorn, Johann Gottfried. *Einleitung in das Alte Testament*. 1781. Leipzig: Weidmann, 1803.

Elfenbein, Andrew. *Byron and the Victorians*. Cambridge: Cambridge University Press, 1995.

Eliot, T.S. "Tradition and the Individual Talent." 1919. *Selected Essays of T.S. Eliot*. New Ed. New York: Harcourt, Brace and World, 1964, 13–22.

Ellis, Sarah Stickney. *Daughters of England, Their Position in Society, Character & Responsibilities*. London: Fisher, n.d. (1842).

Elmore, Phyllis. "Elizabeth Barrett Browning: Argumentative Discourse in *Sonnets from the Portuguese*." Ph.D. dissertation, Texas Women's University, 1989. *DAI* 51 (1990): 861.

Elwood, Anne Katherine. *Memoirs of Literary Ladies of England*. 2 vols. London: Henry Colburn, 1843.

Erdman, David V. "The Dawn of Universal Patriotism: William Wordsworth Among the British in Revolutionary France." In *The Age of William Wordsworth*. Ed. Kenneth R. Johnston and Gene W. Ruoff. New Brunswick: Rutgers University Press, 1987.

Erickson, Lee. *The Economy of Literary Form*. Baltimore: Johns Hopkins University Press, 1996.

Esterhammer, Angela. *Creating States: Studies in the Performative Language of John Milton and William Blake*. Toronto: University of Toronto Press, 1994.

Ezell, Margaret J.M. *Writing Women's Literary History*. Baltimore and London: The Johns Hopkins University Press, 1993.

Falk, Alice. "Elizabeth Barrett Browning and Her Prometheuses: Self-Will and a Woman Poet." *Tulsa Studies in Women's Literature* 7 (1988): 69–85.

Fane, Violet. *Denzil Place: A Story in Verse*. London: Chapman and Hall, 1875.

———. "Lancelot and Guinevere," *From Dawn to Noon*. 1872. London: Longmans; New York: Carlton, 1881.

———. *Poems by Violet Fane*. 2 vols. London: John C. Nimmo, 1892.

Faxon, Frederick W. *Literary Annuals and Gift Books: A Bibliography 1823–1903*. 1912. Repr. with supplementary essays by Eleanore Jamieson and Iain Bain. Middlesex: Private Libraries Association, 1973.

Faÿ-Hallé, Antoinette and Barbara Mundt. *Porcelain of the Nineteenth Century*. New York: Rizzoli, 1983.

Feldman, Paula R. Introduction to *Records of Woman With Other Poems*. Ed. Paula R. Feldman. Lexington: University of Kentucky Press, 1999, xi–xxix.

———. "The Poet and the Profits: Felicia Hemans and the Literary Marketplace." *Keats–Shelley Journal* 46 (1997): 148–76.

Finneran, Richard J., ed. *The Literary Text in the Digital Age*. Ann Arbor: University of Michigan Press, 1996.

Fletcher, Loraine. *Charlotte Smith: A Critical Biography*. New York: St. Martin's Press, 1998.

Flint, Kate. *The Woman Reader 1837–1914*. Oxford: Clarendon, 1993.

Fox, J., Jr. Preface to *Santa Maria*. London: Kearsley, 1797.

Fyfe, James Hamilton. "Mrs. Norton." *Temple Bar* 52 (January 1878): 101–10.

Gabler, Neal. *Life: The Movie*. New York: Random House, 1998.

Genette, Gerard. *Paratexts: Thresholds of Interpretation*. Tr. Jan E. Lewin. New York: Cambridge University Press, 1997.

Gérin, Winifred. *Charlotte Brontë: The Evolution of Genius*. Oxford: Clarendon, 1967.

Gettman, Royal A. *A Victorian Publisher: A Study of the Bentley Papers*. London: Cambridge University Press, 1960.

Gill, Stephen. *William Wordsworth: A Life*. Oxford: Oxford University Press, 1990.

Gorham, Deborah. *The Victorian Girl and the Feminine Ideal*. Bloomington: Indiana University Press, 1982.

Goslee, David. *Tennyson's Characters: "Strange Faces, Other Minds."* Iowa City: University of Iowa Press, 1989.

Greer, Germaine. "The Tulsa Center for the Study of Women's Literature: What We Are Doing and Why We Are Doing It." *Tulsa Studies in Women's Literature* 1, 1 (1982): 5–26.

Hagen, June Steffensen. *Tennyson and His Publishers*. University Park: The Pennsylvania State University Press, 1979.

Hall, Anna Maria. "A Sketch." *The Keepsake* for 1849. Ed. the Countess of Blessington. London: Bogue, 1848, 35–43.

Hall, Anna Maria. "The Wild Rose of Rosstrevor." *The Keepsake* for 1850. Ed. the Countess of Blessington, London: Bogue, 1849, 254–68.

Hall, Samuel Carter. *Retrospect of a Long Life: From 1815 to 1883.* New York: Appleton, 1883.

Hamilton, Catherine J. *Women Writers: Their Works and Ways.* London: Ward, Lock & Bowden, 1893.

Haney, Janice. L. "'Shadow-Hunting': Romantic Irony, *Sartor Resartus,* and Victorian Romanticism." *Studies in Romanticism 17* (1978): 307–33.

Harding, Anthony John. *Coleridge and the Inspired Word.* Kingston: McGill-Queen's University Press, 1985.

Harrison, Antony H. *Victorian Poets and Romantic Poems.* Charlottesville: University Press of Virginia, 1990.

Harrison, William Henry. "The Island Bride." *The Keepsake* for 1845. Ed. the Countess of Blessington. London: Longman, 1844, 16–31.

Haydon, Benjamin Robert. *The Diary of Benjamin Robert Haydon.* 5 vols. Ed. Willard Bissell Pope. Cambridge, MA: Harvard University Press, 1963.

Hays, Mary. *The Victim of Prejudice.* London: Joseph Johnson, 1799. Vol. 2. Facsimile of the first edition. Intro. by Terence Allan Hoagwood. Delmar, NY: Scholars' Facsimiles and Reprints, 1990.

Hazlitt, William. "A Letter to William Gifford, Esq." (1819). *The Complete Works of William Hazlitt.* Ed. P.O. Howe. London: J.M. Dent and Sons, 1932. Vol. 9.

Hector, Anne. "Mrs. Norton." *Women Novelists of Queen Victoria's Reign.* London: Hurst & Blackett, 1897.

Hemans, Felicia. "A Spanish Lady." *The Literary Souvenir; Or, Cabinet of Poetry and Romance.* Ed. Alaric A. Watts. London: Longman, Rees, Orme, Brown, and Green; and John Andres, 1827, 120.

Herbert, George. *The Temple: Sacred Poems and Private Ejaculations.* Cambridge: Printed by Thomas Buck and Roger Daniel, printers to the Universitie, 1633.

Herder, Johann Gottfried von. *The Spirit of Hebrew Poetry.* Tr. James Marsh. Burlington: E. Smith, 1833. Rpt. Naperville, IL: Aleph Press, 1971.

Herring, Terrell Scott. "Frank O'Hara's Open Closet," *PMLA* 117, 3 (2002): 414–27.

Herstrom, Ward. *On the Poems of Tennyson.* Gainesville: University Press of Florida, 1972.

Hewlitt, Dorothy. *Elizabeth Barrett Browning: A Life.* New York: Knopf, 1952.

Hilbish, Florence. *Charlotte Smith: Poet and Novelist.* Philadelphia: University of Pennsylvania Press, 1941.

Hill, Draper, ed. *The Satirical Etchings of James Gillray.* New York: Dover, 1976.

Hoagwood, Terence Allan. *A.E. Housman Revisited.* New York: Simon and Schuster Macmillan, 1995.

———. *Byron's Dialectic: Skepticism and the Critique of Culture.* Lewisburg, PA: Bucknell University Press, 1993.

———. "Keats, Fictionality, and Finance." *Keats and History.* Ed. Nicholas Roe. Cambridge: Cambridge University Press, 1995, 127–42.

———. *Politics, Philosophy, and the Production of Romantic Texts.* DeKalb: Northern Illinois University Press, 1996.

———. *Prophecy and the Philosophy of Mind: Traditions of Blake and Shelley.* Tuscaloosa: University of Alabama Press, 1985.

———. *Skepticism and Ideology: Shelley's Political Prose and Its Philosophical Contexts From Bacon to Marx.* Iowa City: University of Iowa Press, 1988.

Hoagwood, Terence Allan, ed. Materialism and Textuality, *Studies in the Literary Imagination* 30, 1 (Spring 1997).

Hoagwood, Terence Allan and Kathryn Ledbetter. "Life of Letitia Landon." "L.E. L.'s 'Verses' and *The Keepsake* for 1829." *Romantic Circles* scholarly Web site. <http://http://www.rc.umd.edu/editions/contemps.lel/keepcov.htm>

Horkheimer, Max and Theodor Adorno. *The Dialectic of Enlightenment.* Tr. John Cumming. New York: Continuum, 1994.

Horne, Thomas Hartwell. *An Introduction to the Critical Study and Knowledge of the Holy Scriptures.* 3 vols. London, 1818–21.

Housman, A.E. *"The Name and Nature of Poetry" and Other Selected Prose.* Ed. John Carter. 1961. New York: New Amsterdam Books, 1989.

Howitt, William. *Homes and Haunts of the Most Eminent British Poets.* London: Bentley, 1847. [Hughes, Harriet]. *The Works of Mrs. Hemans: With a Memoir of Her Life, by Her Sister. In Six Volumes.* Edinburgh: William Blackwood and Sons; London: Thomas Cadell, 1839.

Hughes, Linda K. *The Many Facéd Glass: Tennyson's Dramatic Monologues.* Athens: Ohio University Press, 1987.

Hulbert, Ann, and Judith Rich Harris. "Raising the American Child." *The Wilson Quarterly* 23, 1 (Winter 1999): 13–37.

Hunt, Leigh. *The Story of Rimini.* Edinburgh, 1816.

Huston, Nancy. "A Tongue Called Mother." *Raritan* 9, 3 (1990): 99–108.

Ingelow, Jean. *A Story of Doom and Other Poems.* London: Longmans, Green, 1867; Boston: Roberts, 1867.

Irigaray, Luce. *Speculum of the Other Woman* (1974). Tr. Gillian C. Gill, Ithaca, NY: Cornell University Press, 1985.

Jacobsen, Martin M. "Orality, Literacy, Cyberdiscursivity: Transformations of Literacy in Computer-Mediated Communication." Ph.D dissertation. Texas A & M University, May 1999.

Jameson, Frederic. "The Ideology of the Text." *The Ideologies of Theory: Essays 1971–1986. Volume I: Situations of Theory.* Minneapolis: University of Minnesota Press, 1988.

Jeffrey, Francis. Rev. of *Records of Woman* and *The Forest Sanctuary. Edinburgh Review* 50 (October 1829): 47 and *passim.*

Jerdan, William. *The Autobiography of William Jerdan with His Literary Political, and Social Reminiscences and Correspondence During the Last Fifty Years.* 4 vols. London: Arthur Hall, Virtue & Co., 1852–53.

Johnson, Heidi. "'Matters That a Woman Rules': Marginalized Maternity in Jean Ingelow's *A Story of Doom.*" *Victorian Poetry* 33, 1 (Spring 1995): 75–88.

Johnson-Eilola, Johndan. *Nostalgic Angels: Rearticulating Hypertext Writing.* Norwood, NJ: Ablex, 1997.

Johnston, Kenneth R. *The Hidden Wordsworth: Poet, Lover, Rebel, Spy.* New York: Norton, 1998.

Jones, Ernest. "The March of Freedom." *The Northern Star and National Trades Journal,* (18 March 1848).

Jordan, John O., and Robert L. Patten. *Literature and the Marketplace.* Cambridge: Cambridge University Press, 1995.

Joseph, Gerhard. "Commodifying Tennyson: The Historical Transformation of 'Brand Loyalty.'" *Victorian Poetry* 34 (1996): 133–47.

Jowett, Benjamin, et al. *Essays and Reviews.* London: Parker and Son, 1860.

Jump, Harriet Devine. "'The False Prudery of Public Taste': Scandalous Women and the Annals, 1820–1850." *Feminist Readings of Victorian Popular Texts: Divergent*

Femininities. Ed. Emma Liggins and Daniel Duffy. Aldershot: Ashgate, 2001, 1–17.

Kabbani, Rana. *Imperial Fictions: Europe's Myths of Orient*. New York: Macmillan, 1986.

Kelly, Gary. *The English Jacobin Novel 1780–1805*. Oxford: Clarendon Press, 1976.

Kemble, Frances Ann. *Records of a Girlhood*. New York: Henry Holt, 1879.

Kevles, Daniel J. *In the Name of Eugenics: Genetics and the Uses of Human Heredity*. New York: Knopf, 1985.

Kincaid, James R. *Tennyson's Major Poems: The Comic and Ironic Patterns*. New Haven: Yale University Press, 1975.

Labbé, Jacqueline. *The Romantic Paradox: Love, Violence and the Uses of Romance, 1760–1830*. New York: St. Martin's Press, 2000.

Lackey, Michael. "'God's Grandeur': Gerard Manley Hopkins' Reply to the Speculative Atheist," *Victorian Poetry* 39, 1 (Spring 2001): 83–90.

Lamb, Charles. *Letters of Charles Lamb*. 2 vols. Ed. W. Carew Hazlitt. London: Bell, 1886.

———. *The History of the Lyre, The Poetical Works of Letitia Elizabeth Landon*. Ed. William B. Scott. London: George Routledge and Sons, 1873. Facsimile reproduction with an introduction and additional poems. Ed. F.J. Sypher. Delmar, NY: Scholars' Facsimiles, 1990.

Landon, Letitia Elizabeth. "The Lily of the Valley." *Fisher's Drawing Room Scrap-Book* for 1836. London: Fisher, 1835, 9.

———. *The Troubadour* (1825). *The Poetical Works of Letitia Elizabeth Landon: A New Edition*. 3 vols. London: Longman, Orme, Brown, Green, and Longman, 1839.

Landow, George Paul. *Hypertext: The Convergence of Contemporary Critical Theory and Technology*. Baltimore: Johns Hopkins University Press, 1994.

Lanyer, Aemilia. *Renaissance Women: The Plays of Elizabeth Cary and the Poems of Aemilia Lanyer*. Ed. Diane Purkiss. London: Pickering and Chatto, 1994.

Ledbetter, Kathryn. "'BeGemmed and BeAmuletted': Tennyson and Those 'Vapid' Gift Books." *Victorian Poetry* 34, 2 (Summer 1996): 235–45.

———. "'The Copper and Steel Manufactory' of Charles Heath." *Victorian Review* 28, 2 (2002): 21–30.

———. "Domesticity Betrayed: *The Keepsake* Literary Annual." *The Victorian Newsletter* 99 (Spring 2001): 16–24.

———. "L. E. L.'s 'Verses' and *The Keepsake* of 1829." Hypertext edition of a *Keepsake* poem (and commentary), with Terence Allan Hoagwood and Martin Matthew Jacobsen. *Romantic Circles* scholarly Web site (Fall 1998). <http://www.rc.umd.edu/editions/lel/keepcov.htm>

———. Lucrative Requests: British Authors and Gift Book Editors." *Papers of the Bibliographical Society of America* 88, 2 (June 1994): 207–16.

———. "White Vellum and Gilt Edges: Imaging *The Keepsake. Studies in the Literary Imagination* 30, 1 (Spring 1997): 35–49.

Leighton, Angela. "Stirring a Dust of Figures: Elizabeth Barrett Browning and Love." *Browning Society Notes* 17 (1988): 11–24.

———. *Victorian Women Poets: Writing Against the Heart*. Charlottesville: University Press of Virginia, 1992.

Lewes, G.H. "The Condition of Authors in England, Germany, and France." *Fraser's Magazine* 35 (1847): 285–95.

———. "Our Survey of Literature and Science." *The Cornhill Magazine* 5 (January 1863): 132–44.

Linley, Margaret. "A Centre that Would Not Hold: Annuals and Cultural Democracy." In *Nineteenth-Century Media and the Construction of Identities.* Ed. Laurel Brake, Bill Bell, and David Finkelstein. New York: Palgrave, 2000, 54–74.

"Literary 'Lions': Countess of Blessington." *Hunt's London Journal* 19 (November 9, 1844): 235.

Lockhart, J.G. *The Life of Sir Walter Scott, Bart.* Edinburgh: Black, 1879.

———. Rev of Tennyson's *Poems. Quarterly Review* (April 1833).

Lootens, Tricia. "Hemans and Home: Victorianism, 'Internal Enemies,' and the Domestication of National Identity." *PMLA* 109 (1994): 238–53.

———. *Lost Saints: Silence, Gender, and Victorian Literary Canonization.* Charlottesville: University Press of Virginia, 1996.

———. "Receiving the Legend, Rethinking the Writer: Letitia Landon and the Poetess Tradition." *Romanticism and Women Poets: Opening the Doors of Reception.* Ed. Harriet Kramer Linkin and Stehen C. Behrendt. Lexington: The University Press of Kentucky, 1999, 242–84.

Lukacs, György, *Studies in European Realism.* Tr. Edith Bone. New York: Grosset and Dunlap, 1964.

Lyotard, Jean-Francois. *The Postmodern Condition: A Report on Knowledge.* Tr. Geoff Bennington and Brian Massumi. 1979. Rpt. Minneapolis: University of Minnesota Press, 1997.

Macready, William Charles. *Diaries of William Charles Macready, 1833–1851.* Ed. William Toynbee. London, 1912. Vol. 1.

Madden, R.R. *The Literary Life and Correspondence of the Countess of Blessington.* 2 vols. New York: Harper, 1855.

Maginn, William. "Gallery of Literary Characters. Lady Morgan." *Fraser's Magazine* 11 (May 1835): 529.

———. "Regina's Maids of Honour. List the First." *Fraser's Magazine* (January 1836): 80.

Manning, Peter J. "Wordsworth in the *Keepsake*, 1829." In *Literature in the Marketplace: Nineteenth-Century British Publishing and Reading Practice.* Ed. John O. Jordan and Robert L. Patten. Cambridge: Cambridge University Press, 1995, 44–73.

Marks, Patricia. "Harriet Martineau: *Fraser's* 'Maid of [Dis]Honour." *Victorian Periodicals Review* 19, 1 (Spring 1986): 28–34.

Martineau, Harriet. *Harriet Martineau on Women.* Ed. Gayle Graham Yates. New Brunswick, NJ: Rutgers University Press, 1985.

———. Rev. of "A Letter to the Queen on the State of the Monarchy" by a Friend of the People. *The London and Westminster Review* 32 (April 1839): 455–75.

Mayhew, Henry. *London Labour and London Poor* (1851). Rpt. New York: Dover, 1968.

McFarland, Thomas. *Originality and Imagination.* Baltimore: Johns Hopkins University Press, 1985.

McGann, Jerome. *The Beauty of Inflections: Literary Investigations in Historical Method and Theory.* Oxford: Clarendon Press, 1985.

———. *A Critique of Modern Textual Criticism.* Chicago: University of Chicago Press, 1983.

———. *Dante Gabriel Rossetti and the Game That Must Be Lost.* New Haven: Yale University Press, 2000.

———. "Literary History, Romanticism, and Felicia Hemans." *Re-Visioning Romanticism: British Women Writers 1776–1837.* Ed. Carol Shiner Wilson and Joel Haefner. Philadelphia: University of Pennsylvania Press, 1994.

McGann, Jerome. *The Poetics of Sensibility*. Oxford: Clarendon Press, 1996.

———. "The Rationale of Hypertext." Posted 6 May 1995 and accessed 11 November 2001. <http://www.iath.virginia.edu/public/jjm2f/rationale.html>

———. "Rethinking Romanticism." *ELH* 59 (1992): 750.

———. *The Romantic Ideology*. Chicago: University of Chicago Press, 1983.

———. *Social Values and Poetic Acts: The Historical Judgment of Literary Work*. Cambridge, MA: Harvard University Press, 1988.

———. *The Textual Condition*. Princeton: Princeton University Press, 1991.

———. *Towards a Literature of Knowledge*. Chicago: University of Chicago Press, 1989.

McGann, Jerome, ed. *Black Riders: The Visible Language of Modernism*. Princeton: Princeton University Press, 1993.

———. *The New Oxford Book of Romantic Period Verse*. Oxford: Oxford University Press, 1993.

———. *The Rossetti Archive*. <http://jefferson.village.virginia.edu/rossetti/index.html>

McGann, Jerome and Daniel Riess, eds. *Letitia Elizabeth Landon: Selected Writings*. Peterborough, Ontario: Broadview, 1997.

McKenzie, D.F. "The Book as an Expressive Form." *The Book History Reader*. Ed. David Finkelstein and Alistair McCleery. London: Routledge, 2002, 27–38.

McSweeney, Kerry. *Tennyson and Swinburne as Romantic Naturalists*. Toronto: University of Toronto Press, 1981.

Meggs, Philip B. *A History of Graphic Design*. 3rd ed. New York: John Wiley, 1998.

Mellor, Anne K. *Romanticism and Gender*. New York: Routledge, 1993.

Mermin, Dorothy. *Elizabeth Barrett Browning: The Origins of a New Poetry*. Chicago: University of Chicago Press, 1989.

———. *Godiva's Ride: Women of Letters in England, 1830–1880*. Bloomington: Indiana University Press, 1993.

Merriam, Harold G. *Edward Moxon: Publisher of Poets*. New York: Columbia University Press, 1939.

Meynell, Alice. "Christ in the Universe." 1901. *Collected Poems*. London: Burns and Oates, 1913.

Mill, John Stuart. Rev. of Tennyson's *Poems, Chiefly Lyrical* (1830) and *Poems* (1832). *London Review* 1 (July 1835): 402–24. Rpt. *Tennyson: The Critical Heritage*. Ed. John D. Jump. London: Routledge and Kegal Paul; New York: Barnes and Noble, 1967.

———. *Utilitarianism* (1863). Rpt. Buffalo, NY: Prometheus Books, 1987.

Miller, J. Hillis. *Illustration*. Cambridge, MA: Harvard University Press, 1992.

Millgate, Michael. *Testamentary Acts: Browning, Tennyson, Hardy*. Oxford: Clarendon Press, 1992.

Milton, John. *The Complete Poetry of John Milton*. Ed. John T. Shawcross. Rev. ed. Garden City, NY: Doubleday, 1971.

Mitchell, Sally. "Sentiment and Suffering: Women's Recreational Reading in the 1860s." *Victorian Studies* 21 (1977): 29–45.

Mitford, Mary Russell. *Letters of Mary Russell Mitford*. 2 vols. Ed. Henry Chorley. London: Bentley, 1872.

Morgan (Lady), Sydney Owenson. *Lady Morgan's Memoirs: Autobiography, Diaries and Correspondence*. Ed. Geraldine Jewsbury and Hepworth Dixon. London: William H. Allen, 1862. Volume 2.

Moore, Thomas. *The Journal of Thomas Moore.* 6 vols. Ed. Wilfred S. Dowden. Newark: University of Delaware Press, 1983.

Morison, Stanley. *John Bell, 1745–1831: Bookseller, Printer, Publisher, Typefounder, Journalist.* Cambridge: Cambridge University Press, 1930.

Morlier, Margaret M. "'The Dead Pan': Elizabeth Barrett Browning and the Romantic Ego." *Browning Institute Studies* 18 (1990): 131–55.

Morpeth (Lord), George William Frederick Howard. "The Lady and the Novel." *The Keepsake* for 1835. Ed. Frederic Mansel Reynolds. London: Longman, 1834, 27–28.

Morris, William. *The Defense of Guenevere and Other Poems.* London: Bell & Daldy, 1858.

Mumby, Frank Arthur. *Publishing and Bookselling: A History from the Earliest Times to the Present Day,* 3rd ed. London: Jonathan Cape, 1954.

Murray, John. *A Publisher and His Friends: Memoir and Correspondence of the Late John Murray.* 2 vols. Ed. Samuel Smiles. London: John Murray, 1891.

Nead, Lynda. *Myths of Sexuality: Representations of Women in Victorian Britain.* Oxford: Blackwell, 1988.

Nicolson, Harold. *Tennyson: Aspects of His Life, Character, and Poetry.* Boston: Houghton Mifflin, 1923.

Nochlin, Linda. *Women, Art, and Power and Other Essays.* New York: Harper, 1988.

North, Christopher (John Wilson). "Tennyson's Poems." *Blackwood's Edinburgh Magazine,* 31 (May 1832): 721–41.

Norton, Caroline. "The Dream." *The Dream and Other Poems.* London: Henry Colburn, 1841, 3–76.

———. "The Future." *The Undying One and Other Poems* (1830). *Selected Writings of Caroline Norton.* Facsimile reproduction. Ed. James O. Hoge and Jane Marcus. Delmar, NY: Scholars' Facsimiles & Reprints, 1978, 201–06.

———. "The Haunted Wood of Amesoy." *Katie Bouverie, and Other Tales and Sketches, in Prose and Verse.* 2 vols. Philadelphia: Carey & Hart, 1836, 1:171–84.

———. "Lawrence Bayley's Temptation." *The Keepsake* for 1834. Ed. Frederic Mansel Reynolds. London: Longman, 1833, 142–61.

———. "Marriage and Love." *The Sorrows of Rosalie and Other Poems.* 1829. *Selected Writings of Caroline Norton.* Facsimile reproduction. Ed. James O. Hoge and Jane Marcus. Delmar, NY: Scholar's Facsimiles & Reprints, 1978, 119.

———. *Some Unrecorded Letters of Caroline Norton in the Altschul Collection of the Yale University Library.* Ed. Bertha Coolidge. Privately printed by Yale University Library, 1934.

Onslow, Barbara. *Women of the Press in Nineteenth-Century Britain.* Basingstoke, Hampshire and New York: Palgrave Macmillan, 2000.

Paine, Thomas. *The Age of Reason.* London: R. Carlile, 1819.

Parker, Rozsika and Griselda Pollock. *Old Mistresses: Women, Art and Ideology.* New York: Pantheon, 1981.

Pascoe, Judith. Introduction. *Mary Robinson: Selected Poems.* Peterborough, Ontario: Broadview, 2000.

———. "Mary Robinson and the Literary Marketplace." In *Romantic Women Writers: Voices and Countervoices.* Ed. Paula R. Feldman and Theresa M. Kelley. Hanover and London: University Press of New England, 1995, 252–68.

Patten, Robert L. *Charles Dickens and His Publishers.* Oxford: Clarendon Press, 1978.

Pearce, Lynne. *Woman/Image/Text: Readings in Pre-Raphaelite Art and Literature.* Toronto and Buffalo: University of Toronto Press, 1991.

Pearsall, Ronald. *Tell Me, Pretty Maiden: The Victorian and Edwardian Nude.* Exeter, England: Webb, 1981.

Perkins, Jane. *The Life of Mrs. Norton.* London: John Murray, 1909.

Perry, Anne. "Sexual Exploitation and Freedom: Religion, Race, and Gender in Elizabeth Barrett Browning's 'The Runaway Slave at Pilgrim's Point.'" *Studies in Browning and His Circle* 16 (1988): 14–27.

Peters, Maureen. *Jean Ingelow, Victorian Poetess.* Totowa, NJ: Rowman and Littlefield, 1972.

Peterson, Linda H. "Becoming an Author: Mary Robinson's *Memoirs.*" In *Revisioning Romanticism: British Women Writers, 1776–1837.* Ed. Carol Shiner Wilson and Joel Haefner. Philadelphia: University of Pennsylvania Press, 1994.

———. "Rewriting *A History of the Lyre*: Letitia Landon, Elizabeth Barrett Browning and the (Re) Construction of the Nineteenth-Century Woman Poet." In *Women's Poetry, Late Romantic to Late Victorian: Gender and Genre, 1830–1900.* Ed. Isobel Armstrong and Virginia Blain. London: Macmillan, 1999, 115–32.

Peterson, William S. *The Kelmscott Press: A History of William Morris's Typographical Adventure.* Berkeley: University of California Press, 1991.

Pfeiffer, Emily. *Women and Work. An Essay.* London: Trübner & Co., 1888.

———. "Personifying the Poetess: Caroline Norton, 'The Picture of Sappho.'" In *Women's Poetry, Late Romantic to Late Victorian: Gender and Genre, 1830–1900.* Ed. Isobel Armstrong and Virginia Blain. New York: St. Martin's Press, 1999, 50–67.

Prins, Yopie. *Victorian Sappho.* Princeton: Princeton University Press, 1999.

Psomiades, Kathy Alexis. *Beauty's Body: Femininity and Representation in British Aestheticism.* Palo Alto: Stanford University Press, 1997.

Radway, Janice. *Reading the Romance: Women, Patriarchy, and Popular Literature.* Chapel Hill: University of North Carolina Press, 1984.

Ragg, Laura Marie Roberts. *The Women Artists of Bologna.* London: Methuen, 1907.

Regaignon, Dara Rossman. "Instructive Sufficiency: Re-Reading the Governess through *Agnes Grey,*" *Victorian Literature and Culture* 29, 1 (2001): 85–108.

Reiman, Donald H. *Romantic Texts and Contexts.* Columbia: University of Missouri Press, 1987.

Renier, Anne. *Friendship's Offering: An Essay on the Annuals and Gift Books of the 19th Century.* London: Private Libraries Association, 1964.

Rev. of *A Drama of Exile* by Elizabeth Barrett. *New Monthly Magazine* 107 (July 1856): 369–78.

Rev. of *A Drama of Exile* by Elizabeth Barrett. *New Quarterly Review* 5 (1845): 84–97.

Rev. of *A Drama of Exile* by Elizabeth Barrett. *The Spectator* 17, 843 (24 August 1844): 809–10.

Rev. of *A Drama of Exile* by Elizabeth Barrett. *The Sun* (9 September 1844): 3.

Rev. of *A Drama of Exile* by Elizabeth Barrett. *Tait's Edinburgh Magazine* ns 23 (January 1856): 14–20.

Rev. of *The Keepsake* for 1850. *The Literary Gazette* 1713 (17 November 1849): 842–44.

Rev. of *Lady Morgan's Memoirs: Autobiography, Diaries, and Correspondence. The Westminster Review* 23 ns (April 1863): 490.

Rev. of *The Undying One and Other Poems* by the Hon. Mrs. Norton. *Edinburgh Review* 53 (June 1831): 361–69.

Richards, I.A. *Practical Criticism: A Study of Literary Judgment*. London: Kegal Paul, Trench, Trubner, 1929.

———. *Principles of Literary Criticism*. London: Kegan Paul, Trench, Trubner; New York: Harcourt Brace, 1925.

Ricks, Christopher. *Tennyson*. New York: Macmillan, 1972.

Riess, Daniel. "Letitia Landon and the Dawn of English Post-Romanticism." *SEL: Studies in English Literature 1500–1900*, 36, 4 (Autumn 1996): 807–27.

Roberts, Emma. "Memoir of L. E. L." *The Zenana and Minor Poems of L. E. L.* London: Fisher, 1839.

Robinson, Henry Crabb. *Diary, Reminiscences, and Correspondence of Henry Crabb Robinson*. 2 vols. Ed. Thomas Sadler. Boston: Houghton, Mifflin, 1877.

Robinson, Mary. *Lyrical Tales*. Intro. Jonathan Wordsworth. Oxford: Woodstock Books, 1989.

———. *Memoirs of the Late Mrs. Robinson, Written by Herself*. 4 vols. (1801). Rpt. London: Hunt and Clarke, 1826.

———. *Sappho and Phaon*. Intro. Rebecca Jackson and Terence Allan Hoagwood. Delmar, NY: Scholars' Facsimiles, 1994.

Robinson, Mary Darby. *A Letter to the Women of England, on the Injustice of Mental Subordination*. Ed. Adriana Craciun et al. *Romantic Circles* scholarly Web site. <http://www.rc.umd.edu/editions/contemps/robinson/cover.htm>

Roe, Nicholas. *John Keats and the Culture of Dissent*. Oxford: Oxford University Press, 1997.

———. *Wordsworth and Coleridge: The Radical Years*. Oxford: Clarendon Press, 1988.

Rogers, Katharine. "Fanny Burney." *A Dictionary of British and American Women Writers 1660–1800*. Ed. Janet Todd. Totowa, NJ: Rowman and Littlefield, 1987.

Rossetti, Christina. *The Face of the Deep: A Devotional Commentary on the Apocalypse*. London: Society for the Promotion of Christian Knowledge, 1892.

Sadleir, Michael. *The Strange Life of Lady Blessington*. Boston: Little, 1933.

Saint Augustine. *On Christian Doctrine*. <http://www.iclnet.org/pub/resources/text/ipb-e/epl- 01/agdoc-02.txt>

Scheckner, Peter. *An Anthology of Chartist Poetry: Poetry of the British Working Class, 1830s–1850s*. Cranbury, NJ: Fairleigh Dickinson University Press, 1989.

Scott, William Bell. *Autobiographical Notes of the Life of Willam Bell Scott*. Ed. W. Minto. 2 vols. New York: Harper, 1892. Volume 1.

Searle, Geoffrey Russell. *Eugenics and Politics in Britain*. Leyden: Noordhoff, 1976.

Searle, John. *Speech Acts: An Essay in the Philosophy of Language*. Cambridge: Cambridge University Press, 1969.

Shaffer, E.S. "The Hermeneutic Community: Coleridge and Schleiermacher." In *The Coleridge Connection: Essays for Thomas McFarland*. Ed. Richard Gravil and Molly Lefebure. New York: St. Martin's, 1990.

———. *"Kubla Khan" and "The Fall of Jerusalem": The Mythological School in Biblical Criticism and Secular Literature*. Cambridge: Cambridge University Press, 1975.

Shaw, Marion. "Tennyson and His Public 1827–1859." *Tennyson*. Ed. D.J. Palmer. London: Bell, 1973, 52–88.

Shelley, Percy Bysshe. *The Complete Works of Percy Bysshe Shelley*. Ed. Roger Ingpen and Walter E. Peck. London: Ernest Benn, 1926–30.

Shteir, Ann B. "Mary Robinson." *A Dictionary of British and American Women Writers 1660–1800*. Ed. Janet Todd. Totowa, NJ: Rowman and Littlefield, 1987.

Sigourney, Lydia. Prefatory essay. [Harriet Hughes]. *The Works of Mrs. Hemans; With a Memoir of Her Life, by Her Sister. In Six Volumes*. Edinburgh: William Blackwood and Sons; London: Thomas Cadell, 1839.

Simons, Judy. "Behind the Scenes: The Early Diary of Elizabeth Barrett Browning." *Diaries and Journals of Literary Women from Fanny Burney to Virginia Woolf*. Iowa City: University of Iowa Press, 1990.

Smith, Albert. "Regnier's Vengeance." *The Keepsake* for 1848. Ed. the Countess of Blessington. London: Bogue, 1847, 238–50.

Smith, Charlotte. *The Emigrants* (1793). *The Poems of Charlotte Smith*. Ed. Stuart Curran. New York: Oxford University Press, 1993. Book 1.

Smith, Elizabeth. *The Brethren: A Poem in Four Books*. Birmingham: Printed for the Author by Pearson and Rollason, 1787. Rpt with intro. by Terence Allan Hoagwood. Delmar, NY: Scholar's Facsimiles, 1991.

Snow, Edward. "Theorizing the Male Gaze: Some Problems." *Representations* 25 (Winter 1989): 30–41.

Stephenson, Glennis. *Elizabeth Barrett Browning and the Poetry of Love*. Ann Arbor: UMI Research Press, 1989.

———. "Letitia Landon and the Victorian Improvisatrice: The Construction of L. E. L." *Victorian Poetry* 30, 1 (Spring 1992): 1–17.

———. *Letitia Elizabeth Landon: The Woman Behind L. E. L.* Manchester: Manchester University Press, 1995.

Stevens, Wallace. "The Snow Man," *Harmonium*. New York: Knopf, 1923.

Stillinger, Jack. *Coleridge and Textual Instability: The Multiple Versions of the Major Poems*. New York: Oxford University Press, 1994.

———. *Multiple Authorship and the Myth of Solitary Genius*. New York: Oxford University Press, 1991.

Strauss, David Friedrich. *The Life of Jesus, Critically Examined*, 4th ed. Tr. George Eliot. London: Chapman, 1846.

Sweet, Nanora. "The Bowl of Liberty: Felicia Hemans and the Romantic Mediterranean." *DAI* 54, 7 (1994): 2593A.

———. "Corinne and the Woman as Poet in England: Hemans, Jewsbury, and Barrett Browning." In *The Novel's Seductions: Stael's Corinne in Critical Inquiry*. Ed. Karyna Symurlo. Lewisburg, PA: Bucknell University Press, 1999, 204–20.

———. "History, Imperialism, and the Aesthetics of the Beautiful: Hemans and the Post-Napoleonic Moment." In At the Limits of Romanticism: Essays in Cultural, Feminist, and Materialist Criticism. Ed. Mary Favret and Nicola Watson. Bloomington: Indiana University Press, 1994, 170–84.

———. "'Lorenzo's' Liverpool and 'Corinne's' Coppet: The Italianate Salon and Romantic Education." *Lessons of Romanticism: A Critical Companion*. Ed. Thomas Pfau. Durham, NC: Duke University Press, 1998, 244–60.

Sweet, Nanora and Julie Melnyk. "Introduction: Why Hemans Now?" *Felicia Hemans: Reimagining Poetry in the Nineteenth Century*. Ed. Nanora Sweet and Julie Melnyk. Houndmills and New York: Palgrave (St. Martin's), 2001.

Swindells, Julia. *Victorian Writing and Working Women: The Other Side of Silence*. Minneapolis: University of Minnesota Press, 1985.

Tanselle, G. Thomas. *A Rationale of Textual Criticism*. Philadelphia: University of Pennsylvania Press, 1989.

Taplin, Gardner B. *The Life of Elizabeth Barrett Browning*. New Haven: Yale University Press, 1957.

Tennyson, Lord Alfred. *The Letters of Alfred Tennyson*. Ed. Cecil Y. Lang and Edgar F. Shannon, Jr. Cambridge, MA: Harvard University Press, 1981. Volume 1.

————. *Poems by Alfred Tennyson*. London: Moxon, 1833.

————. *The Poems of Tennyson in Three Volumes*. Ed. Christopher Ricks. 2nd ed. London: Longman; Berkeley: University of California Press, 1987.

Tennyson, Charles. *Alfred Tennyson*. London: Macmillan, 1950.

Tertullian. *On the Apparel of Women. The Anti-Nicene Fathers*. Vol. 4. <http://www.ccel.org/fathers>.

Tetreault, Ronald, ed. The Lyrical Ballads *Bicentenary Project*, <http://www.dal.ca/~etc/lballads/welcome.htm>

Thackeray, William Makepeace. "A Word on the Annuals." *Fraser's Magazine* 16 (1837): 757–63.

Thiry, Paul Henri, Baron d'Holbach. *Christianity Unveiled*. London: R. Carlile, 1819.

————. *The System of Nature; or, Laws of the Moral and Physical World*. 1835. 2 vols. Tr. H.D. Robinson. Boston: Mendum, 1853. Rpt. Kitchener: Batoche Books, 2001.

Thrall, Miriam M.H. *Rebellious Fraser's: Nol Yorke's Magazine in the Days of Maginn, Thackeray, and Carlyle*. New York: Columbia University Press, 1934.

Timperley, Charles H. *A Dictionary of Printers and Printing, with the Progress of Literature, Ancient and Modern*. London, 1839.

————. *Encyclopedia of Literary and Typographical Anecdote*. London, 1842.

Toulmin, Camilla (Mrs. Newton Crosland). "A Tale That Was Told to Me." *The Keepsake for* 1848. Ed. the Countess of Blessington. London: Bogue, 1847, 22–37.

Trudgill, Eric. *Madonnas and Magdalens: The Origins and Development of Victorian Sexual Attitudes*. New York: Holmes, 1976.

Tucker, Herbert. "Of Monuments and Moments: Spacetime in Nineteenth-Century Poetry." *Modern Language Quarterly* 58, 3 (1997): 269–97.

————. *Tennyson and the Doom of Romanticism*. Ithaca: Cornell University Press, 1988.

Tyson, Gerald P. *Joseph Johnson: A Liberal Publisher*. Iowa City: University of Iowa Press, 1979.

Underwood, Ted. "Romantic Historicism and the Afterlife," *PMLA* 117, 2 (2002): 237–51.

Untitled. *The Age* (19 July 1836):196.

Vasari, Giorgio. *The Lives of the Artists* (1568). Tr. Julia Conaway Bondanella and Peter Bondanella. 1991. Rpt. Oxford: Oxford University Press, 1998.

Vendler, Helen. *The Art of Shakespeare's Sonnets*. Cambridge, MA: Harvard University Press, 1997.

————. *The Given and the Made: Strategies of Poetic Redefinition*. Cambridge, MA: Harvard University Press, 1995.

Vicinus, Martha. "The Perfect Victorian Lady." *Suffer and Be Still: Women in the Victorian Age*. Ed. Martha Vicinus. Bloomington: Indiana University Press, 1972.

Viscomi, Joseph. *Blake and the Idea of the Book*. Princeton: Princeton University Press, 1993.

Voltaire, Francois. *Philosophical Dictionary*. Tr. anon. London: Leigh Hunt and John Hunt, 1824.

Ward, Mrs. "Letty Bloomfield." *The Keepsake* for 1854. Ed. Marguerite Power. London: Bogue, 1854, 119–32.

Watts, Alaric Alfred. *Alaric Watts: A Narrative of His Life. By His Son*. 2 vols. London: Richard Bentley and Son, 1884.

Wells, H.G. "Comment of Francis Galton's Eugenics: Its Definition, Scope, and Aims." *American Journal of Sociology* 10, 1 (July 1904).

Whitman, Walt. "Song of the Exposition." *Leaves of Grass: A Textual Variorum of the Printed Poems.* Ed. Sculley Bradley et al. New York: New York University Press, 1980.

Whittemore, Reed. *Pure Lives: The Early Biographers.* Baltimore:Johns Hopkins University Press, 1988.

Wilde, Jane. "The Countess of Blessington." *Dublin University Magazine* 45 (1855): 333–53.

Willis, N.P. *Pencillings by the Way.* London: Bohn, 1846.

Wise, Thomas J. *A Bibliography of the Writings in Prose and Verse of Elizabeth Barrett Browning.* London: Printed for Private Circulation only, 1918.

Wolfson, Susan. "'Domestic Affections' and 'the Spear of Minerva': Felicia Hemans and the Dilemma of Gender." In *Re-Visioning Romanticism: British Women Writers, 1776–1837.* Ed. Carol Shiner Wilson and Joel Haefner. Philadelphia: University of Pennsylvania Press, 1994.

———. Note to "Juana." *Felicia Hemans: Selected Poems, Letters, Reception Materials.* Princeton: Princeton University Press, 2000, 388.

Wollstonecraft, Mary. Rev. of *Man as He Is. Analytical Review* 24 (October 1796): 398–99.

———. *A Vindication of the Rights of Woman* (1792). Ed. Carol H. Poston. New York: Norton, 1975.

Wordsworth, William. "The Country Girl." *The Keepsake* for 1829. Ed. Frederic Mansel Reynolds. London: Longman, 1828, 50–51.

———. The *Lyrical Ballads* Bicentenary Project. Ed. Ronald Tetreault. <http://www.dal.ca/~etc/lballads/welcome.htm>

———. Preface to second edition of *Lyrical Ballads* (1800; rev. 1802, 1836, and rpt. 1850). *William Wordsworth: Selected Prose.* Ed. John O. Hayden. Harmondsworth: Penguin, 1988.

———. *The Thirteen-Book Prelude.* Ed. Mark L. Reed. Ithaca, NY: Cornell University Press, 1991.

Žižek, Slavoj. *Welcome to the Desert of the Real.* London: verso, 2002.

Index